Mindfulness and Meaningful Work

Dedicated to Jack Fitzwater

The nonstudent
visits the nonteacher
and they talk about nothing.

OTHER BOOKS BY CLAUDE WHITMYER

Running a One-Person Business, with Salli Rasberry (Berkeley: Ten Speed Press, 2d ed., 1994)

In the Company of Others: Making Community in the Modern World, Editor (New York: Tarcher/Perigee, 1993)

MINDFULNESS AND MEANINGFUL WORK

EXPLORATIONS IN RIGHT LIVELIHOOD

Edited by
CLAUDE WHITMYER

Parallax Press
Berkeley, California

A NOTE ON LANGUAGE

Given the efforts we have made in the last twenty years toward equality of the sexes, we should by now have devised a better way of handling the neutral gender in the written word. Unfortunately we have not. For this reason, I apologize in advance for the archaic use of the masculine forms "he," "his," "him," and "a man," which designate hypothetical individuals throughout these copyrighted excerpts, especially in the older pieces.

Many of the essays in this collection were previously printed elsewhere, and we have retained the usages of each piece, including masculine gender.

Parallax Press
P.O. Box 7355
Berkeley, California 94707

Cover design by Legacy Media, Inc.
Text layout adapted from a design by Barbara Pope.
Cover is from Shih-tê, 13th century, attributed to Yen Hui,
ink and colors on silk; used with permission of the Tokyo National Museum.

Library of Congress Cataloging-in-Publication Data

Mindfulness and meaningful work : explorations in right livelihood /
    edited by Claude Whitmyer.
       p.   cm.
    ISBN 0-938077-54-6 (pbk.) : $16.00
    1. Eightfold Path.   2. Religious life—Buddhism.   I. Whitmyer,
Claude.
BQ4320.M56   1994
294.3'564—dc20   94-16096
                                        CIP

5 6 7 8 9 10 / 01 00 99 98 97

Contents

ERNEST CALLENBACH

Foreword

Before the Fall, presumably, all livelihood was right, all work meaning-ful. There was no exploitation among humans and no nonsustainable exploitation of nature. The Garden was fruitful, and provided every-thing needed for human survival. Or, to turn Christian myth into prehistorical speculation, our gatherer-hunter ancestors must have had a sense that the universe provided them with what was necessary. But to find it and know what to do with it—that must have required the same fierce, direct, mindful intensity about finding food, constructing shelter, and reproducing themselves that we may observe (if we are attentive) in the wild animals that still share our habitats.

In such circumstances, action and satisfaction were intimately con-nected, not rerouted through "the cash nexus" which sometimes seems to be the only thing that truly links us now. Nature does not forgive mistakes. Things had to be done right, and a vast oral culture of plant and animal lore, social history, and spiritual discipline ensured that they were. It worked; researchers now believe that for gatherer-hunter tribespeople the provision of food, shelter, and other necessities occu-pied (and still occupies, for those remnant tribes still with us) some-thing like twenty hours per week. And this human pattern, we must remember, endured for hundreds of thousands of years. Our industrial epoch of punching time clocks has only endured a few generations, and appears increasingly shaky.

We can see some hints of what "work" must have been like in the gatherer-hunter age by studying films of the Huaranis, contemporary Amazon rainforest dwellers. We notice the patient craft required to make a hunting blowgun perfect for its task of shooting monkeys in the canopy 200 feet above, the careful radial arrangement of firewood logs so that they can be inched inward to keep a cooking fire just hot enough, the ingenious arrangement whereby a dead monkey's tail is tied to its leg to provide a carrying sling for the trip home through the jungle.

Later, as anthropologist Jared Diamond has it, came the Fall—settled agriculture, which required subjugation of human life to the requirements of fixed plots of land, the perennial needs of domesticated animals, the tending of seed stores. Agriculture could feed more human mouths than gathering and hunting; that is why people ultimately came to tolerate it. But it also made possible the appropriation of surplus food by armed men, the raising of vast armies, the building of gilded temples (and universities, and jails), and in short the hierarchized, alienated age that we call Civilization. And it began the long processes of deforestation and habitat destruction, leading to mass extinction of other species, that make our species unique in its relation to the Earth—and multiply our difficulties in inventing livelihoods that do not contribute to the degradation of the natural order.

We learn from Ester Boserup, a historian of early peoples, that gatherer-hunter humans resisted agricultural life with every ounce of their instinct and strength. It took many centuries before they were grudgingly broken to it. The burdens that farming laid on formerly free-ranging peoples of miserable repetitive toil, of fixity amounting almost literally to enslavement in place, of unreliable outputs from limited food plants, first posed for human beings the basic question being wrestled with in this book: are we gaining our livelihood in the right way? And if not, what can we do about it?

There was of course another revolution after the agricultural one, and its consequences for human freedom and happiness were no less dire: the industrial revolution. In this era, so much clearer to us and more accessible to documented historical study, the surprising amount of religious holiday time allowed in the European Middle Ages was done away with, along with piety, in the name of profit; child labor and the fourteen-hour day were considered normal; peasants whose lives before the enclosures (which drove them off the land, into the factory cities) had at least provided the variety of tending animals, sowing and reaping, seeking firewood and game in the common woods, and enjoying village life, were now reduced to machine-tending automatons. (We recognize them as fellow victims, for instance, in photos of rows of factory girls at their cloth-weaving looms, where we can only wonder at the wildness of the Huarani.) Under such circumstances, it is questionable whether any livelihood except on the fringes of society can offer much in the way of rightness. Some of us seek peace in those fringes, which can be beautiful and valid habitats; others look ahead instead, to a post-industrial, ecological age, and do what we can to hasten its coming.

Buddhism, richly represented in this book, distinguished itself at an early date by grappling with the spiritual aspects of work, and did so in a free-spirited and nonhierarchical doctrine for which I have great respect. The achievement of a kind of ecological Buddhism, hints of which were outlined by E.F. Schumacher, may be the next great challenge of Buddhist thought. But, to remain with the thinkers represented in this volume, Robert Aitken notices that on the Earth "we are all eating each other," and sees in compassion—a sense of the suffering of others, included in that wonderful Buddhist phrase "all beings"—the root of wisdom. Yet I miss, in some Buddhist thinking, a biological sense of our common existence here on the planet, a species gone amok, industriously subjugating each other and what is left of nature, preparing some unimaginable ecocatastrophe in which nature—which bats last, as Stephanie Mills reminds us—will probably have to reduce our numbers and our impacts to levels that she can support.

Looking back, the industrial revolution sharply decreased the rightness of most livelihoods. The pace of environmental destruction grew enormously; human degradation on the job was almost unimaginable, especially through the monotony and ferocious pace of factory work; the enclosure and destruction of the commons removed people's sense of sharing a natural world of forest and grassland; a relentless division of labor removed all sense of meaning from the production process. Even now, when we are supposedly protected by laws, regulations, and union contracts, few other animals would put up with living as we live, confined and boxed and cabined; indeed many species, when captured and put in zoos, literally die first.

Another biological sign of our lack of right livelihoods is the charac-teristic and pathetic helplessness of most modern people, who cannot fix their own plumbing or even grow their own tomatoes. (Or face the moral and ecological questions in eating meat, much less kill animals themselves.) If we cannot perform such essential work to provide for ourselves, we become dependent, in a way that would be despised by any peasant or tribesperson, or by the resourceful Pennsylvania hillbil-lies among whom I grew up. What we call work today fits us for unbe-lievably narrow competences; we are good only at securing money, not at producing what we need. To provide our necessities, we must hire specialists, and then wonder why we feel that our lives are out of con-trol. It is no wonder that so many of us feel that work is something we must do in order to afford a vacation and that no work could possibly truly feel right.

The essays in this book offer many important insights about atti-tudes through which work can become an important spiritual discipline. And they often ingeniously suggest strategies by which we can arrange our individual work lives so that they are less demeaning, less damaging to ourselves and others and the environment, more productive of solid satisfactions and joys. They offer recommendations for what I once called "interstitial living"—finding small habitats where we might be happy, nestled inside the general desolation. But I want to worry a more gen-eral and underlying problem: Is it possible to imagine widely shared work patterns, not just the achievements of a lucky few, that would really be fitting for creatures like us, without "going back to the stone age"?

It is not only Buddhists, of course, who have noticed the work prob-lem. The early French socialist Fourier charmingly thought that even the nastiest work would find takers in his egalitarian communes (chil-dren who liked to play in the muck could carry away the garbage). In the thinking of Marx and the Marxists we can sense an attempt to see how oppressive work could, like the state itself, someday dissolve away in what we might now call an automated classless society perhaps made up of people "following their bliss" in Joseph Campbell's injunction. The poisoning of work by wages and wage relationships has been a neglected yet always recurrent theme in social thought.

If our objective is, within the perspective of an ecologically sustain-able future, to recapture the interpersonal supportiveness and the directness and importance and liveliness and variety and conviviality of "primitive" work—to make work feel right again—how might we manage it? How can we satisfy the natural needs of head, hand, and heart? Perhaps, in designing and redesigning whatever jobs are really essential to attain a satisfying civilization, we can find and stick to some useful—and practical—principles.

One I would recommend is that no job should be exclusively nonmanual. "Executives" have lately learned to move their fingers on keyboards without suffering status shock; it would be salutary if everybody was expected to have a certain amount of competence and responsibility for mechanical things. Buddhists have regarded manual labor (even cleaning toilets) as essential to enlightenment for a thousand years. And it is a joy to use our astounding physical capacities and do physical things well, so our jobs should make such satisfactions possible.

Another principle stems from the fact that, as Japanese companies have found, regular rotation of personnel from job to job builds a more flexible, versatile, and resilient cadre of employees—who may also be less bored and more loyal; so people should not be expected to remain in any one job slot for more than, say, a year. Humans are spontaneous, playful, irregular creatures; the discipline that nature has equipped us for is not that of maximum efficiency and profitability, but the discipline of mixed survival strategies, and it must be possible to give work variety, so that it reflects this heritage. Make the erratic and fortuitous quality of gathering and hunting behavior part of work life, not just of shopping!

Yet another principle (surely not the last) is that of shared responsibility in work. Humans can be individualistic, but we are also a species very good at teamwork, and it has a deep fascination for us. No job, therefore, should make its holder work alone for long; at the least, there should be alternations of joint and solitary activity. And in a larger sense, the ultimate in teamwork is worker-ownership of enterprises, which is spreading rapidly through the wreckage of large-corporation business. It seems to me a promising development from a human point of view, since it cuts through the pretense of management-controlled "empowerment" programs and gives owner-employees real power and responsibility. Moreover, an employee-owned and controlled company can sometimes be a little like a tribal village in itself, reducing the gulf between work and the rest of life which has such a schizoid effect on us, and reminding us that one of the chief "products" of an industrial enterprise is the quality of life that it provides for its inhabitants.

If sizable numbers of people begin to think that these principles (or something like them) ought to apply to their jobs, society will ultimately have to respond, just as it has had to begin to respond, painfully and grudgingly, to our demands for gender neutral pay scales, for cigarette-smoke-free air on the job, for the reduction of job safety hazards, and so on. That will make it easier to begin making livelihoods right in the spiritual sense as well. Both kinds of concern, it seems to me, are essential if we are to make our society appropriate for the kinds of beings we are.

Doing Well by Doing Good

Man matures through work
Which inspires him to difficult good.
                    —Pope John Paul II

Joyful is the accumulation of good work.
                    —The Buddha

CLAUDE WHITMYER

Doing Well by Doing Good

I emerged from the shower, greeted by the smell of freshly brewed coffee. I dressed, a bit reluctant to put on yesterday's clothes again, but
having no real choice until payday. I had landed a job as an apprentice
civil engineer, which meant days divided between drawing plot plans in
the office and laying them out in the field so the bulldozers could begin
grading.

I threw the bed covers up over the pillow and double checked my
pockets for wallet, knife, and the few bills of lunch money I had left for
the week. I made my way into the kitchen just as my older brother turned
off the stove to let the percolator come to a halt. We had enjoyed mornings like this, my brother and I, since I had joined the ranks of the working men in my family. Up early to share a quick breakfast, and then off
to the work of the day. Sometimes it was work that required thinking,
sometimes it required sweat. It helped support our family, and gave us a
kind of status. We worked, we made a contribution, and we were proud.

FINDING RIGHT LIVELIHOOD

Work is something I've always done. For me, working is basic, like eating and sleeping. I've never considered for a moment that I wouldn't

work. If I had all the money I needed or could do whatever I wanted, I know I would still work. For me, working is a way of being fully alive. It is more than the identity by which others know me. Work is the place in time and space where I am most fulfilled. And work provides me with most of the opportunities I have to practice mindfulness.

In the beginning, work meant spending-money and parental approval. My earliest memories of work go back to when I was eight years old. In the winter and spring I sold greeting cards door to door, and in the summer and fall I mowed lawns. By the time I was twelve, making money became more important than receiving praise, although that was still important too. I began to discriminate between jobs on the basis of how much they paid, even if the work was embarrassing. Baby-sitting, for example, always paid much better than yard work. So I baby-sat, even though boys weren't "supposed" to.

I began regular work when I was fourteen, as a grocery bagger and produce clerk at the corner market near my family home. I worked every day after school until eight at night, earned $1.17 an hour, and gave all my weekly paychecks to my mother. This little ritual marked a kind of coming of age, a passage into manhood. I worked every day and paid my way. This is what men did, and now I was doing it too. It didn't matter that my mother gave me most of the money back as a kind of allowance. In my mind, I paid rent. I bought groceries. I was a working man.

During the next ten years I held more than two dozen jobs, and I approached each one with the same "beginner's mind" of openness and eagerness to learn. I found this approach both alluring and rewarding, and, accidentally, in what I thought was a search for better pay, I began to leave jobs when they no longer excited or challenged me. Soon, the strategy became an almost purposeful quest for new challenges that would bring back that experience of "beginner's mind." By the time I was twenty-five and out of graduate school, I had worked as a coffee shop busboy, gas station attendant, bookstore clerk, librarian's assistant, office clerk, supply clerk, museum assistant, day-care teacher, apprentice civil engineer, swimming pool cleaner, motel desk clerk and night auditor, data analyst, research assistant, teaching assistant, shipping clerk, animal health technician, apprentice wild animal trainer, apprentice cabinetmaker, carpenter's helper, graphic artist, and cosmetic compounder.

Often, after a short time on the job, I would be promoted to some sort of supervisory position. In this capacity I worked as the inventory manager in a bookstore, crew boss on a surveying team, route manager at a swimming pool maintenance company, administrative assistant on a research project, production manager of a soap manufacturing company, general manager of a public warehouse, and corporate manager for a startup computer company.

Thus, I was introduced to the demands and difficulties of working with others. Increased responsibility led to increased challenge, and an increase in the amount of time it took for my "beginner's mind" to fade.

After ten years of working for others, my fantasies about being my own boss began to be too frequent and too strong to ignore. When the opportunity appeared for me to own my own company, I leaped at it, and for the next ten years, I began exploring what it meant to be the one with whom the buck stopped. During this second decade of my working life, I owned and managed my own natural cosmetics manufacturing company, a wood-burning stove distribution company, and an alternative energy/appropriate technology retail store. Many of the strategies I had developed as a worker were still useful to me, especially my supervisory style. But, it soon became clear that the strategy of moving on to a new job when things became boring and tedious simply didn't work when I was the one in charge.

Because of the value I placed on "beginner's mind," I felt encouraged to find a way to experience that state without repeatedly starting over. By this point in my life I had begun an active meditation practice as well as the regular practice of Aikido and T'ai Chi Ch'uan. Mindful sitting contrasted with mindful movement, in a way that allowed me to see how I might carry the "beginner's mind" from the cushion into daily life. I began to experiment with this at home and on the job, and soon developed many specific practices that actively cultivated mindfulness. Mixing, bottling, and labeling cosmetics; ordering, stacking, and delivering woodstoves; taking inventory; stocking shelves; dealing with customers; working with employees; keeping the books; answering the telephone; making sales calls; every business task I encountered became an opportunity to practice mindfulness.

In the third decade of my working life I became a small business consultant and began learning about the close working relationship of consultant with client. Because of the emphasis I had personally placed on the practice of mindfulness, I was better able to provide advice that was specifically relevant to my clients. I was also able to offer them some guidance, mostly by example, in the use of mindfulness within their own lives. This emphasis on mindfulness practice has become an integral part of my work with clients, and, it seems, I have become known for it.

It was also in this third decade that I was introduced to the relationship of community to right livelihood. In 1974, I became involved with what, at the time, was called the Briarpatch Society, a group of people who had been social activists in the 1960s and who were now entrepreneurs. What drew us together was a shared belief that business did not have to be synonymous with greed, corruption, and profit at any cost. We were among the early pioneers in a movement that has come to be known by the watchwords "environmental preservation" and "social responsibility."

Today the Briarpatch is a loosely affiliated group of about 500 members worldwide. To this day, Briar businesses are either directly involved in the environment, or are operated in a way that greatly reduces their impact on the planet. Briars believe in providing the highest quality product or service and in giving something back to their local community. We share resources—from information and financial statements to shovels and pickup trucks. From the beginning, we have shared a belief that it is important to do all we can to ensure the long-term survival of our businesses and our community. To this end, we donate money to hire a coordinator who arranges technical advice and emotional support for members, as it is needed.

In 1982, I was invited to join the team of volunteers that provided the technical advice to Briarpatch businesses, and in 1984, I was asked to serve as coordinator.

My experience with Briarpatch has clearly illustrated the value of doing work that benefits and is supported by a personal community. By sharing resources and interests in the course of the day-to-day operations of their businesses, members of Briarpatch offer each other a rich source of community-based support that has no geographical boundaries.

Briars value right livelihood. Their first newsletter, *The Briarpatch Review*, was subtitled "A Journal of Right Livelihood and Simple Living." To Briars, right livelihood means not only work that doesn't hurt living beings or the environment, but work that also pays the bills.

In 1974, when the Briarpatch was first organized, a widespread set of stereotypes existed that equated doing good with being poor. A religious cleric was supposed to be "poor as a church mouse." If you were creative, you became a "starving artist." If you wanted to do good, the story went, you had to work for either a church or a nonprofit, and if you did, you worked for peanuts.

After a decade of social activism in the 1960s, Briars found themselves doing business in the 1970s, but doing it in a way that simultaneously offered quality and benefit to the community, and still made an honest profit. By supporting one another, we were supporting all kinds of ethical, virtuous businesses and that these businesses could make a profit and still be run in the context of a personal set of values. The increasing visibility in the mainstream of companies such as Esprit, Ben & Jerry's, Patagonia, The Body Shop, and many others has begun to make this truth apparent.

Throughout my thirty-plus years of work, I have experienced terrific jobs and terrible jobs. It is clear to me now that, while many factors determine whether a job is personally fulfilling, the single most important one is responsibility. The more responsibility I was given, the more fulfilling the work became. Another important factor was creative latitude. When I was allowed to use my own imagination and resources to solve my work challenges, the job was far more rewarding than when I was forced to follow someone else's idea about the "only and best" way of doing things. I guess that's why I just naturally gravitated from working for wages to entrepreneurship, then consultancy, and finally to the work I have discovered that gives me the most latitude, writing.

The relationship of responsibility and creative latitude to job satisfaction held true for me whether or not supervision, management, and, finally, ownership were involved. The few jobs where my bosses were smart enough or lucky enough to have provided me with greater responsibility and a chance to participate in the creative part of the work were also the jobs I found most rewarding. My apprenticeships, in civil engineering, wild animal training, and cabinetmaking, come to mind.

Does this mean that entrepreneurship is the ultimate right livelihood? I think the answer might be yes, if we allow ourselves to redefine entrepreneurship so that it applies to a certain approach to work by employees as well as owners.

The word "entrepreneur" comes from the French *entreprendre*, which means "to undertake." Entreprendre, in turn, comes from the Latin *inter* (between or among) and *prahendere* (to take before, to grasp, to seize, to hold). In its modern connotation, the word "entrepreneur" is taken to mean one who takes an enterprise into his or her own hands.

As we learn more and more about what it takes to make any enterprise work, we learn that the owner can't do it alone. Workers who take things into their own hands are increasingly seen as the key to success in organizations of all sizes. As Tom Peters explains in *Liberation Management*, "Think about your corner grocer. Think about a line worker, or even a middle manager, in a big, traditional firm. The former is a businessperson, no mistake. The latter 'fills a job slot.' What a difference. The most fundamental building block of the new organization is the 'businessperson,' or 'informated individual,' 'case worker,' 'care pair,' 'mass customizer.' Emerging organizational forms will permit—and the market will demand—that each employee be turned into a businessperson."[1]

If you read "entrepreneur" for businessperson, you can see each employee taking things into his or her own hands, being empowered by having access to all the information necessary to make on-the-line, in-the-moment decisions that keep customers satisfied and the corporation accountable to its workers and its community. This is what Peters is saying, and this is the trend that encourages me to think of each of us as an entrepreneur, doing our own right livelihood, taking our lives and our livelihoods into our own two hands, doing well by doing good.

WHAT IS RIGHT LIVELIHOOD?

For most of us today, our identity hinges on what we do to make a living, and the search for meaningful work is becoming a concern for more and more of us. We want work that contributes to the individual and community welfare while doing no harm.

The concept of "right livelihood" originally came to us from Buddhism. It is part of the Buddha's "Eightfold Path" and is intended to guide us in finding our way in life.

THE FOUR NOBLE TRUTHS[2]

The Buddha lived 2,500 years ago in the southern region of present-day Nepal. After years of travel, study, and application of the many forms of spiritual practice available to him, he discovered a life way that produced a clear, calm, centered state of intuitive wisdom and insight into life. The Buddha called his new practice "The Middle Way" to emphasize that the truth about life is found neither in the manic pursuit of sensual gratification nor in the desperate pain of self-mortification. He taught that one should mindfully practice a middle way of moderation.

The Buddha's Middle Way reflects the realization that once human beings have met their basic needs for food, clothing, shelter, and medicine ("the Four Requisites"), then the very biological nature that makes survival possible becomes a barrier to self-discovery and self-realization. This biological nature depends on the biomechanical processes of attraction and repulsion common to all living things. In what scientists call the "more evolved animal forms," these processes have developed into desire and craving, which help us find food when we are hungry, clothing and shelter when we need protection from the elements or danger, and a mate when we feel lust, thus guaranteeing that we live long enough to create more human beings. Without a way to reduce, eliminate, or regulate craving, our biological nature continues to do its job and we continue to experience the attraction and repulsion of everyday life. Thus our biological nature can drag us endlessly along, caught in the treadmill of birth and death, what the Buddha called *samsara*. This profound insight has come to be known as "the Four Noble Truths." Briefly, they are:

1. Suffering exists.
2. Suffering arises from attachment to desire.
3. When attachment to desire ceases, suffering ceases.
4. Freedom from suffering is cultivated by practicing the Noble Eightfold Path of the Middle Way.

Suffering is present in the world, despite our many and varied attempts to deny it and "get on with our life." The deepest, most persistent suffering comes from attachment to our desires, and our inability to accept the inevitability of change. Attachments cease when we let go of our fixed notions about the world and begin to accept things as they are, even while working to change some of them. As a result, suffering ceases. The way to learn to do this, the Buddha tells us, is to practice the Noble Eightfold Path.

The Noble Eightfold Path of the Buddha's Middle Way is more a process than a rigid set of laws or rules. It is meant to help us recognize that there is more to life than survival—that we human beings can grow and experience richer, fuller lives—that each of us has an inner true nature that we realize by listening to our intuitive wisdom.

While right livelihood is specifically mentioned as the fifth of the eight folds,[3] one must practice all eight. Right livelihood arises from the diligent practice of the entire Eightfold Path and cannot be seen in isolation.

THE THREEFOLD PATH OF THE MIDDLE WAY	THE NOBLE EIGHTFOLD PATH
Wisdom	*Right[4] View*
	Right Thought
Morality	*Right Speech*
	Right Action
	Right Livelihood
Meditation	*Right Effort*
	Right Mindfulness
	Right Contemplation

Figure 1. The Noble Eightfold Path as it corresponds to the Threefold Way.

The Middle Way is made up of the Threefold Way of Morality, Meditation, and Wisdom, which correlates with the Noble Eightfold Path (see Figure 1). In the first stage, "Wisdom," we develop an intellectual understanding of the truth about life: that all things are interdependent, that we do not exist apart from the rest of creation, with some special

right to exploit nature for our personal benefit. The Vietnamese Zen
monk Thich Nhat Hanh elaborates:

> If you are a poet, you will see clearly that there is a cloud floating in
> this sheet of paper. Without a cloud, there will be no rain; without
> rain, the trees cannot grow; and without trees, we cannot make pa-
> per. The cloud is essential for the paper to exist. If the cloud is not
> here, the sheet of paper cannot be here either. So we can say that the
> cloud and the paper inter-are. Interbeing is a word that is not in the
> dictionary yet, but if we combine the prefix "inter-" with the verb "to
> be," we have a new verb, inter-be. Without a cloud we cannot have
> paper, so we can say that the cloud and the sheet of paper inter-are.
>
> If we look into this sheet of paper even more deeply, we can see the
> sunshine in it. If the sunshine is not there, the forest cannot grow. In
> fact, nothing can grow. Even we cannot grow without sunshine. And
> so, we know that the sunshine is also in this sheet of paper. The paper
> and the sunshine inter-are. And if we continue to look, we can see
> the logger who cut the tree and brought it to the mill to be trans-
> formed into paper. And we see the wheat. We know the logger can-
> not exist without his daily bread, and therefore the wheat that became
> his bread is also in this sheet of paper. And the logger's father and
> mother are in it too. When we look in this way, we see that without
> all these things, this sheet of paper cannot exist.
>
> Looking even more deeply, we can see we are in it too. This is not
> difficult to see, because when we look at a sheet of paper, the sheet of
> paper is part of our perception. Your mind is in here and mine is also.
> So we can say that everything is in here with this sheet of paper. You
> cannot point out one thing that is not here—time, space, the earth,
> the rain, the minerals, the soil, the sunshine, the cloud, the river, the
> heat. Everything coexists with this sheet of paper. That is why I think
> the word inter-be should be in the dictionary. "To be" is to inter-be.
> You cannot just be by yourself alone. You have to be with every other
> thing. This sheet of paper is, because everything else is.
>
> Suppose we try to return one of the elements to its source. Suppose
> we return the sunshine to the sun. Do you think that the sheet of
> paper will be possible? No, without sunshine nothing can be. And if
> we return the logger to his mother, then we have no sheet of paper
> either. The fact is that this sheet of paper is made up only of "non-
> paper elements." And if we return these non-paper elements to their

sources, then there can be no paper at all. Without "non-paper elements," like mind, logger, sunshine and so on there will be no paper. As thin as this sheet of paper is, it contains everything in the universe in it.[5]

Comprehending this interdependence is the activity of the first fold of the Eightfold Path, known as "Right View."

Fold two is "Right Thought," the volitional counterpart of Right View. This refers more to the motives behind what you do, as reflected in your thinking. It might better be understood as right "purpose." Motives or intentions arise from values. The clearer you are about your values, the clearer your vision of life and your personal purpose. Once you have gained an intellectual understanding of interdependence, you can begin to uncover your true inner nature—your values, vision, and purpose. Fold three, "Right Speech," introduces us to the second stage of the Middle Way, the practice of "Morality." Right Speech calls us to avoid lying and deceit, but it also includes the active cultivation of honesty and the elimination of gossip, backbiting, and harsh, rude, or insulting language, and all unnecessary speech.

In fold four, "Right Action," we continue to practice Right View and Right Thought or Purpose in the rest of our behavior. The Buddha provided specific guidelines for Right Action in the form of "the Five Basic Precepts" which invite us to refrain from killing, stealing, irresponsible or inappropriate sexuality, lying, and intoxication from alcohol and drugs.

In fold five, "Right Livelihood," we are encouraged to make our living only in ways that avoid deceit, treachery, trickery, and usury. Five occupations are specifically condemned: trading in arms, living beings, flesh, intoxicants, and poison. Obviously, anyone following the Eightfold Path cannot work in a munitions factory, a butcher shop, a liquor store, a pesticide company, a company whose wastes kill wildlife, a gambling hall, or a brothel. Hunting and fishing would also be prohibited. In short, a Buddhist practicing "right livelihood" can do no work that might hurt living beings or the environment.

Fold six, "Right Effort," advocates cultivation of what is wholesome in thought and action and elimination of what is unwholesome. This includes specific advice against greed, gluttony, hatred, anger, delusions, and fantasies.

With folds seven and eight, "Right Mindfulness" and "Right Contemplation," we move into the third stage of the middle path, "Meditation." Right Mindfulness refers to the ongoing mindfulness of body, feelings, thoughts, and objects of thought. Right Contemplation takes place in four phases. The first phase uses our powers of conceptualization and discursive thinking to let go of unwholesome desires, leaving us in a state of joyful well-being. The second phase involves allowing these mental activities to come to rest until we find ourselves in a centered, focused state of concentration upon the object of our meditation. Our sense of joyful well-being continues. In the third stage, we move beyond joyful well-being. We experience instead a simple alertness and awareness of our surroundings. In the final stage, we lose any sense of a boundary where *we* end and the world begins. At this point, our intellectual understanding of the Eightfold Path evolves into an experiential one. Having overcome the obstacles to the comprehension of life as it really is, we manifest spontaneous, unmotivated action completely appropriate to the present moment.

This newfound comprehension allows us to explore the entire Eightfold Path in a deeper way, and this in turn leads to a richer, fuller life. Not a life free from pain and suffering, necessarily—bad things *can* happen to good people—but a life free from the cravings and attachments that cause so much unnecessary pain and suffering. Life is filled with complexities and difficulties, successes and rewards. We struggle to follow the Middle Way, doing our best and returning again and again to the path whenever we lose our way. Thus, we come to understand life less with our intellect and more with our heart.

RIGHT LIVELIHOOD IN THE TWENTIETH CENTURY

As Socrates said long before the twentieth century, the unexamined life is not worth living. It is obvious that the Middle Way taught by the Buddha is a comprehensive set of practices that allow us to make a thorough examination of our lives, to learn to tell what is helpful to ourselves and others from what is harmful, to identify sources of suffering and ways to transform them.

Buddhism slowly began to enter American life in the late 1800s. By the 1950s, it had arrived in full force, and today it is a major religion in this country. With the assimilation that inevitably occurs when two cultures meet, certain key concepts began to be integrated into the everyday thoughts of Americans. This is especially true with the concept of right livelihood. Buddhist beliefs in honesty and integrity have also had a profound influence on the rediscovery of the Judeo/Christian/Islamic values of honesty and mutual caring. These values, shared by many Americans, had begun to erode under the widespread onslaught of greed, corruption, and consumption that has characterized the twentieth century. But in recent years, more and more people have begun to take a closer look at their lives and their personal values, and more and more are seeking meaning and fulfillment, as reflected in the burgeoning new academic interest in ethics in business, as well as the increasing number of books such as *Work with Passion, Working from the Heart,* and *Living on Purpose,* to name a few. In my personal experience with nearly 200 clients seeking right livelihood guidance in the last four years, I have found the question of values to be one of the primary motivations for seeking a change in work life.

Witness also the phenomenon of "downshifting," whereby busy, successful corporate managers quit their jobs and opt for a slower pace, a lower income, and a simpler life. In addition to a book entitled *Downshifting,* a slew of books with titles such as *Doing Best by Doing Good, Doing Well while Doing Good,* and, most recently, *Doing Well and Doing Good: The Challenge to the Christian Capitalist,* have suddenly appeared. The concern about ethics in business, set off by the profiteering and financial scandals of the 1980s, has increasingly led to the requirement that those seeking advanced business degrees must add ethics to their coursework. Membership in organizations such as the Canadian Centre for Ethics and Corporate Policy has surged to an all-time high as corporations try to integrate morality into the workplace. Concern for an increased presence of spirituality in the workplace has led to a boom in books such as *New Traditions in Business: Spirit and Leadership in the 21st Century* and *Reawakening the Spirit in Work: The Power of Dharmic Management,* as well as a new batch of corporate success stories such as *Body and Soul: Profits with Principles* and *The Republic of Tea: Letters to a Young Zentrepreneur.*

As the concept of right livelihood has been absorbed by twentieth century Western culture, its meaning has expanded beyond the Buddhist idea of doing no harm, to include the ideas that work should make a difference in the world, benefit the community, and be personally fulfilling. As we move toward the twenty-first century, the world of work will undoubtedly be shaped by today's trends. It is our hope that this book can serve to raise the level of the discussion among all who seek meaningful work now and in the future.

Right livelihood is not just a philosophical ideal. It is a practical, achievable reality. Finding and maintaining right livelihood does require regular, consistent action, but the steps are clear and the results immediate. Finding your own right livelihood depends primarily on getting in touch with your "beginner's mind." Mindfulness challenges us to stay with things as they are and to change our lives through action that harms no one. Working together, mindfully and compassionately, we can create a community in which all our livelihoods are "right."

ABOUT THIS BOOK

Included here are contributions from Buddhist commentators and secular contributors alike, a balanced cross section of the best writing on the subject of right livelihood, ranging from essays that clarify key concepts to first-person accounts of the quest for and discovery of right livelihood.

The underlying themes throughout are: (1) it is not necessary to sacrifice one's true self in order to make a living and, therefore, (2) right livelihood *can* be a practical reality.

Many of us today are anxious to find richer, fuller lives that are at the same time simpler and more meaningful. We long to do work that makes a difference and that contributes to our personal welfare, the welfare of those we love, and our community in general. We hunger for clear guidance on how to find work that satisfies our heart and still pays the bills. Finding "right livelihood" is fundamental and will only increase in importance as we enter the twenty-first century.

The essays in this book are organized into eight sections that parallel the divisions of the Eightfold Path. Since the Eightfold Path is made up of interpenetrating, mutually illuminating practices, any collection of writings using this framework should reflect this interpenetration and mutual illumination. It is obvious therefore that most of the essays in this collection could have been placed in more than one section. The choice of how to group them is arbitrary and dictated more by my personal predilection than by any strong argument or aesthetic principle.

In this introduction, "Right View—Doing Well by Doing Good," I have attempted to lay the groundwork, set the tone, and create a direction for the rest of the book.

Contrary to what some people think, spiritual work does not take place only in a monastery or cloister. In fact, most of us in the West are never going to have the opportunity to escape, for more than a few days at a time, to the quiet safety of a retreat center. We must meet our responsibilities as householders and workers—keep our homes, raise our families, do our jobs, pay our bills—and, at the same time, feed our spirits. After all, right livelihood is essentially spiritual work.

Since the concept of "right livelihood" originally comes from Buddhism, it is fitting that Section Two, "Right Thought—A Few Good Words from a Few Good Teachers," samples the voices of several of today's Buddhist teachers, each speaking directly to the subject of right livelihood. The chosen selections represent neither the depth nor breadth of the available teachings; rather, they introduce the *essence* of right livelihood from a Buddhist perspective and lay the conceptual groundwork for the remainder of the book.

Because the principle of "right speech" calls us to avoid lying, deceit, gossip, backbiting, rude language, and unnecessary speech, it is easy to mistake total silence as the goal. We might remember, though, that right speech is a part of the practice of morality, which calls for us to actively cultivate honesty. Right speech is made up of the honest words necessary to living with other human beings.

For me, honest tales of moral behavior are the obvious result of mastery of right speech. Section Three, "Right Speech—Stories and Reflections," is made up of just such tales—the stories of real people doing their best to carry out good and meaningful work. Also included in this section are essays about ways of working and ways of paying attention that help to differentiate work that is "right" from that which is not.

In Section Four, "Right Action—Economics As If People Matter," we look at the bigger picture of right livelihood's economic, social, and ethical implications. The Buddha taught that right action begins with the Five Basic Precepts, which invite us to practice refraining from killing, stealing, irresponsible or inappropriate sexuality, lies, and intoxication from alcohol and drugs. This is why right action is considered by Buddhists to be part of the practice of morality. Like most Buddhist concepts, however, there is much more to right action than appears at first glance. Right action can lead us to a better life. A part of that better life is improved material welfare, not as an end in itself, but to provide the basic level of material security needed to cultivate a rich spiritual life.

Right action is applied to life as a whole, in all its social, economic, and political aspects. The Buddha taught that poverty was the root cause of immorality and criminal behavior, which could be eradicated if economic conditions improved. So, right action also includes working on our economic and social welfare. It means taking action to understand the true purpose and meaning of economics and money as well as taking action to behave in accordance with personal moral behavior in the workplace.

In Section Five, "Right Livelihood—Mindfulness and Meaningful Work," we take a more in-depth look at the nature of work itself to see what makes it "right" or not. In many ways, right livelihood is a narrowing of the focus we obtain by practicing right action. Traditionally, Buddhism encourages us to make our living in ways that avoid deceit, treachery, trickery, and usury. Five occupations are specifically condemned: those that trade in arms, living beings, the flesh of animals, intoxicants, or poison. This recommendation about what constitutes right livelihood is sometimes stated as a resolution to "refrain from doing work that harms other living beings."

As already explained, you cannot practice right livelihood in isolation. Even if you refrain from the five prohibited trades—even if you have a job that does not require deceit, treachery, trickery, or usury—you must still attempt to apply moral guidelines to your thought, speech, action, effort, mindfulness, and contemplation in order for your livelihood to be "right." It is not enough for your job to be deeply meaningful; it must also provide you with the opportunity to practice mindfulness in everyday life.

In Section Six, "Right Effort—Overcoming Obstacles," we examine the obstacles and dangers that can arise in our own work lives and the conditions necessary for the practice of right livelihood. The practice of right effort is the cultivation of what is wholesome and the elimination of what is unwholesome in thought and action. While Buddhist writings include specific cautions about greed, gluttony, hatred, anger, delusions, and fantasies, the essence of right effort is a focus on the inner obstacles to mindfulness—the urges of the body, the entreaty of emotions, and the rationalization and imaginings of the mind. We face these obstacles in two different but equally necessary ways: first, by creating an environment conducive to mindfulness practice, and, second, by diligent efforts to recognize what is helpful and what is harmful in our individual lives, and to cultivate the helpful while eliminating the harmful.

In Section Seven, "Right Mindfulness—Awakening in Daily Life," we examine the actual practice of mindfulness. Right mindfulness is the lifelong practice of staying awake and aware in the present moment. By engaging in gentle, steady mindfulness exercises, we build a personal practice that can lead to a more meaningful work life and way of being—not necessarily a life free from suffering, but one that is rich and full.

Over the past decade, I have had the opportunity to work as guide to hundreds of individuals seeking right livelihood. In Section Eight, "Right Contemplation—Using Mindfulness to Find Meaningful Work," I offer food for thought by summarizing what I have learned from my experience as a right livelihood guide as well as my own three decades of self-study on the application of mindfulness to the discovery and support of personally meaningful work.

HOW TO USE THIS BOOK

The essays in this book are both thought-provoking and practical. I encourage you to allow yourself to engage with the contents of each essay as you read it. Make notes in the margins or a journal or start a discussion group with your friends. When you read an essay that contains practical exercises, please take the time to try them. Engaging with the content of this book will add a dimension of experience that reading alone cannot provide.

This is a book about using mindfulness to find meaningful work. I have come to think of meaningful work as an inherent right. Recent opinion polls reflect a widespread belief that people want the work they do to make a contribution to their community and society. Work is no less necessary for our emotional and physical health than food or shelter. It doesn't take much effort to realize that putting people to work costs a great deal less than housing and feeding the homeless or catching and imprisoning those driven by poverty to commit crime.

My hope is that this book will expand and enhance what you know about finding and maintaining right livelihood and that it will stimulate you to join those of us who are working toward the day when everyone can find meaningful work. I also hope this collection helps reveal the value of mindfulness practice in developing inner peace, an increased sense of self-worth, and deep insight that can help you find your personal purpose. And I hope it will guide you in identifying the kind of work that makes the most sense for you. I also encourage you to use some of the mindfulness techniques offered in this book to awaken a new attitude that might even help your current work become more "right," even while you identify and seek the work you truly wish to do.

The real purpose of work is to give us an opportunity to practice being human—to discover everything we are and all that we can be, both as individuals and as members of a community. As psychologist Marsha Sinetar puts it, "Work can be used, as can anything and everything we do, to communicate our love for self and other. For the rare person who is religiously or spiritually inclined, work even becomes a vehicle for devotion, a way of utilizing one's gifts and talents to serve others, a way of truthful self-expression." This is reminiscent of that famous quote from *The Prophet* by Kahlil Gibran, "When you work you are a flute through whose heart the whispering of the hours turns to music. To love life through labor is to be intimate with life's inmost secret. All work is empty save when there is love, for work is love made visible."

NOTES

[1] New York: Alfred A. Knopf, 1992, p. 227.

[2] Buddhism was passed on as an oral tradition for the first six centuries of its 2,500-year history. Like most oral traditions, the teachings, therefore, are presented in ways that are easy to memorize: hence, the Four Noble Truths, Eightfold Path, etc.

[3] An understanding of the Eightfold Path is fundamental to the understanding and practice of the Buddha's teachings. The word "path" should not be taken literally. It is not meant to suggest that you follow a narrowly prescribed line to reach some goal. In truth, each link in the Eightfold Path arises simultaneously and is inseparably associated with all the other links. This is why, although it is not commonly done, I have chosen to refer to each link of the Eightfold Path as a "fold." To me the Eightfold Path is a garment that covers my entire being. I know the garment as a whole. I can look at each of its folds, but I am protected from the elements by the entire garment. This fact of interconnectedness, or "interbeing," is true of all Buddhist lists. To practice fully any element on any of these lists is to practice all the elements of the whole list. Thich Nhat Hanh calls this the "methodology of interbeing."

[4] "Right" is the most common translation of the Pali prefix samma (Skt. samyak) which is also sometimes translated as "Perfect" or "Complete." "Samma" translates literally as "contact" or "together with" and is used here to give the sense of a wholeness or completeness that can only be obtained by practicing all eight of the folds simultaneously.

[5] The Heart of Understanding (Berkeley: Parallax Press, 1988), pp. 3-5.

A Few Good Words from a Few Good Teachers

> *Those who see worldly life as an obstacle to Dharma see no Dharma in everyday actions; they have not yet discovered that there are no everyday actions outside of Dharma.*
>
> —Eihei Dogen

WALPOLA RAHULA

Buddhism in the "Real World"

The belief that to follow the Buddha's teaching one has to retire from life is a misconception. There are numerous references in Buddhist literature to men and women living normal family lives who successfully practiced what the Buddha taught and realized *nirvana*. Vacchogatta the Wanderer once asked the Buddha straightforwardly whether there were laymen and laywomen leading the family life, who followed his teaching successfully and attained high spiritual states. The Buddha categorically stated that there were not one or two, not a hundred or two hundred or five hundred, but many more laymen and laywomen leading the family life who followed his teaching successfully and attained to high spiritual states.[1]

It may be agreeable for certain people to live a retired life in a quiet place away from noise and disturbance. But it is certainly more praiseworthy and courageous to practice Buddhism living among your fellow beings, helping them, and being of service to them. It may perhaps be useful in some cases for a person to live in retirement for a time in order to improve his or her mind and character, as preliminary moral, spiritual, and intellectual training, to be strong enough to come out later and help others. But if someone lives an entire life in solitude, thinking only of his or her own happiness and salvation, without caring for fellow beings, this surely is not in keeping with the Buddha's teaching which is based on love, compassion, and service to others.

Those who think that Buddhism is interested only in lofty ideals, high moral and philosophical thought, and that it ignores the social and economic welfare of people, are wrong. The Buddha was interested in the happiness of people. To him happiness was not possible without leading a pure life based on moral and spiritual principles. But he knew that leading such a life was hard in unfavorable material and social conditions.

Buddhism does not consider material welfare as an end in itself, but it does recognize the need of certain minimum material conditions favorable to spiritual success. The Buddha did not take life out of the context of its social and economic background; he looked at it as a whole, in all its social, economic, and political aspects. His teachings on ethical, spiritual, and philosophical problems are fairly well known. But little is known, particularly in the West, about his teaching on social, economic, and political matters. Yet there are numerous discourses dealing with these scattered throughout the ancient Buddhist texts. Let us take only a few examples.

The *Cakkavattisihanada-sutta*[2] clearly states that poverty (*daliddiya*) is the cause of immorality and crimes such as theft, falsehood, violence, hatred, cruelty, and so forth. Kings in ancient times, like governments today, tried to suppress crime through punishment. The *Kutadanta-sutta*[3] says that this method can never be successful. Instead the Buddha suggests that, in order to eradicate crime, the economic condition of the people should be improved: grain and other facilities for agriculture should be provided for farmers and cultivators; capital should be provided for traders and those who are engaged in business; adequate wages should be paid to those who are employed. When people are thus provided for with opportunities for earning a sufficient income, they will be contented, will have no fear or anxiety, and consequently the country will be peaceful and free from crime.

Because of this, the Buddha told laypeople how important it is to improve their economic condition. This does not mean that he approved of hoarding wealth with desire and attachment, which is against his fundamental teaching, nor did he approve of each and every way of earning one's livelihood. There are certain trades, like the production and sale of armaments, which he condemns as evil means of livelihood.

A man named Dighajanu once visited the Buddha and said, "Venerable Sir, we are ordinary laymen, leading the family life with wife and children. Would the Blessed One teach us some doctrines which will be conducive to our happiness in this world and hereafter?"

The Buddha tells him that there are four things that are conducive to a man's happiness in this world. First, he should be skilled, efficient, earnest, and energetic in whatever profession he is engaged, and he should know it well (utthana-sampada); second, he should protect his income, which he has thus earned righteously, with the sweat of his brow (arakkha-sampada)—(This refers to protecting wealth from thieves, etc. All these ideas should be considered against the background of the period.); third, he should have good friends (kalyana-mitta) who are faithful, learned, virtuous, liberal, and intelligent, who will help him along the right path away from evil; fourth, he should spend reasonably, in proportion to his income, neither too much nor too little, i.e., he should not hoard wealth avariciously, nor should he be extravagant—in other words, he should live within his means (samajivikata).

Then the Buddha expounds the four virtues conducive to a layman's happiness hereafter: (1) Saddha: He should have faith and confidence in moral, spiritual, and intellectual values. (2) Sila: He should abstain from destroying and harming life, from stealing and cheating, from adultery, from falsehood, and from intoxicating drinks. (3) Caga: He should practice charity and generosity, without attachment to and craving for wealth. (4) Panna: He should develop wisdom which leads to the complete destruction of suffering, to the realization of nirvana.[4]

Sometimes the Buddha even went into details about saving money and spending it, as, for instance, when he told the young man Sigala that he should spend one-fourth of his income on his daily expenses, invest half in his business, and put aside one-fourth for any emergency.[5]

Once the Buddha told Anathapindika, the great banker and one of his most devoted lay disciples, who founded for him the celebrated Jetavana monastery at Savatthi, that a layman who leads an ordinary family life has four kinds of happiness. The first happiness is to enjoy economic security or sufficient wealth acquired by just and righteous means (atthi-sukha); the second is spending that wealth liberally on himself, his family, his friends and relatives, and on meritorious deeds (bhoga-

sukha); the third is to be free from debts *(anana-sukha);* the fourth happiness is to live a faultless and a pure life, without committing evil in thought, word, or deed *(anavajja-sukha).* It must be noted here that although three of these kinds of happiness are economic, the Buddha then reminded the banker that economic and material happiness is not worth one-sixteenth part of the spiritual happiness arising out of a faultless and good life.[6]

From these few examples, one can see that the Buddha considered economic welfare as requisite for human happiness, but that he did not recognize progress as real and true if it was only material, devoid of a spiritual and moral foundation. While encouraging material progress, Buddhism always lays great stress on the development of the moral and spiritual character for a happy, peaceful, and contented society.

The Buddha says, "Never by hatred is hatred appeased, but it is appeased by kindness. This is an eternal truth."[7] "One should conquer anger through kindness, wickedness through goodness, selfishness through charity, and falsehood through truthfulness."[8]

Buddhism aims at creating a society where the ruinous struggle for power is renounced; where calm and peace prevail away from conquest and defeat; where the persecution of the innocent is vehemently denounced; where one who conquers oneself is more respected than those who conquer millions by military and economic warfare; where hatred is conquered by kindness, and evil by goodness; where enmity, jealousy, ill-will, and greed do not infect men's minds; where compassion is the driving force of action; where all, including the least of living things, are treated with fairness, consideration and love; where life in peace and harmony, in a world of material contentment is directed towards the highest and noblest aim, the realization of the ultimate truth, nirvana.

NOTES

[1] *Majjhima-nikaya,* I (Pali Text Society of London edition), pp. 30-31.

[2] *Digha-nikaya,* No. 26, ed. Nanavasa Thera (Colombo, 1929).

[3] Ibid.

[4] *Anguttara-nikaya,* ed. Devamitta Thera (Colombo, 1929) and Pali Text Society of London, p. 786.

[5] *Digha-nikaya*, III, ed. Nanavasa Thera (Colombo, 1929), p. 115.

[6] *Anguttara-nikaya*, ed. Devamitta Thera (Colombo, 1929) and Pali Text Society of London edition, pp. 232-233.

[7] *Dhammapada*, ed. K. Khammaratana Thera (Colombo, 1926), I, 5.

[8] Ibid, XVII, 3.

TARTHANG TULKU

Skillful Means

Working is the natural human response to being alive, our way of participating in the universe. Work allows us to make full use of our potential, to open to the infinite range of experience that lies within even the most mundane activity. Through work we can learn to use our energy wisely so that all of our actions are fruitful and rich.

It is our nature as human beings to be satisfied and fulfilled. Work gives us the opportunity to realize this satisfaction by developing the true qualities of our nature. Work is the skillful expression of our total being, our means to create harmony and balance within ourselves and in the world. Through work we contribute our energy to life, investing our body, our breath, and our mind in creative activity. By exercising our creativity we fulfill our natural role in life, and inspire all beings with the joy of vital participation.

Each of us has a sense of the role work plays in our lives. We know that work can draw on every part of our being, bringing our minds, our hearts, and our senses into full play. Yet it is unusual in these times to become this deeply involved in our work. In today's complex society, we have lost touch with the knowledge of how to use our abilities to lead effective and meaningful lives. In the past, education played an important role in transmitting the knowledge needed to integrate learning and experience, to manifest our inner nature in a practical way. Today, this vital knowledge is no longer passed on. Thus our general understanding of work is limited, and we seldom realize the deep satisfaction that comes from working skillfully, with our total being.

Perhaps because we do not have to exert our full effort to meet our basic needs, we rarely put our hearts and minds fully into our work; in fact, working just enough to get by has become the norm. Most people do not expect to like their work, much less to do it well, for work is commonly considered as nothing more than a means to an end. Whatever our occupation, we have come to think of work as a time-consuming part of our lives, a duty that cannot be avoided.

If there is a strong enough incentive to work hard, we may do so, but if we look carefully at our motivation, we see it is often narrow in scope, directed primarily toward gaining status, increasing personal power and private domain, protecting the interests of name and family. This kind of self-centered motivation makes it difficult to express and develop our human potential through work. Rather than grounding us in the positive qualities of our nature, the working environment fosters qualities such as competition and manipulation.

There are those who, in reaction to this situation, may choose to avoid work altogether. When we take this view, we may believe we are pursuing a higher virtue. But rather than finding a healthy alternative that can increase our enjoyment of life, we actually limit our potential even more. For living without working causes us to draw back from life itself. By denying our energy expression in work, we unknowingly cheat ourselves of the opportunity to realize our nature, and we deny others the unique contribution we could make to society.

Life exacts a price for less than full participation. We lose touch with the human values and qualities that spring naturally from a full engagement with work and life: integrity, honesty, loyalty, responsibility, and cooperation. Without the guidance these qualities give to our lives, we begin to drift, prey to an uneasy sense of dissatisfaction. Once we have lost the knowledge of how to ground ourselves in meaningful work, we do not know where to turn to find value in life.

It is important for us to see that our survival in a broad sense depends on our willingness to work with the full power of our minds and hearts, to participate fully in life. Only in this way will we realize the human values and qualities that bring balance and harmony to our lives, to our society, and to the world. We cannot continue to ignore the effects of selfish motivation, of practices such as competition and manipulation. We need a new philosophy of work based on greater human understanding, respect for ourselves and others, and an awareness of the qualities and skills that create peace in the world: communication, cooperation, and responsibility.

This means being willing to face work openly, to look honestly at our strengths and weaknesses, and to make the changes that will improve our lives. If we genuinely devote our energy to improving our attitude toward work, developing what is truly valuable within us, we can make all of life a joyful experience. The skills we learn while working will set the tone for our growth and give us the means to bring satisfaction and meaning into each moment of our lives, and into the lives of others as well. Working in this way is working with skillful means.

Skillful means is a three-step process that can be applied to any situation in our lives. The first step is to become aware of the reality of our difficulties, not simply by intellectual acknowledgment, but by honest observation of ourselves. Only in this way will we find the motivation to take the second step: making a firm resolve to change. When we have clearly seen the nature of our problems and have begun to change them, we can share what we have learned with others. This sharing can be the most satisfying experience of all, for there is a deep and lasting joy in seeing others find the means to make their lives fulfilling and productive.

When we use skillful means to realize and strengthen our positive qualities at work, we tap the precious resources that lie awaiting discovery within us. Each of us has the potential to create peace and beauty in the universe. When we develop our abilities and share them with others, we can deeply appreciate their value. This deep appreciation makes life truly worth living, and brings love and joy into all of our actions and experience. By learning to use skillful means in all that we do, we can transform daily existence into a source of enjoyment and accomplishment that surpasses even our most beautiful dreams.

JOHN DAIDO LOORI

The Sacredness of Work

Our ordinary daily tasks can become opportunities to practice. When students reach a certain point of maturity in *zazen*, their work, their life, everything they do develops an equivalent clarity and integrity. Work emerges as an active function of zazen and provides an opportunity to examine our habits, our way of doing things.

The selflessness taught and practiced in a monastic environment tends to conflict with the self-indulgence generally encouraged in our society. In the *zendo* (meditation hall), we bow to each other; in the subway, we push each other. In the monastery, we serve; in the world, we take. The monastery can begin to take the form of a sanctuary—but it is more like a furnace within which, through our training, we can forge a life of strength, gracefulness, and self-confidence to meet the situations we each face every day. Our practice is not about isolating ourselves on some mountaintop, dwelling in tranquility while rejecting the busy activity of the world, but manifesting the *buddhadharma* in everything we do, so that the secular is indeed the sacred. This is what we need to see in order to make the practice of work function as an aspect of our Zen training.

There are many ways to practice work. We can look at it as just "a job to be done," or as simply a way to pass the time, to prevent boredom or idleness. We can also look at it as a sacred activity, as a manifestation of the miracle of being alive. What we practice in the zendo is the "heart of the matter," the core that needs to express itself in everything we do. Zazen (meditation) is not just sitting cross-legged on a pillow; it is growing a garden, getting to work on time, getting the job done.

The foundation of work practice is mindfulness, a state of consciousness in which the body is relaxed, the senses are alert, and the mind is clear and focused on the task at hand. This attentiveness is direct experience. Mindfulness is not static; it moves with the events in our daily life. There are times when we need to totally put ourselves into the task at hand: this is "holding fast," single-pointedly concentrating. At other times, it is necessary to "let go," to release and move on. Our tendency is to stick—to move on to the next thing, while still carrying the debris of the last thing with us. Mindfulness develops the ability to flow, concentrate, and remain in the present.

Some people have the misconception that planning and scheduling are not what Zen Buddhists do. But planning is not goal-oriented—it exists right now; scheduling exists right now. Without a plan, our work tends to become scattered, inefficient, and ineffective. We can get caught up in goals and forget that the goal and the process that brings us to that goal are the same reality—just as "good" and "bad" are the same reality, just as heads and tails are two sides of the same coin. Each step, each action that brings us closer to the goal, is the goal itself. One is not before and the other after; both exist simultaneously. When we realize this, our preoccupation with the goal disappears and we are fully aware of the present moment. Then, each step is vivid, and can be experienced totally.

One of the important parts of work practice is preparation, the placing of everything required for the job in a state of readiness. The work, tools, and materials are laid out. A number of years ago I began a process of ritualizing my preparations to photograph by taking very deliberate steps in laying out my camera, film, light meter, and other equipment, putting it all together, getting ready to go out and photograph. I found that the process was also putting my mind in a state of readiness, awareness.

The Zen arts are highly developed forms of work practice. In teaching a Zen art, theory is rarely dealt with. The art is taught and communicated by practice itself. For example, the teacher of *sumi-e* often does not speak a word in his first meeting with his students. The class sits and waits; the master enters, bows to the students, and then proceeds to his work space. There, he carefully lays out his equipment—the paper, the brushes, the ink tray, and the ink stick—and begins to examine the tools to select the ones he will use. Then he adds a bit of water to the tray and begins rubbing the ink stick in the tray very slowly, producing the ink. This process is itself a meditation; each breath corresponds to one stroke in mixing the ink. When the right consistency, thickness, and tone have been produced, he sets the ink stick aside, selects a brush, and carefully examines the blank paper. He sits in the presence of the empty space on the paper, feels the space, realizes the space fully. Then he wets his brush with just the right amount of ink and in a single breath executes a painting, a whole landscape. The entire process may take half an hour to forty-five minutes of preparation and clean-up time, but the actual production of the painting takes place in a single breath. Those who have the opportunity to observe such masters at work can see their single-pointedness of mind and attention to detail. There are characteristics common to all these masters regardless of whether they are painters, masters of the bamboo flute, or martial artists: a kind of spontaneity, professionalism, and free-flowing action is inevitably evident.

Work practice can also be a teacher if we regard it that way. After the work is laid out, the next step is doing it. The art of this step is to really "do what you are doing while you are doing it." In other words, to be fully present. To experience the breath in zazen, be it...be the *koan* ...be zazen itself. To be the work is no different.

When the work is finished, there is a sense of completion, just as there is a sense of completion when you have finished a painting, a photograph, a performance. It is time to let go. Time to bow and acknowledge the teaching. It doesn't matter whether you are bowing to something animate or inanimate; in either case, you are bowing to yourself. There is nothing outside you, unless you put it outside yourself, and you can only do that by the way you use your mind. To really complete it, clean up, put the tools away, pick up the loose ends, "leave no trace." This means the dishes are washed and put away, the counters are wiped, the sink is clean, the floor is swept and mopped, the garbage is emptied. No trace remains that someone has eaten. Everything looks natural and ordinary. Of course, this also means not being excessive about it: "no trace" means no trace.

We also face problems in work practice that function as the koans of our everyday life. They can be handled in the same manner as the koans we work with in zazen. How do you deal with problems that come up when you are sitting in the zendo? When you are sitting, staying with your breath, and you hear a sound that reminds you of something that reminds you of the next thing, and the next thing, and suddenly you are a thousand miles away and the breath has been forgotten while you become immersed in whatever scenario you are developing. When you realize that you are not involved with the breath any longer, but are involved with a thought: you look at the thought, acknowledge it, let it go, and come back to the breath. You don't evaluate it, analyze it, love it, or hate it. If the thought pops up again, you go through the process again: look at it, acknowledge it, let it go, and return your attention to the breath. Each time you bring the attention back to where you want it, you reinforce your power of concentration. And if the thought continues to recur, you let it happen. Be it. If fear keeps coming up, be the fear. Allow it; give it free range. Be the thing itself; don't separate from it. Each time you separate from it, it gets bigger. The more you pull away from it, the more powerful it becomes. Then, after it has exhausted itself, completed its cycle, let it go and return to the breath.

The same process takes place with work practice. Each time you become distracted, you acknowledge what is happening, let the thoughts go, and return your attention to your work. Sometimes in work practice just as in zazen, we get "stuck." This is what interview with the teacher is for. You can use interview as an opportunity to look at and work with the problem in a different way. It becomes a koan. And the koans that rise out of our own sitting or out of our work are often the most powerful koans of our life. A problem is just another name for an opportunity to really put yourself into your practice. It is easy to practice when everything is going smoothly, but to sit hard is to sit when sitting is difficult. It is also the place that generally is the most productive, because the things that are most difficult for us almost always have the most to teach us.

Another aspect to consider in work practice is silence. Silence doesn't mean not speaking when it is necessary, answering the phone or giving instructions, but cutting down on the unnecessary chatter, the talk that is there just for the sake of talking. When it is necessary to speak in order to communicate, we should do so; when it is time to be silent, we should be able to do that, too. This means being not only outwardly silent, but also silencing the inner dialogue, our habit of constant talking to ourselves. Practicing silence and avoiding idle talk helps develop the clarity, receptiveness, and concentration necessary for good work practice.

This way of working is not "spacey," preoccupied, or trancelike. It is very much alive, filled with life's force—awake and alert. It is the mind of the Way itself. Chao-chou once asked Nan-ch'uan, "What is the Way?" Nan-ch'uan answered, "Ordinary mind is the Way." "Then should we direct ourselves toward it or not?" asked Chao-chou. "If you try to direct your self toward it, you go away from it," answered Nan-ch'uan. Ordinary mind is the mind that sleeps when it is tired and eats when it is hungry. This is the buddha mind, the mind of work practice.

Layman P'ang said, "Isn't it wonderful? Isn't it marvelous? I chop wood and carry water." We should see that life itself and all of its activity are the perfect manifestation of the buddhadharma. This very life is the life of the Buddha, and the secular activities of this life are the Dharma itself. But we should be aware, as Master Dogen says, that "to carry the self forward and realize the secular is delusion; that the secular advances and realizes the self is enlightenment." To "carry the self forward" means to separate yourself. That the "secular advances" means to be one with the object of your attention. The secular world itself becomes your life, and its inherent liberation is constantly manifested. If you still do not believe it, consider your breath for a moment. Bring it in from the atmosphere that surrounds you, taste it, fill your body with it, enjoy it. Now let it go, return it to the environment—isn't it a miracle, this life of ours?

ROBERT AITKEN

Right Livelihood for the Western Buddhist

I am large…I contain multitudes.
                    —Walt Whitman

The notion of engaged lay Buddhism, popular among progressive Western Buddhists, is rooted in earlier Buddhist movements, notably the Kamakura Reformation of thirteenth century Japan. Honen, Shinran, Nichiren, and some of the early Zen masters empowered their lay followers with responsibility for the Dharma itself, rather than merely for its support. In this process they made Buddhism more relevant to Japanese needs and expectations.

The acculturation of Buddhism in the West is a process of further empowering laymen and women. Christian, Jeffersonian, and Marxist ideals of equality and individual responsibility and fulfillment are as alive in our hearts as ideals of Confucianism, Taoism, and Shinto were for our Far Eastern ancestors. Our task is to make Buddhism accessible in the context of Western culture, and to be as clear about this task as Shinran and Nichiren were about making Buddhism Japanese.

This task begins with examining what the old teachers said and did not say about their own traditions, and then considering what we might say in turn. For example, Hakuin Ekaku declared that all beings by nature are Buddha, and "this very body is the Buddha." However, he did not say that this very body is a "bodhisattva," a being enlightening the world.

I interpret this omission as a limitation of the Mahayana. There can be something passive in "This very body is the Buddha." It is Shakyamuni simply accepting himself under the Bodhi tree. He is completely enlightened, but nothing is happening. It was not until he arose and sought out his former disciples that he began to turn the Wheel of the Dharma. This is the process that Buddhism itself has followed over the centuries and millennia. It has, for the most part, sat under the Bodhi tree appreciating itself and only gradually come to remember its myriad, faithful disciples.

Yet all those disciples—ordinary people as well as monks and nuns; birds and trees as well as people; so-called inanimate beings as well as birds and trees—are clearly the responsibility of the Mahayana Buddhist, who vows every day to save them. This faith of ours, the great vehicle transporting all beings to the other shore, emerged 2,000 years ago; but strangely enough, so far as I know no teacher has commented on the vows and said in so many words, "You yourself are the Mahayana. You yourself with your modest limitations are responsible for ferrying people, animals, oceans, and forests across." Surely, with the entire Earth in grave danger, it is time that such things be said.

Regrettably, social responsibility has been framed negatively in Buddhism so far. In setting forth "right livelihood," for example, the Buddha was explicit about wrong livelihood, such as butchering, bartending, manufacturing arms, guarding prisoners, and pimping. Yet the pursuit of such harmful occupations is surely just the most basic kind of transgression. It seems to me that the Western Buddhist might be asking what is right livelihood after all? What is "right lifestyle?" What is the great endeavor that fulfills our bodhisattva vows—not just in the monastery but in daily life?

Turning back to our sources, we find the bodhisattva Kuan-yin offering answers. By her very name, Kuan-yin hears the sounds of the world—the sounds of suffering, and the sounds of joy as well. She hears the announcements of birds and children, of thunder and ocean, and is formed by them. In one of her representations she has a thousand arms, and each hand holds an instrument of work: a hammer, a trowel, a pen, a cooking utensil, a vajra. She has allowed the world to cultivate her character, and also has mustered herself to develop the skills to make her character effective. She is the archetype of right livelihood: one who uses the tools of the workaday world to nurture all beings and turn the Wheel of the Dharma.

Nurturing begins with the experience of inclusion. "I contain this new life," the pregnant woman finds, and this experience sustains her as a mother. Like Mary, she knows that she is mother of all. And like Mary, Kuan-yin too contains everyone and everything. To be intimate the way Kuan-yin is intimate, and to walk her path, is to hear the many sounds within my own skull and skin, and to find that my skull and skin are as porous as the starry sky. The starry sky inhabits my skull and skin.

The genius of the *Hua-yen* (Skt. *Avatamsaka) Sutra* uses a starry image to illustrate inclusion. This is the Net of Indra, multidimensional, with each point a jewel that perfectly reflects all other jewels, and indeed contains all other jewels. Another image in that sutra is the Tower of Maitreya, which the pilgrim Sudhana finds to be beautifully adorned, containing an infinite number of other towers. On entering one of those towers, he finds it also to be beautifully adorned, containing an infinite number of still more towers. Here the androgynous nature of Buddhist archetypes seems to break down. Perhaps if Kuan-yin rather than Maitreya had been the final teacher of Sudhana, we might be stepping into the cavern of Kuan-yin, each cavern beautifully adorned, containing an infinite number of other caverns, and each one of those caverns all-inclusive too.

Thich Nhat Hanh's felicitous expression for inclusion is "interbeing." When you experience interbeing personally, then fulfillment of yourself is the fulfillment of all. Your practice of Kuan-yin is turning the Dharma Wheel with your particular skills—not for, but with everyone and everything as a single organism.

The drive for fulfillment is embodied in another archetype: the Buddha as a baby. Taking seven steps in each of the cardinal directions, he announced, "Above the heavens, below the heavens, only I, the World-honored one." This is the cry of every newborn, human and non-human, animate and inanimate. "Here I am! I begin and end here!"

Completely unique! There is no one else with your face—never has been, never will be. This is the "nirmanakaya"—the special self that has come together by mysterious affinities. There is no essence, and each of the affinities depends on all others. Together they form one kind of bundle here, and another kind of bundle there. Now a child, now a fish, now a stone or cloud.

Each bundle is an eager avatar of the great universal potential, each one drinking in the sounds of mother, father, sisters, brothers, animals, wind in the trees, sea on the shore—with personal and particular talent. Fulfillment of that talent is the abiding passion of infants of every species. It continues to be the passion of life as it unfolds with the satisfactions of consummation to the very last breath. Human beings share this passion with all beings, including those that are called inanimate. See how the stone resists destruction, how the soil heals itself.

Yet with dedicated effort the stone can be destroyed and the soil killed, just as human beings can be stifled—and cows, lambs, chickens, trees, and a thousand other beings can be exploited by harmful livelihood. This exploitation is so fierce today that we are using up the world the way a drunk uses up his body—heading for a premature death. This will be not only your death and mine. It will be the death of Shakespeare and Beethoven and Sesshu, of Mary and Kuan-yin, of oceans and forests.

Human beings are solely responsible for creating this headlong drive to destruction, and only human beings can turn it about. The extra turn of DNA in human genes brings forth awareness that we as individuals include all other people, as well as animals and plants, and it brings forth our motive to name them. The drive to realize this awareness and to reify the names can lead to a conspiracy to exploit all beings for the aggrandizement of a single center, or to a conspiracy to let the countless flowers bloom: the Mayan weaver, the duckbill platypus, the *Hibiscus kauaiensis*, the common sparrow. When this uniqueness and variety is given scope it is the forest at climax, the farm burgeoning with vegetables, the city in one hundred festivals, the stars on course.

In the farm or forest or desert or river or ocean, fulfillment of one is the fulfillment of all in a dynamic system of constant destruction, renewal, evolution, and entropy. With diligent cultivation, you and I can find that the Buddha's own experience of containment is, after all, our own. We can find the vast universal process to be the panorama of our own brains. Gradually it becomes clear just how to help maintain the whole universe at climax.

At the same time, of course, we are, all of us, eating each other. Destruction and renewal join in Shiva's dance. Trees died that this book might live. Beans die that I might eat. Even at the kalpa fire, when all the universes are burned to a crisp, the flames of that holocaust will crack the seeds of something; we don't yet know what. Meantime, with minds as broad as can be, my lifestyle and yours will be modest and hearts will be thankful. It will be clearly appropriate to do this and not to do that. Kuan-yin has a boundless sense of proportion.

Proportion is a matter of compassion, and by "compassion" I refer back to the etymology of the word: "suffering with others." Twenty-five years ago I traveled extensively in Asia, and in some countries I observed mansions surrounded by high walls that were topped with broken glass set in concrete. In the United States the walls are more subtle, but there they are: a hundred different styles of exclusiveness. Yet everything is still interdependent. The slums sustain the suburbs. The suburbs sustain Palm Beach. Palm Beach sustains the prisons. Prisons sustain the judges. Wrong livelihood does not disprove the Buddha.

So the question becomes, How does one practice? As early Zen teacher Yung-chia said: "The practice of the Dharma in this greedy world—this is the power of wise vision." Right livelihood is in the middle of the Eightfold Path—the Path that begins with Right Views : "We are here only briefly, and we are parts of each other."

Hui-neng, who was a key figure in the establishment of Zen in China and who was Yung-chia's teacher, said, "Your first vow, to save the many beings, means, I vow to save them in my own mind." Easy to parrot, difficult to personalize—but if they are saved there, really saved, and we move our bottoms from beneath the Bodhi tree and exert ourselves with our own well-developed skills, then there is hope.

Hope, because willy-nilly we are in intimate communication. We are not a scattering of isolated individuals with the same ideas, but an organism, with each cell perfectly containing all other cells. Color one green, and all are green. Your idea is a virus in my blood, mine in yours.

These are not just Buddhist notions, but perennial truths clarified by nearly simultaneous events across the world, bringing the promise of peace, social justice, and genuine concern for the living Earth, where violence, repression, and exploitation ruled before.

STEVEN D. GOODMAN

Transforming the Causes of Suffering

Right livelihood" is a way of earning a living, or using one's energies, that is "in tune with increasing helpfulness for beings and decreasing harmfulness," as it says in the *Dhammapada*. But it is not always easy to determine what is "helpful" and what is "harmful."

In the Buddhist tradition, what is helpful and wholesome (Skt. *kusala*) and what is harmful and unwholesome (Skt. *akusala*) is not defined according to the dictates of society, or family values, nor even according to one's most cherished opinions. What is "helpful" is anything that encourages or empowers an individual or group to discover and then transform the causes of suffering—be they psychological, interpersonal, social, or economic. And "harmful" is anything that discourages, blocks, or disempowers an individual or group from discovering the causes of suffering and their transformation.

A lifestyle dedicated to this transformation is a matter of exploration and discovery. Shakyamuni Buddha was once characterized as the "great analyzer." He said that his observations were not divine commandments for which he had special insight but rather discoveries he made through the hard work of calm and direct inquiry. He was simply sharing them with others, and if people found them useful, if they tested them according to their own standards and the observations held up, then that made them useful. If the observations didn't hold up, then they could try something else.

It is not easy, however, to gain such calm and direct insight into suffering and its causes. In part this is because the "laws," values, and customs of society often serve to control, entrap, and beguile its citizens, mesmerizing them so they are discouraged from seeking out actual sources of suffering. A lifestyle dedicated to a fearless investigation of suffering and the cessation of suffering is very rare.

The Buddhist teaching recognizes that there is a wide latitude in the interest, propensities, and capabilities of people. Some are characterized as the "common, foolish people" (Skt. *balaprtagjana*), who just try to cope with things as they are. Others are "noble" (Skt. *arya*), for they seriously take the challenge to discover and transform suffering, and they begin to regulate their lives accordingly. One of the big differences between these two is the attitude they take toward the relationship between intention and action.

The common, foolish people say: "There is no particular relationship between thought and action. It's all random." Or, they might say: "It doesn't really matter, because we are just a biophysical system, and our consciousness is part of that system, so when we die that's it, everything comes to an end. Therefore, let's just eat, drink and be merry." This attitude is very prevalent in modern society and is actively reinforced in the consumer driven mass media. According to traditional Buddhist values, however, this viewpoint is nihilist. The modern scientific worldview, as heir to the secular traditions of so-called humanism, would also be classed as nihilist, for according to this now dominant view, life and the essentials of being human are just a kind of higher cognitive organization of the biophysical organism, and when the "assembly" breaks down, that's death. Period.

How does this position differ from that of the teachings of Buddhism? I think this is a key question, for we are now experiencing a collision of paradigms, and we have to adjudicate these different worldviews. Buddhists tend to say that there is an intimate relationship between thoughts, intentions, wishes, and urges, on the one hand, and actions and their effects on the other. For better or worse, they say, our intentions, or at least the effects of them, go on forever. Our ability to do good or harm is extremely powerful. Whether one accepts the notion of previous lives or future lives, minimally what one can say about a Buddhist's understanding is that intentions leave their traces.

The context within which we formulate what is healthy or harmful, worthwhile or not, is to a large extent already determined by a nexus of circumstances that we have inherited—psychological, cultural, political. To a large extent, the inherited patterns of which we are a part determine our intentions, lifestyles, projects, and ideas of livelihood. We have inherited these patterns and we have to act within them, but there is, at the same time, a tremendous latitude in which we can foster faculties and sensitivities that ever increasingly develop our ability to discover and transform sources of suffering.

How is this possible? What is it in our makeup that allows us to overcome these predetermining patterns? The Buddhist philosophers developed different metaphors to address this question, but they all seemed to agree on the key point that there are meaningful consequences to one's thoughts, intentions, and actions.

In general, Buddhists say that we have an "inherent" or "unsullied" wisdom, an "insight" that can be cultivated and that makes it possible to overcome the conditions that lead to harmful consequences. Under the right circumstances, we can "decant," and then discard the incidental conditioning that habituates us to aggression, acquisition, and bewilderment. Mahayana Buddhists often use the analogy of dust on a mirror. The dust of conditioning accumulates on the surface of our "inherent wisdom" mirror, yet with effort the dust can be removed. One can learn to live increasingly at the level of the mirror itself, which means bringing out our inherent capacity to accurately reflect "things as they are," freed from the distortions of emotional or cognitive bias.

The discovery that there are such things as "helpful" and "harmful" actions is the preliminary work, and it has a profound effect on what we regard as right versus wrong livelihood. "Helpful" and "harmful" are not values imposed from the outside, they depend on the unique circumstances of each individual. When one has begun to work on oneself, when one takes seriously the notion that intentions radically affect consequences, then through the development of calm observation one can discover there are two types of intention, those that help us uncover sources of suffering, and those that harm us or prevent us from doing so. If we accept this characterization that the existential discovery that "wholesome" and "helpful" intention is whatever empowers an individual to discover sources of suffering, then we are in a position to determine what constitutes right livelihood.

For example, let us say that you are involved in the health care field. As a health worker, your practice of right livelihood might in part involve looking deeply at what you are doing to see which health practices actually "empower" and which "impede" the discovery into sources of suffering. When you help people with their bodily health you are helping create a more stable situation in which they can use their native intelligence to discover wholesome ways of being. When they are not distracted by bodily aches, pains, or worries, they can go about the business of practicing a calmer, more mindful inquiry into circumstances which foster their well-being, and the well-being of those whose lives they touch. This is an example of how our endeavors to engage in right livelihood foster in other people the growing potential for doing the same.

More generally, "right livelihood" is any activity motivated by the intention to bring knowledge about how to discover what is helpful and harmful into a language that people can understand and apply. Using the power of reason, disclosing the actual fact of suffering and its causes, communicating fearlessly, with the intention to reveal the workings of the manifold and powerful systems of contemporary mystification, these are acts which make up right livelihood. Beginning with a loving intention to ameliorate disempowering circumstances, one can discover and communicate information that shows how suppression, beguilement, and mystification take place. This is right livelihood.

There is no room for dogmatism here. What is helpful or harmful depends on the circumstances. Even when you think you are acting in "good" faith, it may turn out later that you have not done any good after all. The main thing is to stay really clear about your intentions through the practice of internal monitoring. The key to right livelihood, I think, is to begin with good intentions and then monitor the results of your actions, changing them when they are harmful. When one discovers disempowering or harmful intention at work, in oneself or in a group, it is important to note it without engaging in animosity, demonization, or scapegoating. Note the fact that abuse or harm is happening, note the sources and conditions that cause this to occur, and broadly communicate this information to the best of your ability.

According to Mahayana Buddhist traditions, all beings without exception, even the great abusers, are the way they are only because they, or the groups to which they belong, have undergone karmic condition-ing which has disempowered them, obscured their mirror of inherent wisdom with the dust of countless harmful intentions and actions. All beings, even serial killers and mass murderers, do have this "mirror"; the capacity to reflect kindness, clarity, and insight. They have the nature of a "buddha," one who has awakened from the sleep of ignorance about the nature of wholesome and unwholesome intentions. This is not to say that we condone the acts of such people, or that we do not act to neutralize the effects of their behavior. While doing so, however, one should be ever mindful not to engage in any wish for harm or injury to them. This is very difficult; only through the calm habit of watching our own intentions can we "separate" such individuals from their ac-tions, so that we might skillfully discover the conditioning forces which led to the harmful behavior, and work to transform those forces.

A major obstacle to right livelihood is confusion about what is right and what is wrong. There are many occasions where there can arise a conflict between what seems truly empowering or disempowering for an individual, and what societal norms dictate. Furthermore, we do not live in a society that encourages individuals to reflect on the potential rela-tionship between intentions and actions in a deep way. We are taught that right and wrong have been divinely revealed as commandments: "Thou shalt not." The guidelines for ethical living as laid down in the earliest Buddhist communities, however, had a very different basis. The formula is: "I voluntarily take training in abstention from...." One is in a training program, which one has consciously and voluntarily chosen. There is no shame or damnation when one's training slips—one notes the failure and continues to train. The Buddhist tradition is rather real-istic about the wide variety of temperaments amongst human beings. The defining characteristic of being human is recidivism—we back-slide, that's our nature. We train, investigate, and we fall back a bit. This is not a sin, this is how we are, and gradually, through trial and discovery, we may find ways of being that are more satisfactory.

Feeling bad about backsliding may reinforce a narrow view of what it is to be a human being: "I did this and I shouldn't have!" What is that "I"? Buddhists say it is actually a nexus of interacting causes and condi-tions. The sense of right and wrong is not something external to our lived situations. Our real work, then, is to continue to investigate and work with other like-minded people who feel it is possible to discover what is helpful and harmful without turning any particular discovery into dogma or self-righteousness.

Differentiating right from wrong is the sacred task of self-discovery, and is right livelihood in the most profound sense. It makes life worth living, a life in which the practice of gentle mindfulness fosters self-discovery. This adventure of discovery may lead one to a way of being that is wise and kind, ever ready to respond to the challenges imposed on us by this most wondrous occurrence called "life."

GARY SNYDER

On the Path, Off the Trail

WORK IN PLACE OF PLACE

Place is one kind of place. Another field is the work we do, our calling, our path in life. Membership in a place includes membership in a community. Membership in a work association—whether it's a guild or a union or a religious or mercantile order—is membership in a network. Networks cut across communities with their own kind of territoriality, analogous to the long migrations of geese and hawks.

Metaphors of path and trail are from the days when journeys were on foot or by horse with packstock, when our whole human world was a network of paths. There were paths everywhere: convenient, worn, clear, sometimes even set with distance posts or stones to measure *li*, or *versts*, or *yojana*. In the forested mountains north of Kyoto I came on mossy stone measuring posts almost lost in the dense bamboo-grass ground cover. They marked (I learned much later) the dried-herring-by-back-pack trade route from the Japan Sea to the old capital. There are famous trails, the John Muir trail on the crest of the High Sierra, the Natchez Trace, the Silk Road.

A path is something that can be followed, it takes you somewhere. "Linear." What would a path stand against? "No path." Off the path, off the trail. So what's *off* the path? In a sense everything else is off the path. The relentless complexity of the world is off to the side of the trail. For hunters and herders trails weren't always so useful. For a forager, the path is *not* where you walk for long. Wild herbs, camas bulbs, quail, dye plants, are away from the path. The whole range of items that fulfill our needs is out there. We must wander through it to learn and memorize the field—rolling, crinkled, eroded, gullied, ridged (wrinkled like the brain)—holding the map in mind. This is the economic-visual-ization-meditation exercise of the Inupiaqand Athapaskans of Alaska of this very day. For the forager, the beaten path shows nothing new, and one may come home empty-handed.

In the imagery of that oldest of agrarian civilizations, China, the path or the road has been given a particularly strong place. From the earliest days of Chinese civilization, natural and practical processes have been described in the language of path or way. Such connections are explicit in the cryptic Chinese text that seems to have gathered all the earlier lore and restated it for later history—the *Dao De Jing,* "The Classic of the Way and the Power." The word "dao" itself means way, road, trail, or to lead/follow. Philosophically, it means the nature and way of truth. (The terminology of Daoism was adopted by early Chinese Buddhist translators. To be either a Buddhist or Daoist was to be a "person of the way.") Another extension of the meaning of dao is the practice of an art or craft. In Japanese, dao is pronounced "do" (doh)—as in *kado* (the way of flowers); *bushido* (way of the warrior); or *sado* (tea ceremony).

In all the traditional arts and crafts there has been customary ap-prenticeship. Boys or girls of fourteen or so were apprenticed to a potter, or a company of carpenters, or weavers, dyers, vernacular pharmacolo-gists, metallurgists, cooks, and so forth. The youngsters left home to go and sleep in the back of the potting shed and would be given the single task of mixing clay for three years, say, or sharpening chisels for three years for the carpenters. It was often unpleasant. The apprentice had to submit to the idiosyncrasies and downright meanness of the teacher and not complain. It was understood that the teacher would test one's pa-tience and fortitude endlessly. One could not think of turning back, but just take it, go deep, and have no other interests. For an apprentice there was just this one study. Then the apprentice was gradually inducted into some not so obvious moves, standards of craft, and in-house working secrets. The apprentice also began to experience--right then, at the be-ginning—what it was to be "one with your work." The student hopes not only to learn the mechanics of the trade but also to absorb some of the teacher's power, the "mana"—a power that goes beyond any ordinary understanding or skill.

In the Zhuang-zi (Chuang-tzu) book, a third-century-B.C. witty radical Daoist text, perhaps a century or so after the *Dao De Jing*, there are a number of craft and "knack" passages:

> The Cook Ting cut up an ox for Lord Wenhui with dancelike grace and ease. "I go along with the natural makeup, strike in the big hollows, guide the knife through the big openings, and follow things as they are. So I never touch the smallest ligament or tendon, much less a main joint....I've had this knife of mine for nineteen years and I've cut up thousands of oxen with it, and yet the blade is as good as though it had just come from the grindstone. There are spaces between the joints, and the blade of the knife has really no thickness. If you insert what has no thickness into such spaces, then there's plenty of room.... That's why after nineteen years the blade of my knife is still as good as when it first came from the grindstone." "Excellent!" said Lord Wenhui. "I have heard the words of Cook Ting and learned how to care for life!"[1]

These stories not only bridge the spiritual and the practical, but also tease us with an image of how totally accomplished one might become if one gave one's whole life up to a work.

The Occidental approach to the arts—since the rise of the bourgeoisie, if we like—is to downplay the aspect of accomplishment and push everyone to be continually doing something new. This puts a considerable burden on the workers of every generation, a double burden since they think they must dismiss the work of the generation before and then do something supposedly better and different. The emphasis on mastering the tools, on repetitive practice and training, has become very slight. In a society that follows tradition, creativity is understood as something that comes almost by accident, is unpredictable, and is a gift to certain individuals only. It cannot be programmed into the curriculum. It is better in small quantities. We should be grateful when it comes along, but don't count on it. Then when it *does* appear it's the real thing. It takes a powerful impulse for a student-apprentice who has been told for eight or ten years to "always do what was done before," as in the production tradition of folk pottery, to turn it a new way. What happens then? The old guys in this tradition look and say, "Ha! You did something new! Good for you!"

When the master artisans reach their mid-forties they begin to take on apprentices themselves and pass their skills along. They might also take up a few other interests (a little calligraphy on the side), go on pilgrimages, broaden themselves. If there is a next step (and strictly speaking there need not be one, for the skill of the accomplished craftsperson and the production of impeccable work that reflects the best of the tradition is certainly enough in one lifetime), it is to "go beyond training" for the final flower, which is not guaranteed by effort alone. There is a point beyond which training and practice cannot take you. Zeami, the superlative fourteenth-century Noh drama playwright and director who was also a Zen priest, spoke of this moment as "surprise." This is the surprise of discovering oneself needing no self, one with the work, moving in disciplined ease and grace. One knows what it is to be a spinning ball of clay, a curl of pure white wood off the edge of a chisel—or one of the many hands of Kannon the Bodhisattva of Compassion. At this point one can be free, with the work and from the work.

No matter how humble in social status, the skilled worker has dignity and pride—and his or her skills are needed and respected. This is not to be taken as any sort of justification for feudalism: it is simply a description of one side of how things worked in earlier times. The Far Eastern craft-and-training mystique eventually reached every corner of Japanese culture from noodle-making (the movie *Tampopo*) to big business to the high-culture arts. One of the vectors of this spread was Zen Buddhism.

Zen is the crispest example of the "self-help" (*jiriki*) wing of Mahayana Buddhism. Its community life and discipline is rather like an apprenticeship program in a traditional craft. The arts and crafts have long admired Zen training as a model of hard, clean, worthy schooling. I'll describe my experience as a *koji* (lay adept) at the monastery of Daitoku-ji, a Rinzai Zen sect temple in Kyoto, in the sixties. We sat cross-legged in meditation a minimum of five hours a day. In the breaks everyone did physical work—gardening, pickling, firewood cutting, cleaning the baths, taking turns in the kitchen. There were interviews with the teacher, Oda Sesso Roshi, at least twice a day. At that moment we were expected to make a presentation of our grasp of the koan that had been assigned us.

We were expected to memorize certain sutras and conduct a number of small rituals. Daily life proceeded by an etiquette and a vocabulary that was truly archaic. A steady schedule of meditation and work was folded into weekly, monthly, and annual cycles of ceremonies and observations which went back to Song-dynasty China and in part clear back to the India of Shakyamuni's time. Sleep was short, the food was meager, the rooms spare and unheated, but this (in the sixties) was as true in the worker's or farmer's world as it was in the monastery. Novices were told to leave their pasts behind and to become one-pointed and unexceptional in all ways except the intention to enter this narrow gate of concentration on their koan. *"Hone o oru,"* as the saying goes— "break your bones," a phrase also used (in Japan) by workingmen, by the martial arts halls, and in modern sports and mountaineering.

We also worked with lay supporters, often farmers, in downright convivial ways. We would stand out back in the vegetable gardens with locals discussing everything from new seed species to baseball to funerals. There were weekly begging walks down city streets and country lanes, chanting and pacing along, our faces hidden under big basket hats (waterproofed and dyed brown with persimmon juice). In fall the community made special begging trips for radishes or rice to country regions three or four ranges of hills away.

But for all its regularity, the monastic schedule could be broken for special events: on one occasion we all traveled by train to a gathering of hundreds of monks at a small but exquisite country temple for the celebration of its founding exactly five hundred years before. Our group came to be kitchen-workers: we labored for days chopping, cooking, washing, and arranging alongside the farm wives of the district. When the big feast was served we were the servers. That night, after the hundreds of guests had left, the kitchen-workers and laborers had their own feast and party, and old farmers and their wives traded crazy funny dances and songs with the Zen monks.

FREEDOM AT WORK

During one of the long meditation retreats called *sesshin*, the Roshi lectured on the phrase "The perfect way is without difficulty. Strive hard!"

This is the fundamental paradox of the way. One can be called on not to spare one's very bones in the intensity of effort, but at the same time we must be reminded that the path itself offers no hindrance, and there is a suggestion that the effort itself can lead one astray. Mere effort can heap up learning, or power, or formal accomplishment. Native abilities may be nourished by discipline, but discipline alone will not get one into the territory of "free and easy wandering" (a Zhuang-zi term). One must take care not to be victimized by one's penchant for self-discipline and hard work. One's lesser talents may lead to success in craft or business, but then one might never find out what one's more playful capacities might have been. "We study the self to forget the self," said Dogen. "When you forget the self, you become one with the ten thousand things." Ten thousand things means all of the phenomenal world. When we are open that world can occupy us.

Yet we are still called on to wrestle with the curious phenomenon of the complex human self, needed but excessive, which resists letting the world in. Meditation practice gives us a way to scrape, soften, tan it. The intent of the koan theme is to provide the student with a brick to knock on the gate, to get through and beyond that first barrier. There are many further koans that work deeper into nondualistic seeing and being—enabling the student (as the tradition would like to have it) to ultimately be mindful, graceful, grateful, and skillful in daily life; to go beyond the dichotomy of natural and "worked." In a sense it's a practice of "an art of life."

The *Dao De Jing* itself gives us the most subtle interpretation of what the way might mean. It starts out by saying this: "The way that can be followed ('wayed') is not the constant way." *"Dao ke dao fei chang dao."* First line, first chapter. It is saying: "A path that can be followed is not a spiritual path." The actuality of things cannot be confined within so linear an image as a road. The intention of training can only be accomplished when the "follower" has been forgotten. The way is without difficulty—it does not itself propose obstacles to us, it is open in all directions. We do, however, get in our own way—so the Old Teacher said, "Strive hard!"

There are also teachers who say: "Don't try to prove something hard to yourself, it's a waste of time; your ego and intellect will be getting in your way; let all such fantastic aspirations go." They would say, at this very moment, just *be* the very mind that reads *this* word and effortlessly knows it—and you will have grasped the Great Matter. Such were the instructions of Ramana Maharshi, Krishnamurti, and the Zen Master Bankei. This was Alan Watts' version of Zen. One whole school of Buddhism takes this position—Jodo shin, or Pure Land Buddhism, which elegant old Morimoto Roshi (who spoke Osaka dialect) said "is the only school of Buddhism that can scold Zen." It can scold it, he said, for trying too hard, for considering itself too special, and for being proud. One must have respect for the nakedness of these teachings and their ultimate correctness. Pure Land Buddhism is the purest. It resolutely resists any and all programs of self-improvement and stands only by *tariki*, which means "other-help." The "other" that might help is mythologically described as "Amida Buddha." Amida is no other than "emptiness"—the mind without conceptions or intentions, the Buddha-mind. In other words: "Give up trying to improve yourself, let the true self be your self." These teachings are frustrating for motivated people in that no real instruction is offered the hapless seeker.

Then there have always been countless unacknowledged Bodhisattvas who did not go through any formal spiritual training or philosophical quest. They were seasoned and shaped in the confusion, suffering, injustice, promise, and contradictions of life. They are the unselfish, big-hearted, brave, compassionate, self-effacing, ordinary people who in fact have always held the human family together.

There are paths that can be followed, and there is a path that cannot. It is not a path, it is the wilderness. There is a "going" but no goer, no destination, only the whole field. I first stumbled a bit off the trail in the mountains of the Pacific Northwest, at twenty-two, while a fire lookout in the North Cascades. I then determined that I would study Zen in Japan. I had a glimpse of it again looking down the aisle of a library in a Zen temple at age thirty and it helped me realize that I should not live as a monk. I moved near the monastery and participated in the meditation, the ceremonies, and the farm work as a layperson.

I returned to North America in 1969 with my then wife and first-born son and soon we moved to the Sierra Nevada. In addition to the work with farms, trees, and politics my neighbors and I have tried to keep up some formal Buddhist practice. We have deliberately kept it lay and nonprofessional. The Japanese Zen world of the last few centuries has become so expert and professional in the matter of strict training that it has lost to a great extent the capacity to surprise itself. The entirely dedicated and good-hearted Zen priests of Japan will defend their roles as specialists by pointing out that ordinary people cannot get into the finer points of the teachings because they cannot give enough time to it. This need not be the case for the layperson, who can be as intent on his or her Buddhist practice as any worker, artisan, or artist would be with their work.

The structure of the original Buddhist order was inspired by the tribal governance of the Shakya ("Oak Tree") nation—a tiny republic somewhat like the League of the Iroquois—with democratic rules of voting.[2] Gautama the Buddha was born a Shakya—hence his appellation Shakyamuni, "sage of the Shakyas." The Buddhist sangha is thus modeled on the political forms of a neolithic-derived community.

So our models for practice, training, and dedication need not be limited to monasteries or vocational training, but can also look to original communities with their traditions of work and sharing. There are additional insights that come only from the non-monastic experience of work, family, loss, love, failure. And there are all the ecological-economical connections of humans with other living beings, which cannot be ignored for long, pushing us toward a profound consideration of planting and harvesting, breeding and slaughtering. All of us are apprenticed to the same teacher that the religious institutions originally worked with: reality.

Reality-insight says get a sense of immediate politics and history, get control of your own time; master the twenty-four hours. Do it well, without self-pity. It is as hard to get the children herded into the car pool and down the road to the bus as it is to chant sutras in the Buddha-hall on a cold morning. One move is not better than the other, each can be quite boring, and they both have the virtuous quality of repetition. Repetition and ritual and their good results come in many forms. Changing the filter, wiping noses, going to meetings, picking up around the house, washing dishes, checking the dipstick—don't let yourself think these are distracting you from your more serious pursuits. Such a round of chores is not a set of difficulties we hope to escape from so that we may do our "practice" which will put us on a "path"—it *is* our path. It can be its own fulfillment, too, for who would want to set enlightenment against non-enlightenment when each is its own full reality, its own complete delusion. Dogen was fond of saying that "practice *is* the path." It's easier to understand this when we see that the "perfect way" is not a path that leads somewhere easily defined, to some goal that is at the end of a progression. Mountaineers climb peaks for the great view, the cooperation and comradeship, the lively hardship—but mostly because it "puts you out there" where the unknown happens, where you encounter surprise.

The truly experienced person, the refined person, "delights in the ordinary." Such a person will find the tedious work around the house or office as full of challenge and play as any metaphor of mountaineering might suggest. I would say the real play is in the act of going totally off the trail—away from any trace of human or animal regularity aimed at some practical or spiritual purpose. One goes out onto the "trail that cannot be followed" which leads everywhere and nowhere, a limitless fabric of possibilities, elegant variations a millionfold on the same themes, yet each point unique. Every boulder on a talus slope is different, no two needles on a fir tree are identical. How could one part be more central, more important, than any other? One will never come onto the three-foot-high heaped-up nest of a Bushy-tailed Woodrat, made of twigs and stones and leaves, unless one plunges into the manzanita thickets. Strive hard!

We find some ease and comfort in our house, by the hearth, and on the paths nearby. We find there too the tedium of chores and the staleness of repetitive trivial affairs. But the rule of impermanence means that nothing is repeated for long. The ephemerality of all our acts puts us into a kind of wilderness-in-time. We live within the nets of inorganic and biological processes that nourish everything, bumping down underground rivers or glinting as spiderwebs in the sky. Life and matter at play, chilly and rough, hairy and tasty. This is of a larger order than the little enclaves of provisional orderliness that we call ways. It is the Way.

Our skills and works are but tiny reflections of the wild world that is innately and loosely orderly. There is nothing like stepping away from the road and heading into a new part of the watershed. Not for the sake of newness, but for the sense of coming home to our whole terrain. "Off the trail" is another name for the Way, and sauntering off the trail is the practice of the wild. That is also where—paradoxically—we do our best work. But we need paths and trails and will always be maintaining them. You first must be on the path, before you can turn and walk into the wild.

NOTES

[1] Burton Watson (trans.), *The Complete Works of Chuang Tzu* (New York: Columbia University Press, 1971), pp. 50-51.

[2] Richard Gard, *Buddhist Influences on the Political Thought and Institutions of India and Japan* (Claremont, California: Phoenix Papers, no. I, 1949).

TONI PACKER

What Is Right Livelihood?

If we want to find out about "right livelihood," where do we start?

Without giving advice or answers, having no fixed point of view, no good ideas, no set of morals or religious precepts, we start with a blank page: We don't really know what right livelihood is.

Can we question together without knowing?

A friend who has been concerned with the problem of right livelihood suggested many questions for this article:

What is helping (or helpful) work?

If I am independently wealthy, should I work? Should I "do my share," or "be of service"?

Is it important to find work that I enjoy? Work that allows me to use my "full potential." How can I find such work?

Is it important to consider the impact of what I do on the world, on other people, on the ecology, on society, etc.? Are certain jobs morally or actually "bad" or "wrong"?

Is it important to use the talents or skills we have to help society? Or is it okay to not use skills or talents one has? Or should they be put to use for the good of humanity?

Is it wrong to want money? Does "right livelihood" mean being involved in service work and not wanting money?

Could something frivolous or playful or beautiful be right livelihood?

Does the advice to "follow your bliss" or "do what you love" mean anything? Is that good advice?

How do I figure out what to do with my life? I want to help people and use my skills and enjoy what I do. What should I do? Is what I'm doing enough?

Are moral guidelines or ideas important?

What is my relationship to the poor and underprivileged? Do I have a responsibility to use the "privileges" I have (money, education, class, health) to help others?

Is it possible to do work that is "helpful" even though one is not totally free from conflict oneself?

What is creative work?

What are we going to do with all these different questions? Shall we attempt to go through them one by one? Or can we just let them be there without immediately trying to find answers?

Before seeking answers, can we look openly, quietly, inwardly, to find out where our questions about right livelihood come from?

Are they coming out of a deep sense of separateness?

Do I feel that I am separate from society, separate from the privileged or the underprivileged, separate from the world, humanity, the environment? Do I feel that life itself is something separate (apart) from me?

When I realize that the question, "What is right livelihood?" arises out of the idea/feeling of being a separate entity with its inevitable feelings of insecurity, insufficiency, discontent, guilt, loneliness, fear, and wanting, doesn't it follow inevitably that I yearn for a livelihood that will compensate me for what I feel lacking and hurting inside?

Not being aware of what motivates my drives and ambitions, won't I compulsively strive for material or human possessions, power, position, fulfillment of my potential, bliss, enlightenment, peace, or the humbleness of self-abnegation and service to others?'

Am I driven to do something helpful for humanity or the endangered planet because I feel deeply, achingly, apart from it all? Do I expect my daily work to bridge the gulf of separation between me, humanity, and nature, in order to bring about feelings of completion, wholeness, goodness, fulfillment? Can whatever work I'm doing really heal separation? Or does it distract from the disease?

Can separation be healed?

Maybe it needn't be healed at all. It may not be true! It may just be a dream dreamt by human beings like you and me from time immemorial.

Can we wake up to the fact that separateness isn't real at all—that it exists only in thoughts, images, feelings? Are we interested in finding out the truth of this? Not believing someone's pronouncements or refuting them with argumentation, but inquiring freely, patiently, deeply, alone as well as with others, into this strong sense of "me"—this "I" that feels so convincingly real and separate from everything else.

In truth we are not separate from each other, from the world, from the whole Earth, the sun, moon, billions of stars—not separate from the entire universe. Listening silently in quiet wonderment, without knowing anything, there is nothing at all but one mysteriously palpitating aliveness.

When our habitual ideas and feelings of separation begin to abate in silent questioning, listening, and understanding, then right livelihood ceases to be a problem. Whatever we may be doing during the twenty-four hours a day, be it work for money or work for fun, service, leisure, creation or recreation, cleaning toilets, or nothing at all, the doing *now*, this moment of no separation, is the fulfillment, and it affects everyone and everything everywhere. Nothing else is more worthwhile. Everyone and everything is inextricably interweaving in this mysterious fabric called life. Can we understand this not just intellectually, theoretically, but experience it profoundly?

Not feeling separate from ourselves, not cut off from each other, from the environment and life in general, but deeply experiencing the togetherness of it all, we will not need moral guidelines or religious precepts to refrain from killing, or hurting, or doing blind damage to the natural environment. I see clearly that hurting you also hurts me as well as others. Caring for you, I care for myself. Attending to what I do, I also attend to you and to the Earth on which we live.

Is what we call our full potential anything but being fully alive this very instant with all there is? Our "bliss" is living immediately, undefendedly open—in touch.

Is this love?

Stories and Reflections

Let your speech be always with grace, seasoned with salt.
    —Paul the Apostle

Speech is human, silence is divine, yet also brutish and dead: therefore we must learn both arts.
    —Thomas Carlyle

Eyesight and speech they wrought
 For the veil of the soul therein,
A time for labour and thought,
 A time to serve and sin;
They gave him light in his ways,
 And love, and a space for delight,
And beauty and length of days,
 And night, and sleep in the night.
His speech is a burning fire;
 With his lips he travaileth;
In his heart is a blind desire,
 In his eyes foreknowledge of death;
He weaves, and is clothed with derision;
 Sows, and he shall not reap;
His life is a watch or a vision
 Between a sleep and a sleep.
    —Algernon Charles Swinburne

FRAN PEAVEY

For the Love of Work

I love to work. When I used to work in institutions I was occasionally criticized by my fellow workers for working too hard, thus showing them up. One of the joys of my present self-employed life is that I can work as hard as I want to, and, even better, I can do it organically. My work fits into my life, not the other way around.

My early work history, when I was in school, had a lot of variety: recycling of clothes hangers (age thirteen), lawn mowing, raising of garden produce and selling it from my red wagon, car hop, coroner's assistant, camp counselor, restaurant work of all kinds, typist, and film booker.

LEARNING ABOUT WORK

On Saturdays when I was a young girl, I went with my father to his insurance office. It was an old office with a revolving door, walls of dark wood, and three strategically placed green spittoons. I typed, took money to the bank, and held the office open while Dad went out to talk with people. I knew what work was because I saw him doing it.

Sometimes he would take me on trips while he supervised about twenty farms for a Dutch land company. He talked to me about each family's concerns. His dual task was to meet the tenant farmer's needs and the company's needs. We measured the hay by throwing a long tape measure over the stack. I would hold one end to the ground and, across the stack, Dad would pull the round spool down to the ground on his side. He would walk into the field, pull up a few spuds, get a salt shaker from his glove box in the car and we would eat slices of raw potatoes. Often as not, we would get some fresh tomatoes or corn or maybe a couple of live chickens in a bag to take home and kill for dinner. We would drink ice water or lemonade on the front porch and talk about the farm, the weather, and politics.

For my father, the relationship was the most important part of the work. I am sure he thought about the bottom line because he made a lot of money, but his family had been in this valley for years, and he expected his children to be there years after him. The motto over his office door was: "Integrity is our business." Each transaction with the farmers was one of respect. "Almost nothing is as insecure as farming. You can work your fingers to the bone and still not make any money if it doesn't rain at the right time. So our goal is to let them know that they are secure on this farm. Then they do the best job they can." We also had to make sure they weren't stealing from the company that owned the land they worked. It was a complex relationship of trust and distrust. Dad was caught between competing interests and he was trying to work it out. I am sure much of what I know about change, people, and society comes from his talking about his goals in the car as we drove from farm to farm.

My mother's work involved much community work, keeping our family organization focused, and developing new and broader goals and skills. She had been a teacher and thought of raising a family as an extension of that career, teaching in the private sector. She determined the work to be done and got all of us to do it with a minimum of grumbling. She did the same thing in our neighborhood and the organizations she belonged to. She also loved to sing and performed musical shows for community groups. My comedy shows, as the Atomic Comic, seem a logical extension of her modeling although I surely never thought of her as a model. But the integration of art with work is an important concept to me.

DON'T DO BORING WORK

My first "adult" job was as a schoolteacher, which I quit after two years because I wanted to "grow up." I loved teaching but I didn't want to ask the principal every time I went to the bank. There followed years of graduate school and professoring in institutions about technological forecasting and change. Finally, almost fifteen years ago, I concluded that institutional work did not give me joy and my love of freedom and curiosity required that I go into "private practice." I was the official change agent for the San Francisco School District. I taught counseling classes on the community level and did "odd jobs" like developing sixty acres of land (building a road, working with the surveyor, splitting the water bonds), selling Christmas trees, designing and selling furniture, and working for Glide Church as a change agent. For a period I wrote scripts for educational films ("Prevention and Care of Bedsores," "Urine and Feces Inspection" (my dirty movie), and "How to Aim and Drive a Tank"). I built a park for street people, worked to get better access to transportation for disabled people, organized in a hotel for Chinese and Filipino senior citizens who were threatened with eviction, remodeled houses and sold them, and, in general, worked at jobs that interested me. In fact, that was one of the guiding principles I can see looking back; I have always worked at things that interested me. I have never been bored for long.

DON'T WORK SOLELY FOR MONEY

Another principle I adopted for myself (although I now think living by principles is bogus and deprives one of a real-time life) was that I would never work for money alone. A job was acceptable that gave me a tool, a skill, or contacts that fit into "my work." My life's work is to understand how change happens. Whatever job I have should fit or contribute to that somehow. Mostly, of course, I did not look for jobs but created the jobs I wanted to do and then figured out how to get money out of such a job.

PACE IS IMPORTANT

From my travels, I know that U.S. workers work very hard—in a semi-driven state. Our insecurity is built into us by our system. If we lose our job, we lose our health insurance—a double threat over our heads. Other places in the world have a more relaxed attitude toward their work. For me the pace of work is very important. I am a steady worker, preferring not to work at a frantic speed. I struggle against the devil of distraction, so working steadily and with complete concentration helps me. This is a principle that helps me determine whether a task is one I should do or pass on to others.

WORKING AS A GUARD AGAINST OLD AGE

I remember starting to worry about my old age in my late twenties. Would I have enough money? Who would care for me? Would I end up a poor old lady living in a small apartment on social security? These worries nagged occasionally at the back of my mind for years. Finally, I sat down to "plan for my old age." I talked with investment counselors, with my banker, and with friends. "If I invested $____ a month for ____ years I would have $____." Then we plotted out rents, hospital bills, etc. Clearly I would have to save and invest a lot or it would have little effect. One illness could wipe it all out. I was single-handedly fighting the odds, which were in favor of my being poor when I was older. Most people are fighting those odds—especially women. Just a few people—those who are able to save, who are able to postpone really living for forty years or so, who are able to refuse to share money saved with poorer relatives or friends, will be able to live the good life when they are old.

I turned to my friend Isobel Bachels. She was in her eighties and one of the most out-front people I knew. I told her about how I worried about spending my old age playing bridge like my grandmothers in Twin Falls, Idaho. Worse yet, I might end up being poor and living in a run-down hotel somewhere, being robbed by young punks, and unable to take care of myself. She asked me how much bridge I played now. When I replied that I didn't know how to play bridge, she said she didn't think I would need to worry much. Then she asked about my feelings of estrangement from the old women who were poor. She encouraged me to find out more about their life. "You have a choice, you can either live a greedy life gathering up any money you can as a defense against being poor or you can figure out how you can live a happy life, no matter what small hotel room you end up in. Most older people in the world are poor. You can put your entire life into not being like them, and always feel that estrangement, or you can learn how to live successfully now within the world of the poor. Then you will be less afraid and be able to live your life for the right now." I set out to make friends with people living that life. What I found was a world that, with a few exceptions, takes care of each other. I could see how I would be able to continue to do my work in that world. Through my work in the International Hotel, I saw how community can be built among the poor. I found happiness and dignity. It seemed callous and unfeeling to claim more privilege in my old age than was available to the majority.

DO WHAT YOU HAVE TO DO

For me "right livelihood" means to do the work that is in front of me to do, to do it well, with joy, and from my whole being. For many years I have not gone out looking for work. It comes. I don't know how it finds me and I don't know how just the right amount comes. I am rarely in the position with too much or too little work. Some years ago I needed to be able to come and go to do my work of social change, so I chose to get my income by driving a taxicab. I would come home and drive a week or two, then go out to work on the Ganges River, do political comedy, consult on a project, or protest some nuclear enterprise. In the early years of the 1980s antinuclear campaign a friend asked me to stop all other work and work on the strategy for stopping nuclear weapons. So I did.

I was urging an Indian friend of mine to undertake an environmental campaign to clean up the Ganges River when he asked me in return to help him with the project. "I will embark on the project if you will help me, Peavey." How could I say no? So I have been doing that work for the last eleven years. I learn more than I teach, gain more in perspective than I share.

In South Africa, my job was to question black leadership about a particular job a friend was thinking about taking. I went about my job (which was more of an excuse to be there for me) with conscientiousness and deliberateness. What I learned about myself and our human tasks is very precious to me. I was the only Caucasian (if you want to think in colors, I prefer to think of myself as pink) person on a street, in a railroad car, or as I was arrested in a black township for being there without a permit. Work is one key we can use to figure out who we are, which is a very important task. Michael Phillips asked me to help him design, build, and maintain a park for street people in San Francisco. Anytime I find myself with people I have been estranged from, I grow tremendously. I learn from their perspective, from confronting my own fears and prejudices, and conquering alienation. The thrill of going into this wilderness inside of myself and doing battle with my own beasts is comparable I am sure to climbing high mountains or discovering something new. For me, it is always new to go where I have been taught not to go, learn from those I have been taught to fear, love people forbidden to me by society. And good work is all about love, really, anyway. Love of all life, love of connection, love of growth, love of learning. Curiosity has its own deep rewards.

KNOW WHAT IS HAPPENING IN YOUR OWN TIME

There are questions about the world that seem to just tug on me until I find a way to go to that place and find out a way to help. Sometimes, as in the case of the Afghan refugees, I went, thoroughly researched the situation, and returned home speaking and writing about what I learned. In the International Hotel, I worked with the tenants to form a tenants' association and fight eviction. In the process, I learned a lot about the day-to-day realities of Chinese and Filipino elders in this country, and about my own racism. The currents of our times are interesting to me. In Vietnam, I was negotiating a television contract with the government but I was really looking at change and the effects of war and ideology on a people that I have come to respect a great deal. More than anything I don't want to have lived and not known what was happening in my own time.

Five wealthy and generous women got together, through a mutual friend, and said to me, "If you will stop driving a cab and work full time at your work, we will pay you a salary. If you want to go to the beach for six months and rest, go ahead. We have confidence in you and your work." So now I am able to work full time at my real work. I have never taken the six months off. I'm not the kind of person who can do that. So now when a group with few resources asks me for help, I can go. I do not have to have a financial exchange be the criterion for what work I do. I usually have some exchange because I think it is healthy for the relationship. A group of Native American women wanted to consult me. They brought a basket. People come for personal social change consultations and I ask them to bring beautiful rocks for my garden. I do what I have to do. When I get an idea of work that I should do, then I have to figure out how to fund it.

WORK IS PLAY

Now, most of the work I do is more like play. I write books. I organize people for campaigns, concerts, and events. I think. I talk about ideas. I make friends with people all over the world who are trying to make this world work, people caring for life in new and powerful ways. I connect people and ideas from one place to another. I am learning all the time. What a time to be alive! There are no ideas that are totally tapped down, no ideology is adequate to the tasks of this time. So it is a time for really alive, innovative people. I have my oar in the water with everyone else. I am rowing in the direction I can. Others work from their own direction. It is great to be alive. I am fifty this year. As I get older I seem more and more content with life and the work and love I have found to do in my life. I wish the same for you.

JANET TALLMAN

Right Livelihood and Vocation

The ascension of the soul is like a cord of silk that enables devout intention,
groping in the darkness, to find the path to the light.
> —Umberto Eco, *Foucault's Pendulum*

I knew the substance of my vocation by the time I was eight years old. By then I was recognized as a serious reader and a regular library patron, and a story I wrote had received an award. I had developed the habit of stepping back from life and watching the world around me, and the labyrinth of my imagination was a familiar and frequented place. The pleasures of reading and writing carried me through to my doctorate, while my habits of watching and conjecturing led me to study anthropology. What I first began to value in childhood became a lifelong preoccupation with intertwining realities of language, culture, and literature.

My path of "right livelihood" became clear only in adulthood, as I sought direction in both secular and spiritual realms. I had drifted into my work as a professor of anthropology, extending my life as a student, but I had no firm commitment to what I did. Not until I was in my thirties did I embrace my path by linking work with spiritual disciplines. What began in my childhood as interest and pleasure became, as I matured, vocation or a calling, as well as the practice of right livelihood. Looking for guidance, I explored both Buddhism and Christianity, where I found ideas and habits that give spirit to what I do today.

THE CORD OF SILK

By birth through my parents I gained membership in the Episcopal Church, and I was carried and led each Sunday to learn the stories of the Christian tradition, and the prayers that were the expression of our faith. For us the church was primarily social, though I learned early to love the rituals of light and music, and the archaic, poetic language of the liturgy.

At sixteen I began to feel the stirring of my own active spiritual life, but college and secular cynicism soon led me away from the church. I shared, with my generation, the pursuits of the counterculture, most especially Eastern spiritual thought, consciousness expansion, and anarchist and socialist politics. Demonstrations and drugs transported me far beyond the restrained spiritual impulses I had felt in our small midwestern church.

Gradually I sought more discipline. I was drawn to Buddhism in its many manifestations, first to its philosophy and secondarily to practice. For several years I studied Buddhism, with teachers and on my own. I often considered taking refuge in the Buddha, but invisible barriers stood in my way. Some part of me remembered I had been baptized and confirmed, and some part of me resisted the foreign nature of Buddhism. I had trouble sitting zazen, Tibetan chants were so bizarre, and how could I share this with my parents? The linguistic and cultural strangeness of Buddhist thought and practice interfered with my understanding and worship, complicating my expression and elaboration of faith.

One Sunday, in a small parish church in Oklahoma, I felt drawn to take communion once again. Eighteen years of estrangement fell away, and I began to seek a community and place to worship. From time to time I visited various services, until I walked into a nearby Episcopal church and felt a coming home. I have gone there every Sunday ever since, continuing to feel the joy and struggle, doubt and trust of living with the spirit.

I returned to the church of my childhood with its deeply embedded language and ritual. Just as I was returning I had a vision of Jesus as a Bodhisattva, and I realized that the light I saw flowing from him was the same light that flowed from the Buddha. With that insight I knew that the form of my spiritual path was less important than the light that I was seeking, and that the traditions I had learned early would guide me toward that light. The words of the liturgy that had echoed in my mind since childhood took on new meaning when I translated them through my Buddhist understanding. I realized that the cord of silk which leads me along has many assorted strands.

DEVOUT INTENTION

Somewhere in mid-career, as I was developing myself as a professor and an anthropologist, I became aware that work without spirit was hollow. Success, money and ambition had carried me to a certain point, but in my early thirties I became overwhelmed with my work's lack of genuine meaning. In retrospect, I have come to understand that what I lacked was devout intention, a commitment to working for purposes which transcend the needs of the day. As I explored first Buddhism and then Christianity, I came across ways of finding and encouraging devout intention.

In Buddhism and from Buddhists I learned the idea of right livelihood, of doing work that came from and developed compassion, work that was based on religious practice, did not harm others, and had as its goal the alleviation of suffering. The concepts, especially of right thought and right speech, began to permeate my teaching, and I slowly examined and changed the nature of my involvement with students, other teachers, and the content of my work. I discovered that my thoughts could evolve from spiritual sources, from inner truth and contemplation. I also learned that by looking carefully at what students brought me, I could see and accept their gifts, giving back teaching that would let them grow. Returning to the church, I explored the Christian notion of vocation, the idea that I had been called to do what I was doing. Slowly I accepted the commitment to be a teacher, choosing this form of labor to offer to the world as I put into practice the gifts I had been given. No longer did I feel that I had become a teacher by default, but I embraced my work with a new awareness of gratitude and joy.

I looked to Buddhism and then Christianity for guidelines of practice in doing my work. Two tenets of belief stood out and gave me the foundation for my action. From Buddhism the exhortation to practice mindfulness became central to my thinking, and from Christianity the idea of the discernment of spirits.

For me mindfulness is an expansion of the methods of anthropology, which require us to stand aside and observe with an open and inquiring mind. With Buddhist mindfulness I have tried to discern not only an objective vision of the world, but a vision that leads me further along toward balance and compassion. Mindfulness has come to mean a searching of heart and action as I look for Buddha nature, for perfection and the light. By practice I have learned that we can grow in faithfulness and understanding, and that our harmful deeds and thoughts can give way to compassionate and healing awareness.

From Christianity I have learned also to seek perfection in life and work, keeping in mind the teaching and example of the words and life of Jesus. Discerning spirit and respecting spirit are the touch-points in my practice. I try to find in others and in myself the Christlike aspects of our thoughts and actions. I look carefully at my more harmful emotions of anger, pride, and depression, measuring them against a Christian ideal, developing a Christian form of mindfulness as I carry out my life. As I acknowledge, forgive, and try to change these emotions in myself, I find I am more accepting of such emotions in others.

Both traditions have encouraged me to seek my inner wisdom, to discover through meditation and prayer that which has been called the higher self. The further I progress along this spiritually infused path, the more I understand that we all have godlike natures, and we only differ in the degree to which we attend to our inner truth.

PATH TO THE LIGHT

From both Buddhist and Christian faiths my work has become infused with meaning, and I have found that the path to the light becomes clearer. From Buddhism I have gained humbleness, from Christianity gratitude—as I go about the business of the day.

Buddhism places the responsibility of awareness and conscious action on me, and teaches me to stop blaming others for what I have done or left undone. It teaches me both my weaknesses and ways of overcoming them and helps me to suspend critical judgment and pride. It gives me the indispensable perspective of dispassionate detachment as I wend my way through the unpredictable turns of my professional career.

From Christianity I have developed an overwhelming sense of gratitude, for the gifts that I have been given and the teaching through which I can share those gifts. I am grateful for the grace which has quickened my spirit, grace that lends me courage and wisdom to teach what I think is true. I am grateful also for the ability to "see into" other people, which has allowed me to help my students in ways I do not really know how to explain.

Both Buddhism and Christianity have given me glimpses of the light, of those moments when all is at peace and in harmony. I so often find myself in that narrow-sighted and anxious condition brought on by a busy life. Frequently, in the middle of such a nervous state, the broader vision and meaning break through. I am filled with joy, and laughter carries me through.

Both faiths have given me wisdom literature of inspirational beauty, and art and music that stir me deeply and inform my teaching and inner development. I could give so many examples from centuries of religious writing and art, but I will restrict myself to two instances, one Christian and one Buddhist.

In a Catholic church in Zagreb, the Yugoslav sculptor Mestrovic created from stone a huge crucifix that is suspended in midair. Looking at the agony on the face of that Christ figure, I came to understand the profound nature of human cruelty. I realized how the crucifixion happens all around us on a daily basis. Ever since then I have been preoccupied with the image of the scapegoat, and I have tried to teach others to recognize their own unconscious hatred and destructive projections.

I love the Buddhist teaching tales, and they often guide my thinking. One which addresses clearing the mind and letting go concerns two monks and a beautiful woman. A teacher-monk and his novice come across a lovely young woman afraid to cross the river. The older monk takes her on his back and carries her across, where she goes off in the opposite direction. The young monk is shocked by such closeness to a woman. After several miles of troubled thought, he questions this act of his teacher. The teacher laughs and answers him: "I myself left that woman at the river, but I see that you are still carrying her."

Finally, from both Buddhism and Christianity I have learned to watch and to pray, to place between intention and action an alert mindfulness. In my teaching I try to create in my students this increased awareness and the ability to judge actions and shape them to conscience. I have found that no matter what the subject of my classes, I can teach an attitude of dispassionate scrutiny which, coupled with introspection, allows students to grow and transform.

As I look at the influence of these two faiths in my work, I see expansion of my spirit and a deep meaning in what I have chosen to do. The further I go in awakening in myself compassion and love, wisdom and understanding, the more my life gives back to me. I still have the success which came early in my career. Much more significantly, I feel my heart opening up, and I see into the wishes and needs of others in ways that allow me to respond to them. Prayer arises in me spontaneously, and constant watchfulness has become a way of life, as well as the center of my teaching. I still catch the light only in glimpses but it seems to be getting stronger, illuminating the direction and the promise of my Christian-Buddhist path.

CAROLYN MEYER

Ironworking

I became a blacksmith because that's what I had to do," says Michael Snyder, an articulate, serious-thinking, hip-talking mountaineer. Jill, Mike's beautiful, long-legged wife, has made a pot of coffee. Enoch, their sixteen-month-old son, is asleep in the next room. Mike, weary after a ten-hour day at his forge, settles down beneath the single naked light bulb in the living room of his West Virginia farmhouse to explain how he came to be where he is.

"There hasn't been a Snyder in his own business since my great-grandfather Enoch Snyder left his blacksmith shop in Harrison County around the turn of the century. He had a shop with an assistant, but when times got lean, he went to smith for the coal mines. And then my grandpa went to work in the mines, too. My father broke that tradition: he was a mold-maker in a glass factory, and that was one of the best trades in town.

"So I was the first Snyder to go to college. West Virginia University. I started out in journalism, but I just couldn't get turned on by it, and I was flunkin' out, so I switched to history. Big fraternity man I was, too. When I graduated in 1962, I was all gnarled up inside. Didn't know what I wanted to do except make money, and I didn't know how to do that. So I went to Europe and learned to ski and stuck my head in a lot of museums, and then I came home again.

"I got a job as a junior account executive for an ad agency in Parkersburg. Went up to Pittsburgh to buy my Brooks Brothers suits, wore a boater with regimental band that coordinated with my tie. And I drove a Porsche.

"Once in a while I'd go down to Charleston to service an account and I got to like the guys around the capitol. They asked me to edit their state travel magazine, and I said okay. But the whole durn place was blanketed in lethargy: folks with their feet up on the radiators, lookin' out the window, secretaries comin' out of the boondocks and sittin' around chewin' gum. After a while I said, 'What am I doin' here? I got to be Ernest Hemingway.' So I quit and decided what I wanted was to live in the mountains where I could fish, and the only way I could do that was to become independent. Then I ran into this German woodcarver friend of mine, Wolfgang Flor, and I told him I was goin' up to New York to study creative writing. Wolfie said, 'Man, you just cool it and come and stay with me for a while in this little place I got up in the hills.' I went up there and slept and swam and fished for about three months. The last night I was there I wrote a short story, and then I left for New York.

"I was so unhappy there. Everybody in the subways looked gray. Nobody ever smiled. I had this place in the East Village, and some characters tore a hole through my door and robbed most of my stuff. I felt so lost up there in New York. Couldn't even find a decent chew o' tobacco.

"Then I went to work for a public relations agency. They thought I could write. I could, but not fast enough. I finally got sent to the Islands with fifty pounds of bumper stickers for a gubernatorial campaign. Soon as I ditched the stickers and the politicos, I took off on a fishin' boat. Just before my boss canned me, he told me he had planned to leave me down there on permanent assignment. I really blew that one.

"So back to New York to look for another job. But common sense finally took ahold of me for the first time. I jumped on a Greyhound bus for West Virginia and I never looked back, and I haven't been back to New York since, and if I ever go back again, it will be too soon."

But that was not the end of Mike Snyder's odyssey. Back home he couldn't find a meaningful job. Wanderlust took over again, and Mike headed west. For the next few years he lived the life of a ski bum in

Aspen, Colorado, earning just enough money at odd jobs to stay on skis in the winter, fly-fish in the summer, and take jaunts to Mexico in the springtime. Next he went to California to work on a newspaper; but California was overwhelming. Back to Colorado; but Colorado wasn't right either.

"It was the late sixties then. There I was, walkin' around in rags, not doin' anything with my life. I had been a taxi driver—you're kind of a free spirit, nobody hassles you. Drivin' a lumber truck is cool while you're in the cab, but you have to unload all this heavy stuff. Tried to dig ditches, but two days of that and I just had to quit. Couldn't handle it— mentally, not physically. So when I was fired from the taxi job, the only guy left for me to see was Jimmy Smith, who had the New Broom Cleaning Service. We cleaned out the johns of rich people, which is what I was doin' when I ran into old Bill Bright one day in a store in Aspen. He and I went to school together. He had a business back in West Virginia, makin' place mats for women's clubs to sell, makin' millions. He offered me a job with him as an executive, goin' to pay me a lot of money. I said I'd have to think it over, because trout season was just startin'. And you know, they had built a big dam on one of my favorite trout streams.

"So, eventually I headed back for West Virginia. When you cross the Ohio River, you're back home, and when you're home, nothin's goin' to bother you anymore. I never had any peace out there in Colorado, except when I was skiin' or fishin'. All values are transitory, nothin' is permanent. Back here I'm somebody. Out there I was nobody.

"I started to work for my old friend Bill, but it just didn't work and after three months we both knew it. Then I got together with a couple of other friends—one had invented a machine for makin' wooden bowls, and, by golly, we went into the bowl-makin' business. What little savings I had I soon lost in that, and when it fell through, I went to see some folks at the Charleston Gazette. I was out of bread, and they hired me on the spot. I stuck it out for one year. I did a pretty fair job, but I didn't handle dull assignments very well, and I'm not very good at workin' by the clock, which kind of bends your superiors out of shape.

"My last assignment before they fired me was coverin' the Billy Graham Associate Crusade—Charleston isn't big enough for Billy himself. I'm sittin' there takin' it all down faithfully like a camera, really gettin' into it, tellin' about the guy in the mustard-colored silk suit who was usin' a stage name and so on, gettin' all this stuff for an exposé that didn't materialize. Meanwhile, this really good lookin' chick with these long legs is sittin' up there in the choir, lookin' at me all the time. Jill looked about nine feet tall, chewin' gum a mile a minute, all this blond hair piled up on her head, but I liked somethin' about her. She was only nineteen, but we started gettin' along real good. After the *Gazette* and I parted company, I got into the strip minin' fight full time. Pretty soon Jill was helpin' out in the office, wearin' an anti-strippin' badge, goin' with me to rallies down in the coal country, stickin' with me through thick and thin."

Strip mining, in which seams of coal running close to the surface of the ground are exposed by the removal of topsoil, is an emotional issue in West Virginia and many other states where it is practiced. Battle lines have long been drawn between those who recognize the cheap convenience and economic advantages of strip mining and the conservationists, who claim that strip mining not only makes the land ugly but permits erosion that ruins the watershed. Moderates request that topsoil be replaced and other measures be taken to control erosion and to prevent the scarring of the land. But abolitionists like Mike Snyder demand the end of all strip mining activities.

"As a reporter I was around this strip minin' stuff all the time. All I had to do was plug in a few wires and stand back. I did, and the roof blew off. The mine owners closed down every strip mine in the state and put the miners on buses and sent them to Charleston. People were comin' in from all over, demonstratin'. The strippers' wives get there and start wailin', 'Our babies are gonna go hungry.' Which is a lot of baloney. All those guys are skilled workers, all heavy-equipment operators. It takes only three of 'em to tear down a mountain. You put them out of work strippin', and they can go get jobs buildin' West Virginia instead of tearin' it down. There's only about five thousand strip miners in the whole state, so you're not talkin' about puttin' a zillion guys out of work, just keepin' some blood money out of the hands of the owners. Anyway, four hundred or so of 'em had me surrounded—me in my trusty Brooks Brothers suit, puffin' on my pipe. They could have killed me easily. Then some friends came and rescued me. But abolition never got off the ground because the West Virginia legislature is dominated by coal interests.

We've still got strip minin', but we do have some more controls on it now."

It was West Virginia's Department of Commerce that helped Mike become a blacksmith, not a specialist in shoeing horses (that is called a farrier, Mike explains), but a worker in traditional wrought iron. Through Don Page, the state arts and crafts director in Charleston, Mike learned about an apprentice program for craftsmen. The corporation that sponsors the Mountain State Arts and Crafts Fair in Ripley, West Virginia, every Fourth of July wanted to find somebody to learn the blacksmithing trade. Mike Snyder, then a thirty-one-year-old college graduate and job-hopper, suddenly discerned a direction to his life, a tradition inherited from his great-grandfather on his father's side and his grandfather on his mother's side. He applied for the program and was accepted.

The sponsors overlooked some old-time West Virginia blacksmiths and sent Mike instead to an ironworking school in Santa Fe, New Mexico. Jill went with him. He was given $300 plus $50 traveling money for the six-week course, an extremely short training period for a man who had never held a hammer or stood at an anvil. If he did not yet have the "feel" at the completion of the course, at least he was acquainted with the many techniques of blacksmithing.

Mike got his first job as a blacksmith in Sandusky, Ohio, where he was hired by a resort enterprise to entertain tourists with demonstrations of his skill at the anvil. Twenty thousand people a day paused in front of the blacksmith shop. But the noise, the pressure, the popcorn-munching crowds, and the lack of privacy were hard on Mike, and before the summer was over he had developed an ulcer. It had been a rough apprenticeship. He and Jill—they were married by then—yearned for West Virginia. Mike wrote to a couple of people he knew in the eastern mountains, believing that was the area in which he wanted to live and work. The Snyders headed home once again.

"I wasn't Mennonite, but these people I contacted were. The night I got to Randolph County I went to a Mennonite meeting, and here was a group of men sittin' in a circle, prayin'. These strangers were prayin' for me—that I'd find a place to live. My whole way of thinkin' changed right then and there. Then a guy pops up and says, 'I know where there's a place.' Next day we drove up here to Laurel Fork River, and I knew right away this was the place."

"And I said, 'Oh, no!'"

This was Jill's first comment. Her practical nature is a contrast to Mike's unflagging romanticism. He knew it would be a good place for his forge and anvil. She knew it would be a hard place to bring up the baby that was due that winter. The setting is beautiful: sheep grazing on green hillsides that slope steeply to the narrow valley cut through by a small river alive with fish. But the buildings are ramshackle. A Warm Morning coal stove provides heat for the whole house in an area where winter temperatures plunge well below zero. Some of the rooms are too cold to use in the winter. There is hot running water, but the pipes tend to freeze in extreme weather. When the septic tank doesn't work, as it often doesn't, the alternative is an outdoor privy. But the Snyders moved in early in September of 1971, six months after Mike had picked up a hammer for the first time. Enoch Snyder, named for his grandfather and great-great-grandfather, was born the following February.

Money was scarce. It still is. As a reporter, Mike was paying for thirty-five acres of land nearby to satisfy his need to own a piece of West Virginia. But economic pressures forced him to sell the land soon after they moved in. Money from the sale plus a few intermittent jobs got them through the first year. Things were moving along much better the second year. But then a shoulder injury stopped Mike from working. In his zeal to do things in the old way, Mike used a hand-operated blower to keep the fire going in his forge. Even after he was able to work again, Jill had to crank the blower for him until he could improvise a foot pedal.

The Snyders are devoutly religious, fundamental Christians who believe in the power of prayer. It wasn't always this way. Mike had shrugged off his own early Sunday school training. Although Jill's father is a preacher, she had drifted away from her religion after she left the Billy Graham Associate Crusade to help Mike. But the kindness, generosity, simplicity, and quiet faith of their Mennonite friends has had a deep effect on them, and they are now members of the Mennonite church and attend regularly.

"Every time we'd get down and out," Mike explains, "we'd pray for the Lord to help us, and a check would come through, or an order."

While Mike couldn't work, neighbors helped: one family, as poor as they, brought the Snyders a fresh caught bass. A farmer donated a hundred pounds of seed potatoes. Their Mennonite friends rallied around to keep them going until Mike was able to get back to his shop again.

Not surprisingly, Mike's designs are as traditional as his tools. Chauvinistically West Virginian, he admits, nevertheless, that much old-time West Virginia ironwork lacks imagination and grace, while in his own designs—chandeliers, andirons, fireplace and kitchen tools—he incorporates both grace and imagination. He grumbles about the West Virginia shops that would rather stock plastic skunks from Hong Kong than the work of native craftsmen to sell to out-of-state tourists. He has a few items, such as a dinner gong, that are staples, to sell at craft fairs and through retail outlets, but most of his work is commissioned.

Sometimes his personal feelings get in the way. A Roman Catholic priest asked him to do some candlesticks for a modern chapel. While they were discussing the job, the priest placed an object on the altar that looked like an icon to Mike. It reminded him that his Mennonite brothers had been persecuted at one time for their desire to worship plainly—without icons. Troubled about whether or not to take the job, because of his uneasy but unspecified feeling about a church that used icons, Mike consulted his Mennonite preacher friend. "Shall I take the job or not?" Mike asked. "Why not?" replied the preacher, more of a pragmatist than Mike. He accepted the commission.

The struggle for survival goes on. Mike worries about setting a fair price for the things he makes. When he figures in his time for commission work, four dollars an hour is the lowest he can charge and still survive. Sometimes he underestimates and adds an apology: "I'm sorry I've got to charge you this, but I've got a baby and all." He worries about getting orders in and getting orders out. He worries about earning enough to support his family. But after years of wondering and wandering, Michael Snyder knows who he is—a blacksmith and a Christian—and he praises God for the simplicity and the richness of his life.

RICK FIELDS, WITH PEGGY TAYLOR, REX WEYLER,
AND RICK INGRASCI

To Work Is to Pray

In *Prosperity Is God's Idea*, Margaret M. Stevens tells the following story:

> [There was] a man who died and found himself in a beautiful place, surrounded by every conceivable comfort. A white-jacketed man came to him and said, "You may have anything you choose: any food, any pleasure, any kind of entertainment."
>
> The man was delighted, and for days he sampled all the delicacies and experiences of which he had dreamed on Earth. But one day he grew bored with all of it, and calling the attendant to him, he said, "I'm tired of all this. I need something to do. What kind of work can you give me?"
>
> The attendant sadly shook his head and replied, "I'm sorry, sir. That's the one thing we can't do for you. There is no work here for you."
>
> To which the man answered, "That's a fine thing. I might as well be in hell."
>
> The attendant said softly, "Where do you think you are?"

This fable strikes a chord, and also suggests an intriguing question: Why is it that so many of us think that not to work would be heaven, or something very close to it? Why do we make such clear distinctions be-tween work and play in our lives, often finding it difficult to bring the same quality of joy and attention to our work as we do to our leisure? And what do we miss out on by holding these attitudes? Very possibly the answer has something to do with the way many of us consider work purely in terms of "making a living." Surely this sense of work as survival is an important part of work, but it is hardly the whole story.

In *Identity, Youth and Crisis*, Erik Erikson writes: "Freud was once asked what he thought a normal person should be able to do well. The questioner probably expected a completed 'deep' answer. But Freud sim-ply said, '*Lieben und arbeiten*' (to love and to work). It pays to ponder on this simple formula; it grows deeper as you think about it."

"Caring about our work, liking it, even loving it, seems strange when we see work only as a way to make a living," writes Tibetan Buddhist teacher Tarthang Tulku in *Skillful Means*. "But when we see work as the way to deepen and enrich all of our experience, each one of us can find this caring within our hearts, and awaken it in those around us, using every aspect of work to learn and grow."

Work, like any other activity in our lives, can be a deeply enrich-ing—and meditative—experience. It all depends on the attitude we carry to it. Approaching work with care and awareness can transform even the most mundane task into an exciting opportunity to reflect and grow. This attitude is reflected in most spiritual traditions.

In the yogic traditions, for example, work is seen as such an integral part of spiritual development that it is called Karma Yoga. In *Creative Work—Karma Yoga: A Western Interpretation*, the philosopher and phi-lologist Edmund Bordeaux Szekely describes the essence of this teach-ing:

> In the highest sense, work is meant to be the servant of man, not the master. It is not so important what shape or form our work may take; what is vitally important is our attitude toward that work. With love and enthusiasm directed toward our work, what was once a chore and hardship now becomes a magical tool to develop, enrich and nourish our lives. "Work makes the man" is an old proverb with much more truth in it than appears on the surface. Work can indeed make the man, if the man will use his God-given powers of reason to transform work into the sacred partnership with the Creator it was originally meant to be.

The idea of action without attachment to the results or fruits of your labor is basic to Karma Yoga. Both the Hindu and Christian traditions stress that all work should be dedicated to God and undertaken to serve others. *"Laborare est orare,"* say the Benedictine monks, "To work is to pray."

"The true husbandman," H.D. Thoreau writes in the "Bean Patch" chapter of *Walden*, "will cease from anxiety, as the squirrels manifest no concern whether the woods will bear chestnuts this year or not, and finish his labor with every day, relinquishing all claim to the produce of his fields, and sacrificing in his mind not only his first but last fruits also."

> When we work in this way, we offer all we really have to offer: ourselves.

This story about three masons illustrates how much difference our attitude about our work makes. Margaret M. Stevens writes:

> You know the story of the three brick masons. When the first man was asked what he was building, he answered gruffly, without even raising his eyes from his work, "I'm laying bricks." The second man replied, "I'm building a wall." But the third man said enthusiastically and with obvious pride, "I'm building a cathedral."

"Blessed is he who has found his work," writes Thomas Carlyle. "Let him ask no other blessedness."

All very well, you may say, but how do you achieve this state of blessedness? How do you find work that is right for you and right for the world?

"Playing into the victim mentality is the biggest cause of people failing to find satisfying work," says Richard Bolles, a minister and the closest thing to an enlightened career counselor America has ever seen. In his book *The Three Boxes of Life and How to Get Out of Them*, Bolles writes:

> The Victim Mentality, simply defined, is that outlook or attitude which says: "My life is essentially at the mercy of vast powerful forces (or a vast powerful force) *out there* and beyond my control. Therefore, I am at the mercy of [Usually at least four are selected]:

My history, my upbringing, my genes, or my heritage.

My social class, my education (or lack of it), or my I.Q. (or lack of it). My parents, my teachers, or an invalid relative.

My mate, my partner, my husband, or my wife.

My boss, my supervisor, my manager, or my coworkers.

The economy, the times we live in, the social structure, or our form of government.

The politicians, the large corporations, or the rich.

Some particular enemy who is out to get me, and who has great power: an irate creditor, an ex-boyfriend or ex-girlfriend, a combine, or the Devil.

The Victim Mentality ultimately discharges you from any responsibility for your life, since clearly what is happening to you is not your fault. You don't have to lift a finger....Now, to be sure, there is a sense in which we are victims, in our culture. We often are at the mercy of forces that we have no control over. A good hurricane or earthquake will remind you forcibly of that fact. So will even a moment's contemplation of what it means to live in the Nuclear Age....

Nonetheless, there is a vast difference between being a victim (which we all are, in some areas of our life) and having the Victim Mentality. Being a victim means there are some areas to my life where I am battling powerful forces, *but I will still do battle with them.* Whereas, having the Victim Mentality means giving up: "What's the use? Why even try? I have no power at all; the things you suggest may help other people, but they can't offer any hope to me...."

I want to state a simple truth, and that is, I believe every individual has more control over his or her life than he or she thinks is the case....no matter how much of our life we perceive to be unchangeable, because it is in the control of someone or something else, there is always that part that is under our control, and that we can work on to change. Be it 2%, 5%, 30% or whatever, it is almost always more than we think.

Danaan Parry, one of the founders of the Holy Earth Foundation and the Earthstewards Network, offers this pragmatic advice on how to move toward "right livelihood" in one's life. If your work does not allow you to express your creativity, your joy, your fullness, your own internal code of rightness, he says, then you have three choices:

> 1. Use your creativity to uncover ways and means to change the system. Introduce concepts of right livelihood in your workplace. Have patience and persistence; gently assist others to find their point of positive service.

> 2. Do nothing, but be honest about it. Admit to yourself that you are more interested in not rocking the boat than in changing your life, because right livelihood demands change for most of us, away from work for security, prestige, and overabundance and toward a positive, right relationship to our labor that is congruent with our roles as planetary stewards.

> 3. Leave this work and seek other work that has the potential of right livelihood. Create a situation wherein you do what you are good at, are who you want to be, and are able to feel what you think is right, all intermingled.

A group of engineers who worked in the nuclear weapons field provide an inspiring example of one innovative way to move toward right livelihood. They had all come to the decision that their work and their spiritual beliefs were out of synch, but, because they all had families to support, they were reluctant to just up and quit their jobs. So they got together and created a group support system. One at a time, the engineers left their jobs; they and their families were supported by the others in the group during the months it took them to find a new job in a more benign field.

In *The Turning Point*, Fritjof Capra suggests that our values about what is worthy work are exactly upside down. The work given the lowest value in our culture, he says, is the most "entropic work"—the work "that has to be done over and over again, without leaving a lasting impact"—while high status is given to jobs that create something that lasts: "skyscrapers, supersonic planes, space rockets, nuclear warheads, and all the other products of high technology."

Entropic work, says Capra, is the key to a spiritual life:

> Doing work that has to be done over and over again helps us recognize the natural cycles of growth and decay, of birth and death, and thus become aware of the dynamic order of the universe. 'Ordinary' work, as the root meaning of the term indicates, is work that is in harmony with the order we perceive in the natural environment....What we need, therefore, is to revise the concept and practice of work in such a way that it becomes meaningful and fulfilling for the individual worker, useful for society, and part of the harmonious order of the ecosystem. To reorganize and practice our work in this way will allow us to recapture its spiritual essence.

Manual labor, called *samu* in Zen, is part of the life of every Zen monk. Every day after breakfast a time is set aside for sweeping, dusting, polishing the floor, scrubbing the toilets, weeding, and gardening.

"Since the time when Pai-chang first instituted it, more than a thousand years ago," Roshi Philip Kapleau writes in *The Three Pillars of Zen*, "manual labor has been an essential ingredient of Zen discipline. It is recorded of Pai-chang that one day his monks, feeling he had grown too feeble to work, hid his gardening tools. When they refused to heed his entreaties to return them, he stopped eating, saying, 'No work, no eating.'"

Samu, explains Kapleau, serves two main functions in Zen training. "First, it points up that zazen is not merely a matter of acquiring the ability to concentrate and focus the mind during sitting, but that in the widest sense zazen involves the mobilization of *joriki* (the power generated by zazen) in our every act. Samu, as a mobile type of zazen, also provides the opportunity to quiet, deepen, and bring the mind to one-pointedness through activity, as well as to invigorate the body and thereby energize the mind."

The object of such work, says Kapleau, "as in every other type of zazen, is the cultivation first of mindfulness and eventually mindlessness." (Mindfulness is awareness in which one is aware that one is aware. "Mindlessness" is, on the other hand, "a condition of such complete absorption that there is no vestige of self-awareness.")

"All labor entered into with such a mind is valued for itself apart from what it may lead to," says Kapleau. "This is the 'meritless' or 'purposeless' work of Zen. By undertaking each task in this spirit, eventually we are enabled to grasp the truth that every act is an expression of the Buddha mind. Once this is directly and unmistakably experienced, no labor can be beneath one's dignity. On the contrary, all work, no matter how menial, is ennobling because it is seen as the expression of the immaculate Buddha nature. This is true enlightenment, and enlightenment in Zen is never for oneself alone but for the sake of all."

GENE LOGSDON

Amish Economics

Amish farmers are still making money in these hard times despite (or rather because of) their supposedly outmoded, horse-farming ways. If they do get into financial jeopardy, it is most often from listening to the promises of modern agribusiness instead of traditional wisdom. The Amish continue to farm profitably not only with an innocent disregard for get-big-or-get-out modern technology, but without participating in direct government subsidies other than those built into market prices, which they can't avoid.

BARN RAISING IN A SINGLE DAY

I first learned about the startlingly effective economy of Amish life when I was invited to a barn raising near Wooster, Ohio. A tornado had levelled four barns and acres of prime Amish timber. In just three weeks, the downed trees were sawed into girders, posts and beams and the four barns rebuilt and filled with livestock donated by neighbors to replace those killed by the storm. Three weeks! Nor were the barns the usual modern, one-story metal boxes hung on poles. They were huge buildings, three and four stories high, post-and-beam framed, and held together with hand-hewn mortises and tenons. I watched the raising of the last barn in open-mouthed awe. Some 400 Amish men and boys, acting and reacting like a hive of bees in absolute harmony of cooperation, started at sunrise with only a foundation and floor and by noon had the huge edifice far enough along that you could put hay in it.

A contractor who was watching said it would have taken him and a beefed-up crew all summer to build the barn if, indeed, he could find anyone skilled enough at mortising to do it. He estimated the cost at $100,000. I asked the Amish farmer how much cash he would have in the barn. "About $30,000," he said. And some of that paid out by the Amish church's own insurance arrangements. "We give each other our labor," he explained. "We look forward to raisings. There are so many helping, no one has to work too hard. We get in a good visit."

Not long afterwards, I gave a speech to an organization of farmers concerned with alternative methods of agriculture in which I commiserated at length with the financially depressed farmers. When my talk was over, two Amish men approached me, offering mild criticism. "We have finished one of our most financially successful years," one of them said. "It is only those farmers who have ignored common sense and tradition who are in trouble." What made his remarks more significant is that he went on to explain that he belonged to a group of Amish that had, as an experiment, temporarily allowed its members to use tractors in the field. He also was making payments on land that he had recently purchased. In other words, he was staring at the same economic gun that's pointed at English farmers and he was coming out ahead. "But," he said, "I'm going back to horses. They're more profitable."

When I helped a neighbor haul hay, I received another lesson in Amish economics. If they need to buy extra feed for their livestock, they almost always choose to buy hay and raise the grain rather than vice versa. The price of the hay is partially regained as manure after passing through the livestock, allowing them to cut down on the amount of fertilizer they need to buy. The greater mass of hay generates a greater mass of manure, adding organic matter to the soil. That is valuable beyond computer calculation. Grain farmers in my area who sold their straw and hay to the Amish were trading their soil fertility for cash of flitting value.

UMBILICAL CORDS TO THE
DANGEROUS OUTSIDE WORLD

Housing is another good example of Amish economy. First of all, the Amish home doubles as an Amish church. How many millions of dollars this saves the Amish would be hard to calculate. Secondly, the Amish home doubles as the Amish retirement village and nursing home, thereby saving incalculably more millions of dollars, not to mention the self-respect of the elderly. The Amish do not pay Social Security, nor do they accept it. They know and practice a much better security that requires neither pension nor lifelong savings.

There is an old Amish quiltmaker who lives near Pfeiffer's Station, a crossroads store and village I often frequent. Her bedroom is just big enough for a bed and quilting frame; her kitchen is equally tiny. The boys of the family keep the walkway stacked with firewood for her stove. She has her own little garden. Children play on her doorstep.

She has her privacy but is surrounded by living love, not the dutiful professionalism of the old folks' home. And she still earns her way. Quilt buyers come, adding to her waiting list more quilts than her fingers, now slowed by arthritis, can ever catch up with. I love that scene. She still lives in the real world. If she were not Amish, she would have languished in some nursing home and no doubt be dead by now—from sheer boredom if nothing else.

There are no telephones in the homes, but the Amish use the telephone booths that dot the roadsides. An Amishman views a telephone wire in the home, like an electric line, as an umbilical cord tying them to dangerous worldly influences. You will not talk so long or often at a pay booth down the road.

Whatever one's views of such fence-straddling religious convictions, they obviously reveal tremendous economizing. In a 1972 study of Illinois Old Order Amish conducted by the Center for the Biology of Natural Systems at Washington University in St. Louis, Amish housewives said they spent $10 to $15 a week on food and non-food groceries. They reported household living expenses from $1,379 per year for a small young family up to $4,700 for a large, better-financed one. My own Amish informants thought that today, that figure might top out at $8,000 for a large family, including transportation by buggy and occasionally renting a car or riding a bus. A horse and new buggy cost about $2,000 and last a good bit longer than a $12,000 car.

Medical costs are the only expenses the Amish cannot control by their subeconomy. Religion forbids education beyond the early teens, so they cannot generate their own doctors and medical facilities, and must pay the same ridiculous rates as the rest of us.

Another surprising element in the Amish economy is the busy social life they lead within a day's ride by buggy or bicycle. We could scarcely schedule a softball game because there was always a wedding, a raising, a sale, a quilting, or church and school doings to attend! I can assure the world that the Amish have just as much fun as anyone, at far less than the cost of weekends made for Michelob.

A LIVELIHOOD ON TWENTY COWS

It is in agriculture that the Amish raise economy to a high art. After the ball games, when talk got around to the hard times in farming today, the Amish said a good farmer could still make a good living with a herd of twenty to twenty-five cows. The Amish farmers all agreed that, with twenty cows, a farmer could gross $50,000 in a good-weather year, of which "about half" would be net after paying farm expenses including taxes and interest on land debt, if any. Deducting $8,000 for family living expenses still leaves a nice nest egg for emergencies, bad years, and savings to help offspring get started in farming.

The most amazing part of the Amish economy to me is that, contrary to notions cherished by old farm magazine editors who escaped grim childhoods on 1930s farms for softer lives behind desks, the Amish do not work as hard, physically, as I did when my father and I were milking 100 cows with all the modern conveniences in the 1960s.

English farmers like to make fun of the Amish for their hairsplitting ways with technology allowing tractors or engines for stationary power tools but not in the fields. But in addition to keeping the Amish way of life intact, such compromises bring tremendous economy to their farming while lightening the workload. A motor-powered baler or corn harvester, pulled by horses ahead of a forecart, may seem ridiculous to a modern agribusinessman, but it saves thousands of dollars over buying tractors for this work. The reasons tractors aren't allowed in the fields is that they would then tempt an Amishman to expand acreage, going into steep debt to do so, and in the process drive other Amish off the land, which is exactly why and how American agriculture got into the trouble engulfing it today.

To satisfy religious restrictions, the Amish have developed many other ingenious ideas to use modern technology in economizing ways. Other farmers should be studying, not belittling, them. When Grade A milk regulations forced electric cooling tanks on dairymen, the Amish adopted diesel motors to generate their own electricity for the milk room, cooler and milk machines. They say it's cheaper than buying electricity and keeps them secure from power outages.

Where Amish are active, countryside and town are full of bustling shops and small businesses, neat homes, solid schools and churches, and scores of roadside stands and cheese factories. East central Ohio even has a small woolen mill, one of the few remaining in the country. Compare this region with the decaying towns and empty farmsteads of the land dominated by large-scale agribusiness. The Amish economy spills out to affect the whole local economy. Some farmers, like Lancie Cleppinger near Mount Vernon, have the great good sense to farm like the Amish even though they don't live like them. They enjoy profits too. When discussing the problems agribusiness farmers have brought on themselves, Cleppinger just shook his head and repeated, "What in the world are they thinking?"

Economics as if People Matter

While carrying your active life on your head,
can you embrace the quiet spirit in your arms and not let go?
While being fully focused on your vital breath,
can you make it soft like that of a newborn babe?
While cleaning your inner mirror,
can you leave it without blemish?
While loving the people and ruling the country,
can you dispense with cleverness?
While opening and closing the gates of Heaven,
can you be like a mother bird?
While penetrating the four quarters with your insight,
can you remain simple?
Help the people live.
Nourish the people.
Help them live, yet lay no claim to them.
Benefit them yet seek no gratitude.
Guide them yet do not control them.
This is called the hidden virtue.
                              —Lao-tzu

In choosing your home look to the land.
In preparing your heart go deep.
In associating with others value gentleness.
In speaking exhibit good faith.
In governing provide good order.
In the conduct of business be competent.
In action be timely.
When there is no strife, nothing goes amiss.
                              —Lao-tzu

DAVID LOY

Buddhism and Money

The modern world is so materialistic that we sometimes joke about the religion of "moneytheism." But this joke is nothing to laugh about: for more and more people, the value system of money is supplanting traditional religions as part of a profound secular conversion we only dimly understand. I think that Buddhism (with some help from the psychoanalytic concept of repression) can explain this historical conversion and show us how to overcome it.

The Buddhist doctrine of no-self implies that our fundamental repression is not sex (as Freud thought), nor even death (as existential psychologists think), but the intuition that the ego-self does not exist, that our self-consciousness is a mental construction. In this case, the repressed intuition "returns to consciousness in distorted form" as all the symbolic ways we compulsively try to ground ourselves and make ourselves real in the world, such as power, fame, and, of course, money.

THE MIDAS TOUCH

If there is to be a psychoanalysis of money, it must start from the hypothesis that the money complex has the essential structure of religion, or, if you will, the negation of religion, the demonic. The psychoanalytic theory of money must start by establishing the proposition that money is, in Shakespeare's words, the "visible god"; in Luther's words "the God of this world."[1]

How can money be both religious and the negation of religion? Because the money complex is motivated by our religious need to redeem ourselves (fill in our "sense of lack"). In Buddhist terms, the demonic results from the "sense of self" trying to make itself real (that is, objectify itself) by grasping the spiritual in this world. This can be done only unconsciously, which means symbolically, and our most important symbol today is money.

Schopenhauer says that money is human happiness *in abstracto*; consequently, he who is no longer capable of happiness *in concreto* sets his whole heart on money. It is questionable whether there is really such a thing as happiness in abstraction, but the second half is true. To the extent one becomes preoccupied with symbolic happiness, one is not alive to concrete happiness. The difficulty is not with money as a convenient medium of exchange, but with the "money complex" that arises when money becomes the desired thing, that is, desirable in itself. How does this happen? Given our sense of lack, how could this not happen?

Money is the "purest" of all symbols, "because there is nothing in reality that corresponds to it."[2] As Midas discovered about gold, money in itself is worthless: you can't eat or drink it, plant it, ride in it, or sleep under it. Yet it has more value than anything else because we use it to define value itself. It can transform into anything. The psychological problem occurs when life becomes focused around the desire for money, and an ironic reversal takes place between means and ends: everything else is devalued in order to maximize a worthless-in-itself goal, because our desires have been fetishized into that symbol. When everything has its price and everyone has his price, the numerical representation of the symbol system becomes more important, more *real*, than the things represented. We end up rejoicing not at a worthwhile job well done, or at meeting a friend, or at hearing a bird, but at accumulating pieces of paper. To find the method in this madness, we must relate it to the sense of self's sense of lack, whose festering keeps us from being able to fully enjoy that bird-song (just *this*!), etc. Since we no longer believe in original sin, what is wrong with us, and how can we hope to get over it? Today, the socially-approved explanation—our contemporary original sin—is that we don't have enough money.

The origin of money is puzzling: how did the transition from barter ever occur? How were human cravings fetishized into pieces of metal? The answer that Norman O. Brown provides is elegant, because it reveals much about the character of money today: money was and still is literally sacred. "It has long been known that the first markets were sacred markets, the first banks were temples, the first to issue money were priests or priest-kings."[3] The first coins were minted and issued by temples as medallions inscribed with the god's image and embodying his protective power. Containing such *mana*, they were naturally in demand, not because you could buy things with them, but vice versa: because they were popular, you could exchange them for other things.

As a consequence, "now the cosmic powers could be the property of everyman, without even the need to visit temples: you could now traffic in immortality in the marketplace." This eventually led to the emergence of a new kind of person, "who based the value of his life—and so of his immortality—on a new cosmology centered on coins." A new system of meaning arose, which our present economic system makes more and more *the* meaning-system.

"Money becomes the distilled value of all existence...a single immortality symbol, a ready way of relating the increase of oneself to all the important objects and events of one's world."[4] Beyond its usefulness as a medium of exchange, money has become modern man's most popular way of accumulating Being, of coping with our gnawing intuition that we don't really exist. Suspecting that the sense of self is a groundless construction, we used to go to temples and churches to ground ourselves in God; now we work to ground ourselves financially.

The problem is that we end up paying a heavy price. The value we place on money karmically rebounds against us: the more we value it, the more we use it to evaluate ourselves. In *The Hour of Our Death*, his great historical study of death in Western culture, Phillipe Aries turns our usual critique upside down. Today we complain about materialism, but modern man is not really materialistic, for "things have become means of production, or objects to be consumed or devoured...the ordinary man in his daily life no more believes in matter than he believes in God. The man of the Middle Ages believed in matter and in God, in life and in death, in the enjoyment of things and their renunciation."[5]

Our problem today is that we no longer believe in things but in symbols; hence, our life has passed over into these symbols and their manipulation. We find ourselves manipulated by the symbols we take so seriously. We are preoccupied not so much with what money can buy, but with its power and status; not with a car in itself, but with what owning a Lexus says about us. Modern man wouldn't be able to endure real economic equality, says Ernest Becker, "because he has no faith in self-transcendent, other-worldly immortality symbols; visible physical worth is the only thing he has to give him eternal life." Or real Being. Our spiritual hunger to become real, or at least to occupy a special place in the cosmos, is reduced to having a bigger car than our neighbors! We can't get rid of the sacred, because we can't get rid of our ultimate concerns, except by repressing them, whereupon we become "the more uncontrollably driven by them."[6]

We tend to view the profit motive as natural and rational (the benevolent "invisible hand" of Adam Smith), but it is not traditional to traditional societies, and in fact has usually been viewed with fear. For us, the desire for profit defines economic activity, but in archaic society there is no clear division between that sphere and others. Polanyi notes:

> Man's economy, as a rule, is submerged in his social relationships. He does not act so as to safeguard his individual interest in the possession of material goods; he acts so as to safeguard his social standing, his social claims, his social assets. He values material goods only insofar as they serve this end....The economic system will be run on non-economic motives.[7]

Primitive man had no need for a financial solution to lack, for he had other ways to cope with it. Tawney brings this home to us by discovering the same truth in the history of the West:

> There is no place in medieval theory for economic activity which is not related to a moral end, and to found a science of society upon the assumption that the appetite for economic gain is a constant and measurable force, to be accepted like other natural forces, as an inevitable and self-evident datum, would have appeared to the medieval thinker as hardly less irrational and less immoral than to make the premise of social philosophy the unrestrained operation of such necessary human attributes as pugnacity and the sexual instinct.[8]

The crucial transformation evidently began at the end of the Middle Ages. Once profit became the engine of the economic process, the tendency was for gradual reorganization of the entire social system and not just of the economic element, since, as Polanyi implies, there is no natural distinction between them. According to Tawney, "Capital had ceased to be a servant and had become a master. Assuming a separate and independent vitality it claimed the right of a predominant partner to dictate economic organization in accordance with its own exacting requirements."[9]

"Happiness is the deferred fulfillment of a prehistoric wish," Freud said. "That is why wealth brings so little happiness: money is not an infantile wish." Then what kind of wish is money? "Money is condensed wealth; condensed wealth is condensed guilt."[10] The most brilliant chapter of Brown's *Life Against Death*, "Filthy Lucre," links money to guilt. "Whatever the ultimate explanation of guilt might be, we put forward the hypothesis that the whole money complex is rooted in the psychology of guilt." The psychological advantage of archaic man is that he "knew" what his problem was and therefore how to overcome it. Belief in sin allowed the possibility of expiation, which occurred in seasonal rituals and sacrifices. "The gods exist to receive gifts, that is to say sacrifices; the gods exist in order to structure the human need for self-sacrifice."[11] For Christianity, that sacrifice is incarnated in Christ, who "takes our sins upon him." Religion provides the opportunity to expiate our sense of lack by means of symbols, e.g., the crucifix, eucharist, the mass whose validity is socially agreed and maintained. In such a context, we do feel purified and closer to God after taking Holy Communion.

But what of the modern "neurotic type," who "feels a sinner without the religious belief in sin, for which he therefore needs a new rational explanation"?[12] How do you expiate your sense of lack when there is no religious explanation for it? The main secular alternative today is to experience our lack as "not yet enough." This converts cyclic time (maintained by seasonal rituals of atonement) into linear time (in which the atonement of lack is reached for but perpetually postponed, because never achieved). The sense of lack remains a constant, but our collective reaction to it has become the need for growth: the "good life" of consumerism (but lack means the consumer never has enough) and the gospel of sustained economic growth (because corporations and the GNP are never big enough). The heart (or rather blood) of both is the money complex. Writes Weston LaBarre, "A dollar is…a codified psychosis normal in one subspecies of this animal, an institutionalized dream that everyone is having at once."[13] Brown is almost as damning:

> If the money complex is constructed out of an unconscious sense of guilt, it is a neurosis.…The dialectic of neurosis contains its own "attempts at explanation and cure," energized by the ceaseless upward pressure of the repressed unconscious and producing the return of the repressed to consciousness, although in an increasingly distorted form, as long as the basic repression (denial) is maintained and the neurosis endures. The modern economy is characterized by an aggravation of the neurosis, which is at the same time a fuller delineation of the nature of the neurosis, a fuller return of the repressed. In the archaic consciousness the sense of indebtedness exists together with the illusion that the debt is payable; the gods exist to make the debt payable. Hence the archaic economy is embedded in religion, limited by the religious framework, and mitigated by the consolations of religion above all, removal of indebtedness and guilt. The modern consciousness represents an increased sense of guilt, more specifically a breakthrough from the unconscious of the truth that the burden of guilt is unpayable.[14]

The result of this is "an economy driven by a pure sense of guilt, unmitigated by any sense of redemption," which is "the more uncontrollably driven by the sense of guilt because the problem of guilt is repressed by denial into the unconscious."[15] Nietzsche said that it's not only the reason of millennia but their insanity too that breaks out in us; today's version is the cult of economic growth, which has become, in effect, our religious myth. "We no longer give our surplus to God; the process of producing an ever-expanding surplus is in itself our God.…To quote Schumpeter: 'Capitalist rationality does not do away with sub- or super-rational impulses. It merely makes them get out of hand by removing the restraint of sacred or semisacred tradition.'"[16]

If so, we can see what the problem is: money and economic growth constitute a defective myth, because they can provide no expiation of guilt—in Buddhist terms, no resolution of lack. Our new "holy of holies," the true temple of modern man, is the stock market, and our rite of worship is communing with the Dow Jones average; in return, we receive the kiss of profits and the promise of more to come, but there is no atonement in this. Of course, insofar as we have lost belief in sin, we no longer see anything to atone for, which means we end up unconsciously atoning in the only way we know, by working hard to acquire all those things that society tells us are important and will make us happy; and then we cannot understand why they don't make us happy, why they don't resolve our sense of lack. The reason can only be that we don't yet have enough. "But the fact is that the human animal is distinctively characterized, as a species and from the start, by the drive to produce a surplus....There is something in the human psyche which commits man to nonenjoyment, to work." Where are we all going so quickly? "Having no real aim, acquisitiveness," as Aristotle correctly said, "has no limit." Not *to* anywhere but *from* something, which is why there can be no end to it as long as that something is our own "lack-shadow." "Economies, archaic and civilized, are ultimately driven by that flight from death which turns life into death-in-life."[17] Or by that flight from emptiness that makes life empty: by an intuition of nothingness which, when repressed, only deepens my sense that there is something very wrong with me. If money symbolizes becoming real, the fact that we never quite become real means that we end up holding pure deferral in our hands. Those chips we have accumulated can never be cashed in, for the moment we do so, the illusion that money can resolve lack is dispelled, and we are left more empty and lack-ridden than before, deprived of our fantasy for escaping lack. We unconsciously suspect and fear this; the only answer is to flee faster into the future.

I think this points to the fundamental defect of any economic system that requires continual growth not to collapse: it is based not on needs but on fear, for it feeds on, and feeds, our sense of lack. In sum, our preoccupation with manipulating these symbols, which we suppose to be the means of solving the problem of life, turns out to be a symptom of the problem.

Curiously, the best analogy for money may be *sunyata*. Nagarjuna warns that there is no such thing as sunyata; it is a heuristic device demonstrating the interdependence of things, that nothing self-exists, but if we misunderstand this, the cure is more dangerous than the disease. Although also nothing in itself, also merely a symbol, money is indispensable, because of its unique ability to convert anything into another; but woe to those who grab this snake by the wrong end.

If this critique of the money complex is valid, what solution is there? The same solution that Buddhism has always offered: not any quick fix that can be "conditioned" into us, but the personal transformation that occurs when we make the effort to follow the Buddhist path, which means learning how to let go of ourselves and "die."

Once we are good and dead, once we have become nothing and realize that we can be anything, we see money for what it is: not a symbolic way to make ourselves real, to measure ourselves by, but a socially-constituted device that expands our freedom and power. Then we become truly free to determine our attitude towards getting it and using it. If we are really "dead," there is nothing wrong with money: not money but love of money is the root of evil. However, if we are truly "dead," we also realize that there is no question of our essential nature getting better or worse; just as it does not come or go, so it has nothing to gain or to lose. This means that, for those who have realized their essential nature, which is no nature, who do not experience themselves as separate from the world, the value of money becomes its ability to help alleviate suffering. Those who do not crave it and are also not afraid of it know how to use it.

NOTES

[1] Norman O. Brown, *Life Against Death: The Psychoanalytic Meaning of History*, [hereafter *LAD*] (New York: Vintage, 1961), pp. 240-241.

[2] *LAD*, 271.

[3] *LAD*, 246.

[4] Ernest Becker, *The Escape from Evil* [hereafter *EE*] (New York: The Free Press, 1973, 1975), pp. 76, 79, 80-81.

[5] Phillipe Aries, *The Hour of Our Death* (Harmondsworth: Penguin, 1981), pp. 136-137.

[6] *EE*, 85.

[7] K. Polanyi in *LAD*, 262.

[8] R.H. Tawney, *Religion and the Rise of Capitalism* (New York: Harcourt, Brace, 1926), p. 31.

[9] *Religion and the Rise of Capitalism*, p. 86.

[10] Sigmund Freud, *The Origins of Psychoanalysis*, ed. M. Bonaparte, et al. (New York: Basic Books, 1964), p. 244; *LAD*, 266.

[11] *LAD*, 265.

[12] Otto Rank, *Beyond Psychology* (New York: Dover, 1958), p. 194.

[13] Weston LaBarre, *The Human Animal* (University of Chicago Press, 1954), p. 174.

[14] *LAD*, 270-271.

[15] *LAD*, 272.

[16] *LAD*, 261.

[17] *LAD*, 256, 258, 285.

RAMI G. KHOURI

Islamic Banking

*Al-Barr: the Source of All Goodness, the messenger of Allah (Peace and Bless-
ings of Allah be upon him) has said, "Allah does not take into account your
figures or your wealth. He looks and values your hearts and deeds."*

Millions of people avoid banks as institutions. Some are simply wary
of organizations not rooted in their own villages. But many are professional and business people, and it is not suspicion, but Islamic beliefs
that bar them from financial dealings they define as usurious. Yet Muslims need banking services as much as anyone. Nor are they averse to
legitimate profit: the Prophet Muhammad himself was a successful busi-
nessman. But today's financial world is tightly knit, linking Muslim and
non-Muslim. In this world, can Muslims find rooms for the principles of
their religion? The answer comes with the rise of international Islamic
banking.

As oil prices increased after 1974, a number of Arab and Muslim
countries experienced a rise in income and became dissatisfied with the
rigid requirements of commercial banks (mostly Western) and the banks'
view of interest-earning activities as their central reason for being. The
best response, for both individuals and communities, seemed to be rein-
vigoration of the principles of Islam.

Several Qur'anic passages admonish the faithful to shun *riba*, or fixed
interest payments: "Fear God and give up what remains of your demand
of usury, if ye are indeed believers." Riba is prohibited on the tenet that
money is only a medium of exchange, a way of defining value; it has no
value in itself, and should not give rise to more money simply by being

put in a bank or lent. The human effort, initiative and risk involved in a venture are more important than the money used to finance it.

According to the Shari'a, or Islamic law, the provider and the user of capital should equally share the risk of business ventures. Translated into banking terms, the depositor, the bank and the borrower should all share the risks and rewards of business ventures, unlike the interest-based commercial banking system where all the pressure is on the borrower, who must pay back the loan and the agreed interest regardless of the success or failure of the venture. Islamic economics also requires investments to support only practices or products that are not forbidden or discouraged by Islam. Trade in alcohol or arms, for example, would not be financed by an Islamic bank. Nor could money be lent to other banks at interest.

Islamic banks have devised creative, flexible variations on the risk-sharing, profit-sharing principle. A group in Jordan, for example, had the land for a community college, but not the money to build it. An Islamic bank built the college and agreed to be repaid with 30 percent of tuition fees. But after the school opened, the government raised admission standards; the number of students—and the college's cash flow—fell to half of predicted levels. The bank responded by stretching out the repayment period. Another Islamic bank finances individuals' car or taxi purchases by *murabaha*, buying the vehicle and transferring ownership to the client, who repays the cost over thirty-six to forty months. If the client cannot repay on the original, or a revised schedule, the bank agrees with the client to sell the car secondhand, whether or not the proceeds cover the outstanding balance of the original debt.

The public's acceptance of Islamic banking has been quicker and greater than its advocates had anticipated. The banks initially attracted depositors whose religious beliefs had caused them to shun commercial banks' interest-bearing savings accounts. (Islamic banks also offer a full spectrum of the normal services of modern banking that do not involve interest payments.) Once they had proved their viability and safety, the Islamic banks attracted others who preferred the less pressured style of profit-sharing dealings, or who shared the precept that wealth should be invested in socially and economically productive ventures rather than idly earning money in interest-bearing accounts.

The first of the contemporary Islamic banks, the Dubai Islamic Bank, was founded in 1975. Between that year and 1983 most new Islamic banks were established in Arab countries. In the past four years Islamic banking has spread more widely, to Asia, Africa and Europe. Today there are more than one hundred Islamic banks and financial institutions throughout the world, and several multinational banking companies. In countries other than Iran and Pakistan, which have required their banking systems to apply Islamic practices, Islamic and interest-based commercial banks operate side by side; increasingly, they cooperate with one another on principles acceptable to both.

In most cases, Islamic banks have paid dividends and profits that compare well with the rates of commercial banks. Islamic bankers shun this sort of comparison, insisting that their clients consider both financial criteria and the satisfaction of conducting their business in accord with religious dictates and ethical traditions. Indeed, some Islamic banking practices are not designed to make a profit, such as *gard hassan*, or social-purpose loans, extended to poor or needy individuals at no charge. "Our clients are not motivated solely by financial gain," General Manager Musa Shihadeh, of the Jordan Islamic Bank, said in a recent interview, "Their two main criteria are to honor their deeply-held religious beliefs, and to deal with banks that offer confidence and minimum risk."

SHUNRYU SUZUKI

On Money

Much of the confusion in our society comes from a lack of understanding about the material world. Having labor as the most important element when you determine the value of work is, I think, a kind of arrogance of human beings. Before we count the value of labor, we must think about all of the other things that are given to us and not ignore the Buddha nature that everything has. If we notice this, our system of life will change a lot. Labor only makes sense when we work with respect. That is its true nature. To count only the labor without having a deep respect for what is worked on is a big mistake. When we work with respect, we experience our human life in its truest sense.

So, we pay for the labor, but we also pay for the things that are given to us by God, or by Buddha. When we have this understanding, our economic system will change. I am not an economist, but this is the way I feel. Money should be treated this way also. You pay with respect for the work done, and money is exchanged. Behind the money there is respect—respect for the things that are given to us by Buddha. And there is respect for the labor, the effort someone made.

To exchange is to purify. We may feel that if we have paid for something with money, we don't owe anything else. But something is missing in that idea. Even though we have paid for the labor, there is something we cannot pay for. We cannot pay the true value of what has been given to us by the Buddha. Only when we pay with respect for the things that are given to us, or for the result of someone's labor, can we purify our life within the activities of exchange. Without this, after we pay for the items we have, we still owe something. That is why we must have great respect for things—for money and for labor. This is Dogen Zenji's idea of everyday life. Our money is not ours. It belongs to society.

Because we think the money is ours, we sometimes think that money is dirty. But it is our understanding that is dirty. Money purifies our world. It is important that we take care of it and respect it. It is only when we don't respect money that it becomes dirty. It doesn't matter how much you have. Even if you have very little money, you should respect it and make the best use of it. The best use of it, I think, is to help our society.

Some people are too attached to money. But to accumulate some money can be allowable, for example, to be ready to enter the hospital or prepare for death. A funeral can cost $5,000 or $10,000. But to rely on the power of money is wrong. During the time of the Buddha, the monetary system was not so strong, so he said don't accumulate things— just live on the food that is offered to you and don't beg for more food than will suffice for the next meal. The Buddha understood economics. The reason we have money is for exchange. We should not stop the flow of the money. The Buddha's first principle is that everything changes.

Money is not a symbol. It expresses the value of things that change. If things are valuable because we can eat them or live on them, then the flow of money should not stop. If money stops flowing, that causes a business depression. If money is flowing slowly throughout the society, the society is healthy.

Before we study Buddhism, we should know what we are doing and how we survive. This is a part of our practice. We do not reject people just because they have no money. We are ready to help each other, but each one of us should purify our practice, even with money. That is why each of us must pay something. If you give us some money, someone will take good care of it. We should not accumulate money for Buddhism. Buddha didn't like to accumulate anything.

MICHAEL PHILLIPS

The Social Dimensions of "Rightlivelihood"

The concept of "rightlivelihood," as summarized by Aldous Huxley in his *Perennial Philosophy*, is that a morally proper life includes work which is rewarding because (a) it serves other people, (b) it deepens the person through continual learning experience, and (c) it does both of these with as little "harm to others" as possible. Buddhists would add that it should encourage moment-to-moment awareness. Other religious teachings suggest that it be a "path with heart."

Relating this vague concept to contemporary life, I would say that ninety-five percent of all jobs come close to total failure on each of the main points. Salaried jobs are usually rotten, to put it mildly, and most others aren't much better.

The relevant religious question is not "What is rightlivelihood?" but "How do we measure the failure of most jobs to have any rightlivelihood at all?"

I propose here to offer a measurement of the degree that any job fails to offer rightlivelihood. Let us take the worst job imaginable and give it a zero. This would be an 800 number telephone operator, who sits at a computer, in a warehouse in Iowa, taking orders for *Time* magazine subscriptions from customers who heard the "get a free Walkman with your new subscription" ad on TV. This job falls down completely on each of the three dimensions I propose for contemporary rightlivelihood measurement: *pace control, consequences, and vulnerability*.

PACE CONTROL

The way we handle time is very relevant to how we lead our moral and ethical lives. If we schedule everything tightly and crowd each appointment very closely together, we leave little time for the unexpected, intense conversation of a desperate friend or time to free a butterfly from a plastic barb. A life filled with hectic movement would not meet even modest humane measurements.

The human in religious terms requires a personalized sense of time. The slave must accept the time of the master, the prisoner of his jailer. The religious response to these circumstances throughout the history of religious zealots being enslaved and put in jail, is to focus on the slave's and the prisoner's *internal* time schedule. We have been taught that the uncontrollable slave/jail circumstances can be used to free the internal clock. Once freed, the internal clock permits the slave/prisoner to contemplate moral issues to achieve *satori*, grace, and nirvana. (Picture Jesus, the mythic image of a jailed slave, forgiving his tormentors.) The point is that our time, our pace becomes less and less ours in many working situations, particularly where we interact with machines.

As I write this on a computer, my pace is directed by the machine, my sensibilities are kinesthetically directed by the keyboard-screen interactions. Picture nine-year-old children trying to do the same thing. They couldn't do it because they have not trained their muscles, their motor energy (which makes them want to jump up and run to open a package in the mail), or their emotional temperament to do it.

Two obvious machines that dictate our pace and focus are a chain saw and an airplane. Imagine using either one while in a genuinely intense mood of sorrow; you'll cut off a leg or neglect to tell the airport control tower that you are making a right turn on takeoff. These machines dictate our pace, our focus and timing. So do other machines to different degrees. A bulldozer driver is kinesthetically clumsy and ferocious; such a person cannot be directly sensitive to the small plants being backed over that a hand shovel operator might notice.

To the extent that machines take away our personal sense of time, our fundamental humanness, they also dictate our timing and shape the pace and focus of our daily lives. To that same extent they determine how much our work fails us on the "pace control" dimension.

Using a scale of 0 to 10 for this dimension alone, the job of a dentist, crane operator, airline pilot, and truck driver would get close to zero, while a university administrator, trial lawyer, Tupperware salesperson, or a minister might get closer to a 10.

CONSEQUENCES

The second dimension is that of "consequences," as in "what are the consequences of this work?" Do people downstream get poisoned by our factory's discharges? Do soldiers use our product to kill noncombatant villagers? Do we perpetuate the eviction of elderly widows from their homes?

Most wise people, and even some ordinary folks, recognize that we cannot know the consequences of our actions. "Doing good" can unpredictably result in bad outcomes. A generous gift of a house to a poor person results in their welfare check being cut off. Helping a man get the job promotion he desperately wanted makes him cocky enough to divorce his wife and leave their children for a beautiful woman in his new department.

So if we can't know consequences, what can we know? We can know consequences as far as we can see downstream in our lives. If we can see several stages of future consequences, the effluent going into the river, the fish downstream dying, and the people eating the fish getting sick, then we can see pretty far. And we might be able to act with some knowledge of our consequences.

Compare our ability to view the consequences, with our own eyes, in a situation where we are in top management reviewing technical reports on effluent and interrogating the expert, versus a lower level job that we leave at 5 p.m., where our bosses tell us that "the effluent is clean, the company experts know there is nothing to worry about."

The ability to see down the stream of consequences further gets a higher mark on this dimension of rightlivelihood. It is assumed that being able to see longer range consequences is in itself a sufficiently positive measure because it gives the moral individual greater opportunity to change behavior. A very moral person, locked in a metaphorical corporate closet, who can't see the consequences of their own actions, can make far more harmful decisions than a morally weak person who might see quite far down the stream of consequences.

Looking carefully at typical jobs, at the companies and institutions in which they are mired, we can readily find a simple rule of thumb.

An employee's ability to see the consequences of their own actions increases in direct proportion to (1) the openness of the institution, (2) the availability of reports on what management is doing, (3) the degree of decentralization in management, and (4) the closeness of the institution to its final customers, community, and suppliers.

The ability to see consequences decreases in circumstances of (1) secrecy (where there is a lack of financial and management information), (2) highly centralized, pyramidal hierarchies of management (such as the military or CIA), and (3) isolation from other workers, customers, and related peers involved in the final use of the institution, product, or service.

High scoring jobs in the consequence dimension would be top managers who work directly with customers, dentists (on this dimension they score high because they see the consequences of their work), residential care nurses, and accountants who have their own businesses. Jobs with close to zero scores in "consequence" would be a low-level machine operator manufacturing an unrecognizable part in a secret project, a clerk who spends full time checking signatures of check endorsements against signature cards, and a truck driver carrying unknown cargo for a large company.

Companies with job rotation, a practice that increases employees' knowledge and experience, do well on this dimension, as do companies where a broad base of employees are involved in decision making, and where many people deal directly with customers.

VULNERABILITY

The third dimension of "vulnerability" is the easiest to understand but not so obvious at first glance.

Why? Because when a moral person sees something going wrong in their work environment (such as acid pouring down the drain) that person has to have the freedom to act positively or stop doing what they are doing *at their own discretion.* If what they are doing is polluting the river, then they need the right to argue with management to stop doing it, do more research, and even to report it to the local press *without being fired or punished.*

Vulnerability is a dimension that measures how much freedom to exercise moral choice exists in any institutional circumstance. If the employee can raise strong objections to working conditions and retain their job and their dignity it is obviously desirable from a rightlivelihood vantage point. If they can be fired for raising even the slightest question, then it scores poorly. Most workers in the U.S. can be fired on the whim of their boss and many more can see their wages and opportunities for promotion frozen for the slightest criticism.

I recall a farm worker who was told to set the gauge on a pesticide dispensing implement much higher than was reasonable and after protesting about it to the field manager was told to "forget it and get back to work." Knowing he would be fired for even mentioning it again, he didn't.

Unions are a big help in this respect as is Civil Service. Jobs rank high on this dimension in companies with grievance and internal appeals processes.

A GRIM PICTURE

All in all, having looked at these three tangible measurements of rightlivelihood in contemporary society, the reader can understand why most work comes off so poorly. As I said in the beginning, five percent of all work might qualify as rightlivelihood.

Few jobs would score 10 in each of the three dimensions to get a total of thirty, but some would. Most self-employed occupations that involve direct contact with customers and little machinery would do well: massage therapists, midwives, and stand-up comedians. Their great advantage is the very direct feedback in their businesses. They can readily see many of the consequences of their actions as well as retain the morally valuable discretion to change or stop any behavior they wish to.

Good scores would also go to jobs in companies and institutions that stay small, that are completely open in every way (financially and otherwise), that rotate employees, give them significant decision making power, and have good job protection rights.

By adding this three-dimensional measurement to the concept of rightlivelihood, an old and wonderful religious idea becomes meaningful in contemporary life.

SULAK SIVARAKSA

A Buddhist Model of Society

The Buddhist sangha, in its pure state, is independent of the fashions of a particular historical period. Its ideals—cooperation, propertylessness, egalitarian democracy—have remained intact for two and a half millennia. Even its robes and eating utensils have stayed the same. In spreading peace and stability throughout their societies, the monastic sangha has guided its followers using a code of nonviolent ethics and social welfare.

Although, since the death of the Buddha, sectors of the sangha have become dependent on state patronage for their well-being and have become more centralized and hierarchical, there remains a core of propertyless and familyless radical clergy who practice the methodology of the Buddha. Communities of Buddhists like these continue to function today in disregard of the elite "State Buddhists."

The modern sangha need not be confined to bhikkhus (monks). It should embrace everyone who follows or respects the way of the Buddha. In the Pali Canon, the Buddha refers to the Four Assemblies of Buddhist society—monks, nuns, laymen, and laywomen. In fact, the sangha includes anyone who is of good conduct.[1]

To create a Buddhist model of society, we must first look into traditional Buddhist notions of social order and social justice. It is worthwhile to begin by examining the Buddhist scriptures regarding secular leadership.

In early Buddhism, a king was said to have ten duties. Two of these concerned foreign policy: commitment to peace and prevention of war. The other eight involved relationship to the people: honesty, gentleness, austerity, self-sacrifice, charity, freedom from enmity, tolerance, and non-obstruction of the will of the people. Early Buddhism clearly mandated that the path to social peace involved holding the government to high standards.

Many people think that Buddhism regards poverty as a desirable quality. They equate poverty with the Buddhist virtues of simplicity and non-indulgence. But poverty, as such, was in no way praised or encouraged by the Buddha. What he regarded as important was how one gained one's wealth and how one used it. The Buddha taught not to be attached to wealth, for this creates craving and suffering.

A praiseworthy Buddhist layperson seeks wealth rightfully and uses it for the good and happiness of herself and others. She devotes much of her wealth to support the sangha and to alleviate the suffering and poverty of others. She also enjoys spiritual freedom—not being attached to, infatuated with, or enslaved by the wealth.

In an ideal Buddhist society, under righteous and effective administration, there would be no poverty. Everyone would enjoy economic self-sufficiency, except for the monks and nuns, who would intentionally be sustained by the surplus material resources of the lay society, so that the laypeople could be guided by the monks' lifestyles and spiritual progress. In the old days, such an ideal society may not have existed anywhere, but Buddhist countries had a tradition of righteous rulers who tried to adhere to Buddhist virtues and qualities. Using the ideal of the righteous ruler, the citizens had a yardstick by which they could measure the successes and failures of their leaders.

In the Buddhist ideal society, ordinary citizens also had responsibilities. The society could function only to the degree that the people were honest, moral, generous, tolerant, and confident. It was important that they be energetic, industrious, and skillful; live in a good environment; associate with good people; have a balanced livelihood; and direct themselves. On the social side, everyone was expected to maintain good relationships with others and to make some contribution to the happiness and well-being of society.

Leaders should use "skillful means," then, for their own happiness and for the happiness of others in creating a world of less greed, hatred, and delusion. Righteousness and ethics are essential. The Buddha said:

> When kings are righteous, the ministers of kings are righteous, brahmans and householders are also righteous, and the townsfolk and villagers are righteous. This being so, moon and sun go right in their course. This being so, constellations and stars do likewise; days and nights, months and fortnights, seasons and years go on their courses regularly; winds blow regularly and in due season; men who live on these crops are long-lived, well-favored, strong and free from sickness.[2]

The Buddha also spoke about an ideal society:

> If people are righteous and mindful, using enlightenment as guidelines for their way of life, they can achieve the desirable society... A righteous Universal Monarch would be born in this kingdom, and the people would live in peace and justice throughout the Earth.[3]

Most Buddhists presume that this kind of ideal state is impossible in our own era, but will come about during the time of Maitreya, the next Buddha. Some post-canonical texts state the teachings of Shakyamuni Buddha will last only 5,000 years. The decline was supposed to have begun 2,500 years after the Buddha's death. If one interprets this literally, things will only get worse in the years and centuries ahead.

Buddhism, like any other world religion, would support the status quo if the society were righteous. In the past, when rulers lost their legitimacy, Buddhism would utilize its prophetic element to encourage social upheaval.

Today's situation calls for the same. It is sad but true that most contemporary leaders even in Buddhist countries can be regarded as failures. Yet despite this, or rather because of it, I believe we will see a rebirth of the prophetic element of religions to challenge injustice and promote morality.

If we Buddhists want to play a meaningful role in reinstating the virtues of peace and justice in the world, we need to be bold enough to question the present violent and unjust structures, not only the single acts of individuals and countries. And we will need to cooperate with

Christians, Hindus, Jews, Muslims, and those of other religions and ideologies, asking questions like, "Why are we so good at producing far too
much and so bad at helping where there is too little?"

There is much less wealth to be made providing basic needs than in
pursuing greed. As a result, precious resources are wasted on arms, luxury
goods, and drug trafficking. We should be able to see through these
things, and, with the help of friends, be able to coax these structures in
other directions. The number of people who call themselves Buddhists
is not particularly important, but the world does need Buddhist ethics,
Buddhist meditation, and Buddhist insight. We all need good friends
from our own and other religious traditions and ideologies if we want to
help in resolving personal and international conflicts, and creating peace
and justice for human beings and for nature. To accomplish this, we
need responsive and responsible international institutions. The United
Nations must become a true world government that represents all people
and cultures and is not just controlled by a few. The narrow concept of
nationalism needs to be rejected and replaced by mutual concern for all.

Only when we all transcend narrow concepts of our own selfish "national interests" will we be able to build a harmonious world in which
every problem is perceived to be a mutual problem calling for collective
responsibility.

I would like to make the following proposals:

A transnational response to the transnationalization of capital. The world
economy has become increasingly unified. Big companies today operate
globally, but political institutions have not kept up with these economic
realities. We need new, powerful institutions capable of taxing and regu-
lating transnational corporations, and we need international unions to
represent workers dealing with global capitalists.

Political and economic solidarity of the South in dealing with the North.
There cannot be world peace without economic justice. Thus, Third
World solidarity is indispensable to the establishment of peace and a
new generation of strong institutions is necessary to consolidate the
power of the South in its negotiations with the North.

Arms control, conflict resolution, and security maintenance. If economic
interdependence provides the carrot for world federalism, the threat of
complete annihilation provides the stick. The world order in the twenty-

first century will have to emerge from the contradictions of the global arms industry, and we can influence its course.

Curbing consumerism. The religion of consumerism emphasizes greed, hatred, and delusion. It teaches people to look down on their own indigenous, self-reliant culture in the name of progress and modernization. We need to live simply in order to subvert the forces of consumerism and materialism.

Democracy, egalitarianism, and international organization. The early Buddhists held that decentralized, egalitarian, democratic structures were the most conducive for the achievement of personal and social liberation. When questions of concern to the entire community had to be decided, the monastic community as a whole would gather and vote. A contemporary Buddhist internationalism might envision institutions designed not to represent the interests of nation-states but rather of human beings. By moving away from its status as a league of nation-states and an institution for solving nation-state conflicts to becoming a true world parliament elected directly by a world citizenry, the United Nations could become an organization that truly reflects the interests of humanity. The current UN General Assembly might be maintained as an "upper house," while a new 500-member world parliament could be established as a "lower house," with electorates of ten million people each. This idea is only possible if support for it is made a priority by those in the progressive movements of the North. Once the decision-making process of UN institutions is viewed as legitimate, we can begin to construct and strengthen international conflict-resolution machinery. This might include four pillars:

A global disarmament administration. Probably connected with an international satellite system monitoring weapons stockpiles, some machinery is necessary to deal with violations and arbitration of disarmament agreements.

A strengthened international judiciary. To adjudicate violations of international law and impose binding sanctions, this would discourage the current double standards whereby powerful countries play by different sets of rules than weaker ones.

A permanent, strengthened, international peacekeeping force. This would have to be recruited independently of existing armies and used to enforce universal rules.

A *Universal Bill of Rights*. This is needed to ensure the basic rights of all people to live in peace and freedom. In many ways this is the key. When Prince Siddhartha saw an old man, a sick man, a corpse, and a wandering monk, he was moved to seek salvation, and eventually he became the Buddha, the Awakened One. The death and destruction throughout the world today compel us to think and act together to overcome all suffering and bring about the awakening of humankind.

To alleviate suffering, we must always go back to our own spiritual depths—to retreat, meditation, and prayer. It is nearly impossible to sustain the work otherwise. It is easy to hate our enemies—the industrialists who exploit us and pollute our atmosphere. But we must come to see that there is no "other." We are all one human family. It is greed, hatred, and delusion that we need to overcome.

When we see this clearly, we will work hand in hand with everyone. This is the lesson of the Buddha, and I try to put it into practice in my life and in my work for society. Without friends, we can accomplish nothing. As a worldwide network of friends, peaceful and loving, we can overcome all obstacles.

NOTES

[1] *Majjhimanikaya*, Volume 1, p. 37.

[2] *Aggañña Sutta*.

[3] *Cakkavatti Sihananda Sutta*.

Mindfulness and Meaningful Work

Orare est laborare, laborare est orare.
[To pray is to work, to work is to pray].
                              —Ancient motto of the Benedictine order

By the work one knows the workman.
                              —Jean de La Fontaine

I am the people—the mob—the crowd—the mass.
Do you know that all the great work of the world is done through me?
                              —Carl Sandburg

I hear America singing, the varied carols I hear,
Those of mechanics, each one singing his as it should be
    blithe and strong,
The carpenter singing his as he measures his plank or beam,
The mason singing his as he makes ready for work, or leaves off work,
The boatman singing what belongs to him in his boat,
    the deckhand singing on the steamboat deck,
The shoemaker singing as he sits on his bench,
    the hatter singing as he stands,
The woodcutter's song, the ploughboy's on his way in the morning,
    or at noon intermission or at sundown,
The delicious singing of the mother, or of the young wife at work,
    or of the girl sewing or washing,
Each singing what belongs to him or her and to none else,
The day that belongs to the day—at night the party of young fellows,
    robust, friendly,
Singing with open mouths their strong melodious songs.
                              —Walt Whitman

SHAKTI GAWAIN

Work and Play

Work and play are the same. When you're following your energy and doing what you want all the time, the distinction between work and play dissolves. Work is no longer what you have to do or play what you want to do. When you are doing what you love, you may work harder and produce more than ever before, but it will feel like play.

The people I work with, in groups and individually, are often wondering what they are "going to be when they grow up." What is it they're going to do, what is their true purpose? I tell them that each one of us has a true purpose and each one of us is a channel for the universe. When we follow the light, everything is fun, creative, and transformational. We make a contribution to the world just by being ourselves in every moment. There are no more rigid categories in our lives such as this is work, this is play. It all blends into the flow of following the universe and money flows in as a result of the open channel that's created. You no longer work in order to make money. Work is no longer something you have to do in order to sustain life. Instead, the delight that comes from expressing yourself becomes the greatest reward. The money comes along as a natural part of being alive. Working and getting money may no longer even be directly related to each other; you may experience that you are doing whatever you have energy to do and that money is coming into your life. It's no longer a matter of, "You do this and then you get money for it." The two things are simply operating simultaneously in your life but not necessarily in a direct cause-and-effect relationship.

In the new world, it's difficult to pin your life's work and true purpose down to any one thing. In terms of looking for a career, our old-world concept told us that when we became adults, we had to decide what our career would be, and then pursue an education or other steps to achieve that career. The career would then be pursued for most or all of our life.

In the new world, many of us are channels for a number of things which may come together in fascinating combinations. Perhaps you haven't found your career because it doesn't exist yet. Your particular and unique way of expressing yourself has never existed before and will never be repeated again. As you practice following the energy in your life, it will start to lead you in many directions. You will begin to express yourself in a variety of ways, all of which will begin to synthesize in some surprising, interesting, and very new, creative way. You will no longer be able to say, "I am a writer (or a fireman or a teacher or a housewife)." You may be a combination of all of those things. You'll be doing what you love, what you're good at, what comes easily to you and has an element of challenge and excitement to it. Whatever you do will feel satisfying and fulfilling to you. It is no longer a matter of doing things now for later gratification: "I will work hard now so that I can get a better job later. I will work hard now so that I can retire and enjoy my life. I will work hard now in order to have enough money and time to have a vacation where I can have fun." It's the fulfillment of what you're doing at this very moment that counts. In being a channel, everything you do becomes a contribution; even the simplest things are significant.

It is the energy of the universe moving through us that transforms, not the particular things we do. When I write a book that has a certain amount of wisdom in it, it's the energy that impacts people. It's the energy of the universe that comes through me and connects to the reader's deeper levels of awareness. The words and ideas are the icing on the cake. They are the things that enable our minds to grasp what has already been changed. It is not so important that I wrote a book. What is important is that I expressed myself, opened up and allowed the creative energy to flow through me. That creative energy is now penetrating other people and things in this world. I had the joy of that energy moving through me and other people had the joy of receiving that energy. That's the transformational experience.

Whether you are washing the dishes, taking a walk, or building a house, if you're doing it with a sense of being right where you want to be and doing what you want to be doing, that fullness and joy in the experience will be felt by everyone around you. If you're building a house and somebody walks by and sees you doing it, they will feel the impact of the fullness of your experience. Their lives will be transformed to the degree that they are ready to allow the energy's impact. Though they may not know what hit them, they will start to experience life differently. It's the same when you're just being. If you walk into a room, feeling one with yourself, knowing who you are, knowing that you're a channel, and expressing yourself in whatever way feels right to you, then everyone in the room will be transformed. Even though they may not recognize it or know anything about it consciously, you will be able to see the direct result of your channel operating. You will see proof of it in watching the changes in people. It is an incredibly exciting and satisfying experience.

You can see that it is no longer an issue of focusing on one particular thing, although you may be led to focus and build structure in a particular area. You may choose to learn certain skills that you will use to allow your channel to function in a way that it wants to function. If you do this, you will be led to it easily and naturally. The process of learning will be just as much fun as the doing. In other words, it is no longer necessary to sacrifice in the moment so that in the future you will be able to have what you want. The learning process will be full of fun, joy, and excitement. You'll experience it as being exactly what you want to be doing at that time. Practicing, learning skills, going to school—all of this can be fun and fulfilling when you are following your intuitive guidance.

Conversely, the work you do will be a learning experience. For example, I teach workshops, not because I've mastered information and I am the teacher and you are the student, but because I love to share myself in this way. This sharing deepens my learning experience. Again, there is no difference between learning and teaching, just as there is no difference between work and play. It all begins to blend into one totally integrated and balanced experience.

Most people do have some sense, at least deep inside, of what they would love to be doing. This feeling is often so repressed, however, that it is experienced only in the form of some wildly impractical fantasy, something you could never do. I always encourage people to get in touch with these fantasies. Observe and explore thoroughly your most incredible fantasy of how you'd like to be and what you'd like to be doing. There is truth in this desire. Even if it seems impossible, there is at least a grain of truth in the image. It is telling you something about who you really are and what it is you really want to be doing.

Your fantasies can tell you how you really want to be expressing yourself. Many times, I've found that people have a strong sense of what they would like to do, yet they take up a career that is very different from their desire. Sometimes they go for the opposite because they feel it is practical or will gain the approval of their parents or the world. They figure it is impossible to do what they really want, so they might as well settle for something else that comes along. I encourage people to risk exploring the things that really turn them on. The following are examples of people I've worked with and their exploration of their true purpose:

1. A brilliant and talented woman I know had been working with sick and dying people for many years. Although she was a great nurse and a powerful healer, it became evident to her that she needed to be where she could express herself more creatively. With encouragement, she started working fewer days as a nurse and began leading workshops and counseling people. Because she's doing this she feels more fulfilled and those around her feel her fulfillment, as well.

2. Joseph, following family tradition, went into business with his father and brothers. He was very successful in real estate and contracting. The problem was, he knew there was something else he wanted to do with his life. After lots of encouragement from the group in one of my workshops, he admitted that he wanted to work in the arts, but knew his family would frown on it. He most wanted to be a dancer. The first step was admitting to himself what he wanted to do. Eventually, he mustered the courage to take dance classes. He had a lot of talent and immediately attracted the attention of the teacher. He continued to explore

this form of artistic expression. When he supported his desires, he actually found that his family was equally supportive.

3. A close friend of mine had three children, no education, and was living on welfare. Her desire was to get into business. She intuitively felt she was going to handle large amounts of money, but considering her situation, this didn't make sense. Nevertheless, she decided to explore some possibilities in the financial district of San Francisco. She was immediately hired as a receptionist in a firm and found the perfect live-in baby-sitter for her children. From receptionist, she went on to be an administrative assistant and continued to rise to higher levels of skill and responsibility. She is moving steadily toward her goal of being a stockbroker. She loves what she's doing and her children are flourishing as well.

4. A woman who came to a recent workshop of mine shared that she'd been a talented pianist with hopes of becoming a concert pianist. Then, for several reasons, the most predominant being a lack of faith in herself, she had given up her dream. She started working in an office and found that between work and her children she had little time for her music. After fifteen years she felt it was simply too late to ever go back to the piano. She felt the time she had lost in not playing rendered hopeless any chance of being great. Despite all her doubts, we encouraged her to at least start playing again. I assured her that if she was doing what she loved it would come back to her easily. As she opened to this idea, she started opening to herself. Her sense of hopelessness was replaced by a renewed sense of power. She called later to say she had been playing the piano and feeling great about it. A friend had asked her to play accompaniment for a choral group and she was feeling very excited about the musical possibilities opening up for her.

MEDITATION

Sit or lie down in a comfortable position. Close your eyes and relax. Take several slow, deep breaths, relaxing your body more deeply with each breath. Take several more breaths and relax your mind. Release and relax all the tension in your body. If you want, imagine that your body is almost sinking into the floor, bed, or chair.

From this very relaxed place inside, imagine that you are doing exactly what you want in your life. You have a fabulous career that is fun and fulfilling for you. You are now doing what you've always fantasized about and getting a tremendous sum of money for it.

You feel relaxed, energized, creative, and powerful. You are successful at what you do because it is exactly what you want to be doing.

You follow your intuition moment to moment and are richly rewarded for it.

EXERCISES

1. Follow any impulses you have in the direction of your true work/play desires. Even if it seems totally unrealistic, follow the impulse anyway. For example, if you're sixty-five years old and have always wanted to be a ballet dancer, go to a ballet class and observe, or if you want, take the class. Watch some ballet and imagine that you're a dancer. While alone at home, put on some music and dance. This will get you in touch with that part of yourself that wants to be expressed that way. You may end up dancing much more than you thought possible, and you may be led to other forms of expression that will feel as good.

2. List any fantasies you've had around work, career, or creativity, and beside that list the action you plan to take to explore this.

3. Write an "ideal scene," a description of your perfect job or career exactly as you would like it to be. Write it in the present tense, as if it were already true. Put in enough description and details to make it seem very real. Put it away somewhere, and look at it again in a few months or even a year or two. Unless your fantasy has changed completely in that time, chances are that you will find you have made significant progress in the direction of your dream.

E.F. SCHUMACHER

Good Work

Traditional wisdom teaches that the function of work is at heart three-fold: (1) to give a person a chance to utilize and develop his faculties; (2) to enable him to overcome his inborn egocentricity by joining with other people in a common task; and (3) to bring forth the goods and services needed by all of us for a decent existence.

I think all this needs to be taught.

What is the current teaching with regard to work? I do not quite know, but, at least until quite recently, I heard it said everywhere that the real task of education was not education for work, but education for leisure. Maybe this extraordinary idea has now been abandoned. Fancy telling young and eager souls, "Now, what I really want you to envisage is how to kill time when you have nothing useful to do."

As our ancestors have known (it has been expressed by Thomas Aquinas), there can be no joy of life without joy of work. This is a statement worth pondering. Laziness, they also know, is sadness of the soul. This, too, is worth pondering. A nineteenth-century thinker said something like this: Just watch it a bit. If you get too many useful machines you will get too many useless people. Another statement worth pondering.

The question is raised: How do we prepare young people for the future world of work? and the first answer, I think, must be: We should prepare them to be able to distinguish between good work and bad work and encourage them not to accept the latter. That is to say, they should be encouraged to reject meaningless, boring, stultifying, or nerve-racking work in which a man or woman is made the servant of a machine or a system. They should be taught that work is the joy of life and is needed for our development, but that meaningless work is an abomination.

A sensitive British worker wrote this:

> It is probably wrong to expect factories to be other than they are. After all, they are built to house machines, not men. Inside a factory it soon becomes obvious that steel brought to life by electricity takes precedence over flesh and blood. The onus is on the machines to such an extent that they appear to assume human attributes of those who work them. Machines have become as much like people as people have become like machines. They pulsate with life, while man becomes a robot. There is a premonition of man losing control, an awareness of doom.

It is probably wrong to expect, he says, good work. He has been conditioned not even to expect it! He has been conditioned to believe that man himself is "nothing but" a somewhat complex physico-chemical system, "nothing but" a product of mindless evolution—so he may suffer when machines become like men and men become like machines, but he cannot really be surprised or expect anything else.

It is interesting to note that the modern world takes a lot of care that the worker's body should not accidentally or otherwise be damaged. If it *is* damaged, the worker may claim compensation. But his soul and his spirit? If his work damages him, by reducing him to a robot—that is just too bad. Here we can see very clearly the crucial importance of metaphysics. Materialistic metaphysics, or the metaphysics of the doctrine of mindless evolution, does not attribute reality to anything but the physical body: why then bother about safety or health when it comes to such nebulous, unreal things as soul or spirit? We acknowledge, and understand the need for, the development of a person's body; but the development of his soul or spirit? Yes, education for the sake of enabling a man or woman to make a living; but education for the sake of leading them out of the dark wood of egocentricity, pettiness, and worldly ignorance? At the most, this would be a purely private affair: does it not smack of "copping out" and "turning one's back on reality"? Materialistic meta-physics, therefore, leaves no room for the idea of good work, that work is good for the worker. Anyone who says, "The worker needs work for the development and perfection of his soul," sounds like a fanciful dreamer, because materialistic metaphysics does not recognize any such need. It recognizes the needs of the body; that they can be met only by somebody's work is an unpleasant fact and perhaps automation will soon abolish it. Meanwhile, the work needs to be done. Let's get on with it, but make sure the body doesn't get hurt.

If we see work as nothing but an unpleasant necessity, it is no use talking about good work, unless we mean less work. Why put any good-ness into our work beyond the absolute minimum? Who could afford to do good work? What would be the point of making something perfect when something imperfect would do as well? Ananda Coomaraswamy used to say: "Industry without art is brutality." Why? Because it damages the soul and spirit of the worker. He could say this only because his metaphysics is very different from that of the modern world. He also said: "It is not as if the artist were a special kind of man; every man is a special kind of artist." This is the metaphysics of good work. How, then, could there be education for good work?

First of all, we should have to alter the metaphysical basis from which we proceed. If we continue to teach that the human being is nothing but the outcome of a mindless, meaningless, and purposeless process of evolution, a process of "selection" for survival, that is to say, the out-come of nothing but utilitarianism—we only come to a utilitarian idea of work: that work is nothing but a more or less unpleasant necessity, and the less there is of it the better. Our ancestors knew about good work, but we cannot learn from them if we continue to treat them with friendly contempt—as pathetic illusionists who wasted their time wor-shipping nonexisting deities; and if we continue to treat traditional wis-dom as a tissue of superstitious poetry, not to be taken seriously; and if we continue to take materialistic scientism as the one and only measure of progress. The best scientists know that science deals only with small isolated systems, showing how they work, and provides no basis whatso-ever for comprehensive metaphysical doctrines like the doctrine of mind-less evolution. But we nevertheless still teach the young that the modern theory of evolution is part of science and that it leaves no room for divine guidance or design, thus wantonly creating an apparent conflict between science and religion and causing untold confusion.

Education for good work could then begin with a systematic study of traditional wisdom, where answers are to be found to the questions such as: What is man? Where does he come from? What is the purpose of his life? It would then emerge that there is indeed a goal to be reached and that there is also a path to the goal—in fact, that there are many paths to the same summit. The goal can be described as "perfection" ("Be ye therefore as perfect as your father in heaven is perfect") or as "the king-dom," "salvation," "nirvana," "liberation," "enlightenment," and so forth. And the path to the goal? Good work. "Work out your salvation with diligence." Don't bury your talents and don't let anybody else bury them. He who has been given much, of him much will be demanded. In short, life is some sort of school, and in this school nothing counts but good work, work that ennobles the product as it ennobles the producer.

In the process of doing good work the ego of the worker disappears. He frees himself from his ego, so that the divine element in him can become active. Of course, none of this makes sense if we proceed from the basic presuppositions of materialistic scientism. How could the prod-uct of mindless evolution, whose abilities are only those selected by blind nature for their utilitarian value in the universal struggle for survival—how could such a product of chance and necessity free itself from its ego, the center of its will to survive? What a nonsensical proposition! And the assumption of the existence of a divine element in man is, of course, entirely pre-scientific!

"The world of work," as seen and indeed created by this modern meta-physics, is alas! a dreary place. Can higher education prepare people for it? How do you prepare people for a kind of serfdom? What human quali-ties are required for becoming efficient servants, machines, "systems," and bureaucracies? The world of work of today is the product of a hun-dred years of "de-skilling"—why take the trouble and incur the cost of letting people acquire the skills of a craftsman, when all that is wanted is a machine winder? The only skills worth acquiring are those which the system demands, and they are worthless outside the system. They have no survival value outside the system and therefore do not even confer the spirit of self-reliance. What does a machine winder do when

(let us say) energy shortage stops his machine? Or a computer program-
mer without a computer?

Maybe higher education could be designed to lead to a different world
of work—different from the one we have today. This, indeed, would be
my most sincere hope. But how could this be as long as higher education
clings to the metaphysics of materialistic scientism and its doctrine of
mindless evolution? It cannot be. Figs cannot grow on thistles. Good
work cannot grow out of such metaphysics. To try to make it grow from
such a base can do nothing but increase the prevailing confusion. The
most urgent need of our time is and remains the need for metaphysical
reconstruction, a supreme effort to bring clarity into our deepest convictions with regard to the questions: What is man? Where does he come
from? and What is the purpose of his life?

ROBERT GILMAN

Emerging Patterns in the Workplace

The key issue facing organizations today is how to combine "empowerment" and "coordination." If people are to be more productive and effective, they need to make more use of their full human potential, they need to feel motivated in their work, and they need to be able to respond to opportunities and changes as they happen. This suggests considerable independence, yet today's complex activities also require a great deal of interdependence, specialization, and coordination. It does indeed seem like a paradox, but there are signs that it is being unravelled, as the following examples illustrate.

The Mondragon Cooperatives in the Basque region of Northern Spain are probably the world's most successful group of employee-owned private companies. Their system encompasses more than 20,000 workers in eighty-five industrial cooperatives, as well as a bank (one of Spain's largest) and a major research institute. To create their remarkable system, they began by redefining the usual rules of ownership to give it a more democratic character. Every employee must contribute significant capital ($5,000 or more, treated formally as a loan), but control and profit sharing are based on working involvement, not the size of each employee's investment. The board of directors is elected on a one-person/one-vote basis. On the other hand, the day-to-day operation of each cooperative uses an (at least partially) conventional management system that gives managers clearly defined real power. At the production level, however, they work often in self-supervised teams. They have found that, to maintain a close community feeling in each cooperative, it is necessary to keep the size of each group under 500 employee-owners. The relationship between cooperatives within the federation is in some ways like divisions in a large corporation and in other ways like independent units in the marketplace.

Kollmorgan Corporation has turned corporate decentralization into a resounding success. It is a collection of sixteen semi-autonomous divisions that manufacture printed circuit boards, specialty electric motors, periscopes, sophisticated electro-optical equipment, and related products. It has about 5,500 employees and annual sales of $350 million. While not as deeply innovative in its structure as the Mondragon Cooperatives, it is remarkable in American business for the effectiveness with which it has decentralized decision making and built team spirit. From 1970 (when it gave up on its previous attempts at centralized control) through 1982, its sales grew by a factor of eight, yet all this was overseen by a corporate staff of only twenty-five. The basic organizational unit is the product team (typically about fifty people), which has almost total control over the making and selling of their item, and which receives profit-sharing bonuses based on that product's performance (thus bringing direct marketplace feedback to everyone in the business). Overall, Kollmorgan distributes about one-third of its pre-tax profits in such bonuses. Each division, whose size is kept below 500 employees in order to maintain a family atmosphere, is made up of product teams that can share overhead and equipment. Each division's board of directors is made up largely of top executives from the other division's—peers rather than organizational superiors—and decisions are made by consensus. Within each division, monthly "People Meetings" give all employees a voice in running the business. As part of their regular annual review process, employees evaluate their supervisors. While Kollmorgan does have a chain of command, its levels are few, status differences are kept to a minimum, and most decisions are made at the team level.

W.L. Gore & Associates goes even further with no formal ranks or titles at all. Best known as the makers of Gore-tex fabric for rain gear, they also produce a wide range of other products from medical supplies to electronic components to systems for desalinating water and recovering waste oil. Started in 1958, the company now has 4,000 employees, or rather, "associates," in thirty plants around the world and annual sales of over $150 million. They call their system a "lattice organization." When a new associate joins the company, s/he is not assigned a job. Instead s/he wanders around (with friendly help) until s/he finds something that needs doing (not hard to find) and that s/he wants to do. This generally means becoming part of a work team (or creating a new one) in which an already established associate will act as sponsor (not boss) for the new employee. New teams are formed whenever a group of associates has a new direction they want to go in. The leadership within the group is not assigned but comes from whatever natural leadership develops. Objectives are set by those who must make them happen, and tasks and functions are organized by commitments between the associates. Pay is set by compensation teams with sponsors acting as advocates for each associate. Associates (including the Gore family) own ninety percent of the company stock (although without the full employee-ownership structure that Mondragon has), with each associate receiving annually stock equivalent to fifteen percent of their salary. As Bill Gore explains, each plant is kept small to maintain a "we" feeling. The relationships between the plants is a combination of community and marketplace.

Intrapreneuring is not the name of an organization. It is a way to bring innovation into large organizations by encouraging the development of small teams that can operate with almost entrepreneurial freedom. In his book, *Intrapreneuring*, Gifford Pinchot III describes an intrapreneur as someone "who takes hands-on responsibility for creating innovation of any kind within an organization." For intrapreneuring to work, intrapreneurs must be self-selected, they need to be allowed to follow through with their project, and they need to be able to make most of the decisions about its development. The organization needs to provide them with guidelines to work within, resources, and patience. One of Pinchot's most intriguing suggestions is that successful intrapreneurs be rewarded with "intracapital"—effectively an internal bank account funded from the profits of the intrapreneur's successful innovation and available to that intrapreneur as capital for future projects. Such a system would convert today's centrally controlled corporations into confederations of innovative teams backed up and held together by various support staffs.

COMMON THREADS

While there is a lot of diversity within these (and similar) examples, there are also some strong common themes. The keys seem to me to be:

Size. Again and again, the message comes through that effective working units must be small enough to maintain a sense of family, of "we." Whether the upper limit to this is 200 or 500 may depend on the specifics of the situation, but there is no question that somewhere in that range is a very important human systems natural limit. Organizations can be larger than this by federating these units together, but it is essential that each unit be empowered to make the most of its own decisions and that it get direct feedback from the market it serves.

Appropriate Leadership. All of these organizations are held together more through leadership than through tight management. This leadership creates a social architecture within which the business lives rather than attempting to dictate what each employee should do. It emphasizes vision (rather than commands), clear and open communications and procedures (kept simple enough to be effective), trust-building integrity, and a clear confidence in people. These four qualities closely parallel those described by Warren Bennis and Burt Nanus in their book, *Leaders*.

Appropriate Ownership and Control. Although the degree varies among these examples, in each of them profit sharing and a significant voice in decision making are crucial, unavoidable elements essential for cementing the necessary alignment and "we-ness." This is probably the most sensitive area of change, and the one that will be most vigorously resisted by the present business establishment both in management and on Wall Street. (I've noticed that most of the currently popular authors who are writing for the managerial audience about business innovation avoid it like the plague.) Yet, much to the credit of the competitive marketplace, this revolutionary change is moving forward both rapidly and peacefully. Those businesses in which employees do have significant ownership and control prove time and again to be much more productive than the rest.

In their own way, American companies are gradually evolving toward the pattern pioneered by the Mondragon cooperatives almost thirty years ago. In the process, they are developing a wonderful richness of variation that adapts the basic principles to the needs of many different industries and to a diverse culture. At the same time, they are reinforcing the validity of these principles. It is looking increasingly likely that the large business of the future will look more like Mondragon or Gore than like IBM or GM.

JAMES ROBERTSON

The Future of Work

As we reach the final years of the present millennium, we are entering a new phase of human history. The new postmodern patterns of life and thought will reflect the emergence of a one-world human community, in which people will relate in a new way to themselves, to one another, to nature, and to what is larger than all of those and provides the framework and context for them.

Many people today, conditioned as they are by the scientific worldview of the modern age, think of the future as something which already exists. For them the future is there, down the track, waiting to be reached. Their concern about it, if they have one, is to forecast it and prepare for it. But that is not good enough. We humans help to create the future, each one of us, whether we like it or not. We are responsible for choosing between different possible futures, and for helping to realize the future we prefer.

A BRIEF HISTORY OF WORK

When thinking about the future of work and the transformation of work that is now in prospect, it is instructive to look back on how work has been organized in past ages. In ancient societies, such as classical Greece and Rome, most people worked as slaves. In medieval Europe, most people worked as serfs. In modern industrial societies, most people work as employees. At least in a formal legal sense this development reflects some progress towards greater freedom and equality. Nevertheless, in modern, as in ancient and medieval society, the organization of work still reflects and reinforces the domination of subordinates by superiors: then, of slaves by masters and serfs by lords; now, of employees by employers. The assumption still is that most people should work for people and organizations other than themselves and for purposes other than their own.

In the 1980s we heard a lot about the need to shake off a dependency culture. But the way people work, and what they regard as work, is at the heart of a culture. In the 1990s we must confront the need to change the way we organize and understand work, so that most people will no longer be compelled to depend either on an employer to give them work or on the state to give them the dole.

In other words, the postmodern era must be one in which employment is no longer the dominant form of work. The transition to the new era must include a liberation of work. Employment must give way to "ownwork" as the norm to which most people aspire.

Ownwork, as I have said in my book *Future Work*, is "activity which is purposeful and important, and which people organize and control for themselves. It may be either paid or unpaid. It is done by people as individuals and household members; it is done by groups of people working together; and it is done by people, who live in a particular locality, working locally to meet local needs. For the individual and the household, ownwork may mean self-employment, essential household and family activities, productive leisure activities such as do-it-yourself or growing some of one's own food, and participation in voluntary work. For groups of people, ownwork may mean working together as partners, perhaps in a community enterprise or a cooperative, or in a multitude of other activities—with social, economic, environmental, scientific, or other purposes—in which they have a personal interest and to which they attach personal importance. For localities, the significance of ownwork is that it contributes to local self-reliance, an increased local capacity to meet local needs by local work, and a reduction of dependence on outside employers and suppliers."

I am suggesting that the new consciousness and new social order will involve, among other things, a transformation of the dominant form of work from employment to ownwork.

THE CONTEXT FOR THE TRANSFORMATION

The medieval-to-modern transition was from a morally and religiously based worldview and world order to a worldview and world order claiming to be objectively scientific. So modern economic life including people's work choices, and also their consumer choices and investment decisions is supposedly governed by value-free economic laws, not subject to ethical decision. (Don't mix ethics with economics, the economics professors tell their students.)

Now, nature abhors a vacuum, and the resulting ethical vacuum in economic life has been filled with the values of greed and power and competition. Global ecological and social catastrophe now threatens. A fundamental change of direction is necessary to a new path of development. As more and more people have become aware of this, a worldwide "new economics" movement has come into existence in the 1980s, including The Other Economic Summits (TOES) held annually since 1984.

In the next ten or twenty or thirty years, the new economics movement envisages a transformation of economic life and thought. Today's conventional economic approach is amoral, dependency-creating for people, and destructive for the Earth. These characteristics can be traced back to the thinking of the founders of modern thought: Bacon, Galileo, Descartes, Hobbes, Newton, and Adam Smith, though, in my view, it is silly to blame them for it. The new ways of economic life and thought must be enabling for people, conserving if not positively enriching for the Earth, and ethically based. Those are the underlying principles of the new economics. I believe they will form part of a wider new consciousness and social order—ethical, developmental, and (to borrow Albert Schweitzer's phrase) with reverence for Life.

And that, I believe, is the wider context in which we should be aiming to create a new future for work.

REDEFINING WORK AND THE WORKPLACE

There are two important alternative views of the future of work which must be discussed. First is the approach of those who focus on people working in companies, such as the work of economist Fred Blum with Hormel, a meat packing and canning firm in the United States, and the Scott Bader Commonwealth, the common ownership pioneer in Great Britain. Blum's approach reflects the modern view of work as something done in employing organizations. One of the strengths of this approach is that that is how most people still understand work in countries like ours today, as employment, having a job. So, in that sense, it reflects where we actually have to start from.

The other view of the future of work, as typified by the approach I take, emphasizes the need to redefine work to include many kinds of purposeful and useful and rewarding activity, unpaid as well as paid, in addition to work in employing organizations. I think we need to create new opportunities for increasing numbers of people to take up many kinds of ownwork. We need also to ask how it was that the firm or enterprise ever came to be regarded as the basic unit of economic activity and wealth creation. Why, when modern economic ideas took shape, was the household or the local community not regarded as the basic building block in the economy? Why did the term "workplace" come to be attached to factories and offices, and not to households or communities? And how should we now set about turning those industrial-age definitions and assumptions on their heads?

There are, of course, serious difficulties here. Most of the people who concern themselves today with "the world of work" don't understand this approach or see it as practical or relevant. They don't see how it addresses the problems of the many millions of people who are now in unsatisfactory jobs, or who, being unemployed, want jobs. Business, government, and the established foundations are unwilling to support action research into the potential for reconceptualizing and restructuring work in this way.

And yet, surely, only by exploring the possibility of replacing employment with ownwork as the norm shall we be able to understand what a new consciousness and a new social order, that puts people first and focuses on the development of human potential, will actually mean. Because work is such a central feature of social organization and culture, an ownwork society will differ fundamentally from an employment society.

Take the question of men's work and women's work. In preindustrial societies, most men and women worked around their homes and neighborhoods, as part of the local village community. Then, in industrial society the split between men's work and women's work widened. Men became "economically active" members of the "work force," going out to "workplaces" in "the world of work" to do paid, high-status, impersonal kinds of work, more or less unrelated to their own personal and family interests and concerns. Meanwhile, women stayed at home, "dependents" of their menfolk, looking after the home and family—doing unpaid, low-status work, but with much more direct personal involvement and concern. Many of the problems and injustices resulting from this split are still with us today. By contrast, the ownwork society will offer men and women alike a more equal and balanced share in both the formal and informal sectors of this dual economy.

Or, again, take technology. An ownwork society will involve the development of enabling technologies which people—either as individuals, or as cooperatives, or as local communities—can control and use to serve their own purposes. These will also be ecologically conserving technologies. Examples include soft energy and organic farming technologies. By contrast, the employment society develops technologies that dominate people and nature, and are designed to be used by employees in the interest of employers.

The ownwork approach also opens up important questions about money. Because, at least to some extent, ownwork delinks people's work from their incomes, it points towards what is known as the Basic Income Scheme—under which all citizens will receive an unconditional basic income from the community. It points also to the need for wider distribution of capital, so that people will become less dependent on employers to provide them with the means of production—material (including land, premises, and equipment) as well as financial. And it points to the need for some fundamental changes in taxation that will encourage people to take on useful work, unpaid as well as paid.

Then there is the question of people's attitudes to work. In an employment society most people work for purposes other than their own. They work because they have to, to get a living. In such condition, other things being equal, work is something to be minimized. Remember the Caribbean proverb, "If work were a good thing, the rich would have found a way to keep it to themselves." In an ownwork society, on the other hand, in which most people are able to work on their own chosen purposes, work will be what gives meaning to most people's lives—as it is today for the fortunate few. It isn't just because I was brought up in Scotland and Yorkshire with more than my fair share of the puritan work ethic, that I think good work should be a centrally valuable part of human life.

What I am saying, then, is that there are two valid, though in a significant respect different, approaches to creating a people-centered future for work, the one starting from today's work situation, the other from the possibility of a different situation in the future. There is no need to argue that one is right and the other wrong. They complement one another. Together they point the way to a future for work in which increasing numbers of corporate organizations will make human and ecological values central, and also in which increasing numbers of people will be liberated from the need to work in the typical corporate structure of today.

A CHALLENGE TO THE WORLD'S FAITHS

The teachings of all the world's religious faiths are opposed to the amoral economic orthodoxy of modern times. Why is it that they have failed to challenge it more successfully? Why have they shown so much respect for supposedly value-free expert knowledge about economic matters? Why have they failed to halt the onward march of economic imperialism into almost every corner of our lives?

Is it perhaps because the faiths—I'm thinking of Buddhism, Hinduism, Islam, and Judaism, as well as Christianity—have tended to see things in terms of two separate worlds: an ideal spiritual world; and a sinful, delusory "real-life" world which is not important enough to be worth the trouble of transforming?

Of course many Christians have been deeply concerned about work and other economic questions. An example is Pope John Paul's encyclical "Centesimus Annus." Like its predecessors back to "Rerum Novarum" a hundred years ago, this contains many pointers to the kind of future we now need to create for work and economic life. But the fact remains that religious teachings have not yet made significant impact on the way of economic life and thought, and on the path of economic development, which humankind has actually taken in the last few hundred years.

Two factors may now help to change this. The first is the increasingly evident bankruptcy of the modern worldview in the face of the global crisis of environment and development. The second is the collapse of communism and the destruction of its credibility as a transformative ideology. The collapse of communism does not mean the triumph of capitalism or, as one American pundit would have us believe, the end of history. On the contrary, I believe it opens the way for the faiths to participate more actively in a new approach to this worldly transformation.

Some of us in the New Economics Foundation, with the backing of the WorldWide Fund for Nature (WWF) and Christian Aid, are now working to establish a new network of faiths and economic alternatives. This is bringing new understanding to those of us who are not active members of a faith.

I hope it will also be useful to people from the various faiths who want to grapple with the contradictions between their faith's teachings and the secular institutional values that shape most people's work and economic life today.

I hope it will help us all to participate more effectively in the transformation of today's dominant values and institutions for the new era in human history which now beckons.

JOANNA MACY

Sarvodaya Means Everybody Wakes Up

What has religion to do with economic development? Not much, in the eyes of most planners and administrators who design programs to alleviate poverty in the "Third World." Conventional Western economists consider the religious traditions of a given society to be peripheral. Indigenous belief systems and practices are generally viewed as hangovers from a precolonial past that have little relevance for modernization. They have even been seen as obstacles to overcome in freeing people from apparent superstition and passivity, and in transferring the technology that would bring them unencumbered into the marketplace of the late twentieth century.

This transfer of technology has turned out, as we know, to be not so simple a process. Unexpectedly, it boomerangs, exacerbating local inequities, creating patterns of dependence, and leaving behind, along with rusting, unused equipment, an increased sense of frustration and powerlessness.

WHAT IS DEVELOPMENT?

At the end of the second decade of such development efforts, at a meeting of the Society for International Development in Colombo, Sri Lanka, in 1979, these problems were openly acknowledged. In a moving expression of honesty and humility, some economists and planners questioned the very assumptions on which aid programs had been built. "Do we need a new definition of development?" some voices asked. They pressed for understandings that go beyond Western style modernization and industrialization.

Sri Lanka was an appropriate place to raise such questions, for it is the home of Sarvodaya Shramadana Sangamaya, a Buddhist inspired community development movement that, involving over 5,000 participating villages, is the country's largest nongovernmental organization. And this movement, with its extraordinary record of popular participation, has its own definition of development. Having come to Sri Lanka to spend a year with Sarvodaya, I had heard it from trainers and village workers and seen it put into action in many a grassroots project. Now at this international meeting in Colombo, amidst the suits and ties of Western and Westernized development "experts," A.T. Ariyaratne, founder and president of Sarvodaya, mounted the platform in his white cotton shirt and sarong to convey views that were as different from the prevailing mode as was his dress. I found myself wishing that the audience could also hear Sarvodaya's voices from the villages and know that what Ari spoke was not one man's rhetoric but a living reality to many village workers in his Movement.

In my mind I still hear the local Sarvodaya workers, in their village meetings and district training centers: Development is not imitating the West. Development is not high-cost industrial complexes, chemical fertilizers, and mammoth hydroelectric dams. It is not selling your soul for unnecessary consumer items or schemes to get rich quick. Development is *waking up*—waking up to our true wealth and true potential as persons and as a society. That is what the Buddha did under the Bodhi tree and that is what we can do—wake up. Sarvodaya's name conveys that. Originally coined by Gandhi to mean "the uplift or welfare of all," it was adopted by Ari and his colleagues and given a Buddhist twist: for as, in the Sanskrit, *sarva* means "all," *udaya* connotes awakening, as well as being raised up.

So Sarvodaya means "the awakening of all" or "everybody wakes up." "Everybody" includes the landless laborers as well as the farmers, the school dropouts as well as the university trained; the women and children and old people along with the merchants, managers, and civil servants. What they call "awakening" happens when, prompted by local Sarvodaya organizers, they meet together, plan, and carry out joint community projects. They wake up to their real needs, to their capacity to work together, and to their power to change.

In the decade following the Colombo meeting a terrible civil war has racked Sri Lanka. Conflict between the two main ethnic groups of Sinhalese and Tamils erupted in bloody violence—aided by external supplies of arms—and fractured the society at every level. But the Sarvodaya movement has continued its village programs. Because it had, from the beginning, engaged Buddhists and non-Buddhists alike, it has provided intercommunal communication in the midst of the conflict.

THE MOVEMENT

A young woman greeting her friends as she returns to her remote village after attending a training program…families assembling and weaving palm fronds to thatch a roof for a preschool…toddlers learning songs, getting vaccinated, bringing matchboxes of rice to share…mothers preparing food in a community kitchen, starting a sewing class, pooling rupees for a machine…a procession of villagers with picks and banners heading out to cut a road through the jungle…a monk in orange robes calling on government officials in their file-filled offices, inviting them to join a work party and supply the cement for culverts…police cadets in the city coming to training courses on community awakening…prisoners released from jail to work with neighborhood families to clear parks and playgrounds for their children…school dropouts organizing masonry workshops in a corner of a temple compound…monks and laypeople chanting sacred verses as a new community shop is opened, as a mile of irrigation canal is dredged of weeds, as a hand-built windmill is erected and begins to pump while in the temple's preaching hall villagers gather to hear their children sing ancient songs and to discuss the construction of community latrines.

What can such a multiplicity of scenes and actors have in common? Each is a fragment of the larger whole that is Sarvodaya, woven together by a philosophy of development based on indigenous religious tradition, that is, on the Buddha Dharma.

The movement began in 1958 when a young science teacher at a prestigious Buddhist high school in Colombo organized a two week "holiday work camp" in a remote and destitute village. "Ari" demonstrated that people could work together and learn from each other in mutually enriching ways, discovering new dimensions within themselves and new promise for their society. This involved discomfort and hard work, and yet it released an enthusiasm that spread and soon constellated into a nationwide self-help movement. From the outset it engaged Buddhist monks, for the awakening it ignited was spiritual as well as economic, and it took inspiration from the social teachings of the Buddha. It also drew considerable assistance from foreign agencies impressed by this new model of development.

Within a decade it had, from its headquarters and main training center in Moratuwa near Colombo, established a dozen regional centers and lively programs in health, preschool education, agriculture, cottage industry, and village technology. By the time I came to live and work with Sarvodaya, in 1979 and 1980, its full-time volunteers numbered nearly 100,000.

The Movement asserts that development can only be meaningful in terms of human fulfillment. While this fulfillment involves the production and consumption of goods, it entails a great deal more such as unfolding the potential for wisdom and compassion. While contemporary conditions neither reflect nor encourage this potential, it is real and can be awakened.

Since "udaya" means awakening, and "sarva" means all, or total, the Movement's name is given a dual meaning. In addition to the awakening of everybody, it denotes the awakening of the total human personality. Indeed, the transformation of personality—the "building of a new person"—is presented as the chief aim of the Movement.

AWAKENING TO INTERDEPENDENCE

Poverty engenders a sense of powerlessness, and is aggravated by it in turn. The Sarvodaya Movement sees any development program as unrealistic that does not recognize and alleviate the psychological impotence gripping the rural poor. It believes that by tapping their innermost beliefs and values, one can awaken people to their *swashakti* (personal power) and *janashakti* (collective or people's power).

Sarvodaya sees this awakening taking place, not in monastic solitude, but in social, economic, and political interaction. While many capitalists and Marxists take spiritual goals to be quietistic, drawing one off onto private quests, Sarvodaya's awakening pulls one headlong into the "real" world and into the Movement's multifaceted programs to help people meet their basic needs.

Furthermore, in working together to meet these needs, people gain wisdom about the interdependence of life. One's personal awakening (*purushodaya*) is integral to the awakening of one's village (*gramodaya*), and both play integral roles in *deshodaya* and *vishvodaya*, the awakening of one's country and one's world.

As I watched and listened to Sarvodaya organizers at work, I saw them challenge the villagers to become more than they were—in their self-image and in their relations with others.

> Your village may boast of having a post office, telephones, electricity...but that is not what constitutes being developed. Development is in your head, your mind.

> Here you find out what you can become. Leave behind your old conflicts, fears, and laziness, and discover your real strength and unity.

> It's not enough to parrot Sarvodaya philosophy, we've got to live it. Our revolution has got to be spiritual; no amount of tricking will get us there.

This belief in the spiritual nature of the revolution is what appears to distinguish Sarvodaya in the eyes of its own organizers, especially those who were formerly communist.

> I tell my communist friends, I know how you work, because I was one of you. It is all talk, talk, talk. In Sarvodaya we act...now...we make shramadanas, training programs, preschools. We don't divide people, we show them how they can change.

The notion that real social change requires personal change, a notion conveyed in songs, slogans, murals, training courses, and organizing methods, is anchored in Sarvodaya's creative interpretation of traditional religious doctrine. It can be seen as a "social gospel" form of Buddhism, stressing the socioeconomic aspects of the Buddha's teachings and presenting them as a challenge for villagers to take responsibility for their lives.

THE FOUR NOBLE TRUTHS

The Movement's distinctive approach can be seen in the way it features and interprets the Buddha's Four Noble Truths. The dictum of the First Noble Truth, that "there is suffering," is translated concretely into "there is a decadent village" and used as a means of consciousness raising. It serves to help the villagers focus on the actual conditions prevailing in their community, on its poverty, conflict, and disease. The importance of confronting these facts of life is reenacted in Sarvodaya's style of organizing. Instead of coming in to present a predetermined project or "solution" to local problems, organizers first instigate a village gathering where the village people, out of their own experience, consider together their own situation and needs. Meeting with the object of selecting a common work project, the "family gathering" serves as a lens through which all those present can see more clearly—and through each other's eyes as well—the present conditions of the village, including the scope of its needs and internal conflicts.

The Second Noble Truth, which in Scripture declares that craving (*tanha*) is the cause of suffering, is presented by the Movement in terms of the egocentricity, greed, distrust, and competition that erode village energies. Each of these factors comes down to the individual's sense of separateness and selfishness. In the training of village organizers, these human failings are noted as having been exacerbated by the practices and attitudes of former colonial powers and, especially, by the acquisitiveness bred by capitalism.

The Third Noble Truth, as traditionally formulated, affirms that craving, and therefore suffering, can cease. It is the hope at the heart of Buddhism. Sarvodaya presents this hope concretely in affirming that the village can reawaken and find its potential as a vigorous, unified, and caring community. No inexorable fate condemns people to live in apathy, sloth, distrust, or greed; for their actions, like their thoughts and words, are ultimately of their own choice. Action and choice, Ariyaratne reminds his Movement, are the original meaning of karma: just as our lives are conditioned by past deeds, so can they be remade by our present acts. All hinges on our will, on the choice that is present to us moment by moment.

The Eightfold Path, which constitutes the Fourth Noble Truth, offers the principles by which to make such choices. Right Understanding and Right Intention arise as we understand the systemic nature of life, the interdependence between self and other, mind and body; and Right Speech arises as we give expression to this with honesty and compassion. Right Action, Right Livelihood, and Right Effort are no longer abstract notions, but become as immediate and tangible as today's collaboration in cleaning the village well or digging latrines, and Right Mindfulness is given a similarly social thrust. As a Sarvodaya trainer expresses it:

> Right Mindfulness—that means stay open and alert to the needs of the village....Look to see what is needed—latrines, water, road....Try to enter the minds of the people, to listen behind their words. Practice mindfulness in the shramadana camp: Is the food enough? Are people getting wet? Are the tools in order? Is anyone being exploited?

The last aspect of the Eightfold Path, Right Concentration or *samadhi*, is made present to the Movement through the moments of meditation that precede every meeting as well as through the meditation courses offered to its full-time workers.

The Four Noble Truths as reformulated are not taught to the people as a catechism; rather they are presented in symbols and graphics, on murals and posters, as reminders of what the people experience already as they engage in the Movement's activities.

DANA AND THE FOUR ABODES

How do you know if you are waking up? How, for that matter, do you go about that process? You practice *dana*, you enter the abodes.

Even more central to lay Buddhists than the Four Noble Truths is the concept and practice of dana, a venerable term that means generosity, the act of giving, and the gift itself. Considered the most meritorious of all virtues, dana had, over the centuries, come to be identified with almsgiving to the Sangha or Order of Monks. Sarvodaya reclaimed its original scope by interpreting it to include the sharing of one's time, skills, goods, and energy with one's community. Villagers are not given sermons so much as opportunities to experience their own innate generosity. Whether it is a small child bringing her matchbox of rice to the Sarvodaya preschool, or a landowner invited to give right of way for an access road through his tea estate, the operative assumption is that the act of giving empowers the giver and is the soil out of which mutual trust and respect can grow.

> Of course, her family is poor and of course we do not really need her little bit of rice or her betel leaf. But in giving it, she gets a new idea about herself.
>
> —Shramadana organizer

Most frequently on the lips of Sarvodaya organizers and participants, and evoked at village gatherings, are the Four Abodes of the Buddha, the Brahmaviharas. Both the means and the measure of personal awakening, these are *metta* (loving-kindness), *karuna* (compassion), *mudita* (joy in the joy of others), and *upekkha* (equanimity). Like the Four Noble Truths, each of these is portrayed in terms of social interaction.

Metta, or loving-kindness, is presented by the Movement as the fundamental attitude that must be cultivated to develop motivation for service, capacity to work harmoniously with others, and, above all, nonviolence. The Movement promotes it through sermon, song, and slogan, and also through the practice of the metta meditation, which is expected of all participants and accorded silence at the outset of every meeting, be it a community "family gathering" or a committee session on latrines. Summoning participants to develop the "boundless heart" of the Buddha, it serves to ennoble menial tasks, defuse conflict, and inspire the giving of energy.

Metta is taken, furthermore, as an instrument for affecting the behavior of others. A young Sarvodaya-trained monk went to settle and work in a village that had been a communist stronghold. Over half the

villagers initially opposed him through ostracism, open threats, and dep-
redations on the newly reopened temple. His explanation to me of how
he finally won their support did not feature any particular organizing
strategy. Rather, he said,

> It was doing the metta meditation...every day before I went out and
> every night when I came back, sending the power of loving kindness
> to my opponents. After two years, most of the village was with me.

Compassion (karuna) the second Sublime Abode, is seen by the
Movement as the translation of metta into action on behalf of others. It
is concrete service and "self-offering" in tangible projects that improve
the village life.

> Feeling sorry for people is not enough. Act to help them.
> —Shramadana guideline

Mudita, as defined by the Movement, is the joy one reaps in behold-
ing the effects of this service. Whether these results are seen in a completed road to the village or in the altered lives of its inhabitants, they
constitute the most tangible external reward gained by most Sarvodayans.
But the Movement urges its workers not to be dependent on even these
rewards, for their work may fail and is bound, in any case, to displease
some parties and arouse opposition; hence the importance of the fourth
abode, upekkha, equanimity in the face of praise or blame. It is a notion
which helps preserve Sarvodaya workers from "burnout."

> Don't be discouraged if they [villagers] seem not to care. We will teach
> them by our caring.
> —Young trainer

If the Four Abodes are taken as signs and means of personal awakening, the Dharma also specifies four principles of social behavior (Satara
Sangraha Vastu), which Sarvodaya upholds as pathways to community
awakening. In addition to dana, whereby people come alive again to
their capacity to give and receive from each other, these principles include priyavachana, literally translated as pleasant speech. Sarvodaya
takes it to stress the subtle, far-reaching importance of the everyday lan-

guage we use, in helping to avoid divisiveness and violence and in promoting mutual respect and a sense of equality. The third principle, *samanatmatha*, is social equality itself. Ariyaratne, who initiated his Movement in an outcast village, reminds his fellow-Buddhists that discrimination on the basis of caste or class is a moral outrage that was rejected by the Lord Buddha himself. The fourth and last of these ancient principles of social conduct is *arthachariya* or constructive work. Symbolized in the shramadana work camps, the sharing of labor is viewed as essential if persons and communities are to awaken to their potential and capacity for self-reliance.

AWAKENING TO THE POWER OF SELF-RELIANCE

Global economic patterns, with the centralizing effect of their markets, technologies, and capital investments, render rural populations poorer and more dependent; and large-scale assistance programs seem to increase this dependence on external factors. Recognizing these trends, Sarvodaya stresses the importance of local self-reliance and draws on the Dharma to do so.

In Sarvodaya, self-reliance is set within the larger goal of awakening:

> The ideas of self-development, self-fulfillment, and self-reliance, all are understood in the single word "udaya" (awakening)....This is consistent with the Buddhist principle that salvation lies primarily in one's hands, be it an individual or a group.

In appealing to Buddhist principles as fundamental to self-reliance, Ariyaratne is on firm ground. Of the world's great religious teachers, the Buddha was probably the least authoritarian and the most emphatic in urging his followers to rely on their own experience and on their own efforts. Both on the economic level, through his teachings of Right Effort and Right Livelihood, and on the spiritual level through his admonitions to "Come see for yourselves" and "Be ye lamps unto yourselves," he urged people to take responsibility for their lives. These admonitions are echoed now in the words of Sarvodaya trainers—and this despite the traditionally hierarchical cast of Sinhalese culture. To quote one of them, as he expounded Sarvodaya concepts to a group of new trainees,

"Don't take my word for it. Think it out for yourselves. You will see how it works."

To help villagers move out of patterns of apathy and dependence, Movement organizers challenge the villagers, from the moment of the first meeting, to participate in decisionmaking and to take some action—no matter how small or menial—in meeting a local need. When the action is finite enough for its success to be predictable and measurable, it can begin to build a sense of power—both personal power (swashakti) and people's power (janashakti).

> You say you have waited two years for the government to clean that canal. You can keep on waiting, while your fields bake. But where is your power? You won't find it sitting around till the government does it for you. Your power is not in Colombo; it is in you, in your heads and hands.
>
> —Shramadana organizer

Sarvodaya headquarters has been dependent on foreign assistance, and its self-help and appropriate technology programs supported by Dutch, German, and American agencies. So the question arises as to how seriously the Movement takes this matter of self-reliance. In reply to this question, Ariyaratne makes several points. In the light of the structural inequalities at work in our world today, and considering the state of material and psychological dependence existing in the impoverished countries, self-reliance, he says, is a relative term, and not to be equated with financial independence. Until a just economic order prevails, such independence is a chimera, and "for the haves to turn towards the have-nots and tell them to be self-reliant is a very superficial statement."

AWAKENING TO OUR SOLIDARITY

A chief cause of village stagnation, in the eyes of the Movement, lies in the conflicts that fragment human energies and discourage joint action, conflicts bred by caste, class, and especially party politics. Feuding and backbiting, and petty politics at the local level, often mire even the best public programs.

I spoke with villagers in over thirty localities, and I asked how Sarvodaya differs from other organizations. Almost unanimously their replies singled out, as the Movement's most distinguishing feature, its nonpartisan character. It fostered, they said, a sense of community within the village. The Movement's nonpartisan nature is clearly basic to its effectiveness in engaging the trust of the people. This is particularly significant in a country and under a regime where local social and economic efforts are heavily politicized.

> We turned to Sarvodaya and asked the District center to help us organize our rebuilding, because everyone else, including the Gram Sevaka government extension agent at village level, had his own party interests and his own party favorites. The fighting kept us at a standstill. When Sarvodaya came in, we could work together.
> —Member of model village

The high priority Sarvodaya puts on unity stems from its vision of the "awakening of all." Inspiration is drawn from the Buddha, who in his own time assailed social divisions bred by caste or class, by narrow allegiances or doctrinaire opinions. His inclusivity and tolerance are reemphasized as essential to successful community action.

Sarvodaya organizers urge village workers to not get embroiled in party politics:

> Never invite a politician to your first shramadana. Wait till the villagers have a sense of their own power, otherwise he's likely to make them feel dependent on him. No, I never tell villagers how I voted.
> —District coordinators

AWAKENING TO OUR TRUE ECONOMIC NEEDS

Awakening entails economic pursuits that foster self-respect and self-reliance and that serve to integrate, rather than disperse, the energies of the local community. From the perspective of the Dharma, economic goals include not only production and profit, but also their human and environmental impact. The conservation of material resources, their humane use, and their equitable distribution are taken as preeminent concerns.

The Movement is critical of capital-intensive development schemes and free-trade manufacturing zones that draw workers away from their villages. Jobs in remote workplaces are not truly "economic"; for they erode the villagers' true security, which is inseparable from their family and community relations. It is this security, along with the self-respect and harmony generated by constructive work, that is seen by Sarvodaya as the essential value of economic endeavor. The Movement upholds not an economics of growth, with endless and doomed pursuit of an ever-increasing Gross National Product, but an economics of "sufficiency" (to use the term coined in Buddhist Burma and taken up by E.F. Schumacher in his book *Small is Beautiful*). Sufficiency in this context means an economic base adequate to the pursuit of enlightenment. It entails modest consumption, or simple living, and Right Livelihood that contributes to the welfare of all.

The Buddhist and Sarvodaya principle of *arthacharya*, or constructive activity, includes both voluntary and remunerative work. It gives equal dignity to unpaid efforts, and indeed exalts them as dana or gifts to the public weal. Thus it erodes the division between the formal and non-formal sectors of the economy, which has in our time robbed non-remunerated work of its dignity.

THE TEN BASIC HUMAN NEEDS

For training and guidance in its work, the Movement came up with a list of ten basic human needs. Sarvodaya specified these needs in order to help its people keep their intentions clear and their priorities straight, for social and political action, even at the grassroots level, involve hard choices, and these choices in turn involve trade-offs. It's easy, even on the village scene, to get caught up in power plays and party politics. So this roster of human needs was agreed upon, written down, and put to use. I saw it in the hands or heard it on the lips of many a Sarvodaya worker. In English translation it is a small four by five inch pamphlet: *Ten Basic Human Needs and Their Satisfaction* by the Sarvodaya Movement, Sri Lanka.

Recently, years after my sojourn in Sri Lanka, I had occasion to study this pamphlet again for the preparation of an article. Riding in a limousine bus to Los Angeles International Airport, waiting in the air conditioned terminal, and drinking my plastic cup of soda, as the jet lifted up through the smog, I read it and made the following notes.

1. *Environment*–Among the factors conducive to the fullest personality development, a clean and beautiful environment takes pride of place....Well-swept pathways and rooms, gardens and latrines... unpolluted air and soil...freedom from factors such as noise which impede concentration and contribute to mental disturbances. (The airport shuttle inches its way through the fumes and din of downtown traffic, waits bumper to bumper on the freeway ramp.)

2. *Water*–Every individual requires water for drinking, for bathing, for washing clothes, watering the garden....Necessary to sustain life, it can also destroy life, spreading typhoid, cholera, dysentery, hepatitis, if contaminated...so the wells and tanks must be clean. Have a separate rope and bucket for drawing drinking water. (As we take off over Los Angeles, I see through the haze, between the miles on miles of concrete, oasis-like enclaves dotted with turquoise swimming pools, golf courses, and cemeteries kept emerald green by sprinklers. I think of the fight to divert more water from Northern California, of the industrial wastes leaching into the wells, of the leaks from offshore oil rigs.)

3. *Clothing*–Clothing is necessary to protect oneself from heat and cold and from flies and mosquitoes....We believe every individual should be possessed of six sets of clothing: two for daily home wear, two for school or the workplace, one for nightwear and the other for ceremonial wear....See that they are kept clean. If no money is available for soap, dirt can be removed with water mixed with the ash of coconut branches.

4. *Food*–All living beings exist on food. (It's noontime, but no lunch; I consider showing this list to the airline.) Sarvodaya workers should strive to establish conditions to supplement dietary needs of young children, expectant and lactating mothers, invalids and old people. Rice and millet for energy; lentils and dairy for growth; yams and oranges, papaw, pumpkins for protection....(My favorite dish in my Sri Lankan village was pumpkin curry. The stewardess hands me a minuscule packet of peanuts that I can't open; I try tearing the plastic with my teeth.)

5. *Housing*–A house with adequate light and ventilation, affording protection against sun, rain, heat, cold, and mosquitoes is a basic human need. If bricks or stone cannot be afforded, walls can be built of rammed earth or wattle and daub, plastered and lime coated…for roofing, if tiles are too costly, palm-leaf thatching is very adequate…floor of cement or, failing that, rammed earth kept clean with fresh cow dung. (Sleek office buildings rise in my city, their entryways at night littered with rags, papers, huddled figures sleeping.)

6. *Health Services*–Health care activities that can be undertaken at the community level are many and varied. Give priority to training local Health Sevakas (servants) and to preventive and rehabilitational as well as curative measures, especially to the malnourished and the young. Boil the drinking water. Keep hands and utensils spotlessly clean. Include recreation and leisure in daily routine; remain serene and smiling in the midst of any trouble, for mental well-being is essential to physical health.

7. *Communication*–A roadway to every village and at least a footpath to every house is essential. For transport all should have access to bus, and use of cart and bicycle….The media of communication include the temple bell, the conch, bonfires, birds and letters, as well as telephone, radio, television. Place notice boards in public places. Establish a public library to be open at least an hour a day. Disseminate news in the village through a tom-tom beater. Hold village meetings at least once a month to discuss matters of common concern. Train a group of youths to go from house to house and explain relevant matters to the people.

8. *Fuel*–Join in our work to evolve efficient means to generate energy from solar rays, wind and water, methane gas from dung and nightsoil. Meanwhile, to meet the basic needs for heat, light and cooking fuel, we must conserve sawdust and paddy husks for burning in the hearth and plant more trees, such as the "Mara" tree, for eventual firewood. (The pilot announces our descent into Oakland Airport. I look down over denuded hills, see San Francisco Bay appear in the distance and dimly through a brown veil, fed by streams of smoke from the Richmond refineries, the hazy outlines of the city.)

9. *Education*–Lifelong education is a basic human need. Speaking from our Buddhist philosophy, this is an education to liberate oneself from sorrow. From birth to death, all types of experiences a person goes through can be regarded as having an educational value. Begin with programs for children under three years, in cooperation with their mothers, to look after their health and their emotional and social adjustment....A preschool for children between three and six....Adult education programs for those who have missed formal schooling. Create the necessary infrastructure so that community members can educate each other for economic, social, and political growth. Hold lectures and seminars. Provide classes to learn a language other than the mother tongue.

10. *Cultural and spiritual development*–Even when material and social needs are met, human life is incomplete without a cultural and spiritual base....Have the elders perpetuate folklore and folk songs and proverbs to the younger generation. Keep traditions alive with festivals, pageants, drama, and dance....Arrange facilities for learning methods of meditation, and also the essence of other religions as well, giving due respect to those religions.

The plane taxied up to the gate, passengers reached for bags and briefcases, pushed past each other down the aisle, their pace quickening as they moved on out through the airport. I hurried too, by habit, and headed for the parking lot, trying to remember where I left the car. I didn't have a car in Sri Lanka and I didn't hurry either. I had more time.

Is Sarvodaya's list of basic needs too basic for our sophisticated appetites, our complicated comforts and ambitions? Perhaps. But, at the same time, it seems almost utopian. Caught in a rat race that compels us to acquire more and more, we neglect many of our simplest requirements. Safe food, pure water, clean air appear to be scarce luxuries now.

Is it realistic in our modern world to suppose that there is enough to go around? Gandhi said, "There is enough for everyone's need, but not for everyone's greed." Perhaps in our case addiction is a more accurate term than greed. If needs like serenity and community were honored, we might be less compulsive in our patterns of consumption. We might be less inclined to measure our worth in wages and possessions.

Maybe it is not only addictive greed, but denial too that leads us to enslave ourselves to ever-new conveniences and diversions. We may be trying to protect ourselves from confronting the conditions of our world, to block out the knowledge of the figures in the downtown doorways. For even at a subliminal level that awareness hurts. If the hunger and homelessness were not out there, we might relax, might drop the armor and busy-ness that shields us from their pain.

Looking at Sarvodaya's list of basic needs, politicians and lobbyists would find a glaring omission. What about defense? What about national security? It has become axiomatic in our society that military protection and preparedness is a fundamental requirement, clearly more important than schools, housing, health. And here it is not even mentioned by Sarvodaya, even though Sri Lanka is torn by warring factions and terrorist attacks.

Ask a Sarvodaya organizer about this omission and he or she might well answer in terms of what people can awaken to. It is what we are beginning to suspect, as we experience the social, economic, spiritual costs of our military budget. It is that a country's security depends in the last analysis on how well it takes care of its people.

So it seems as relevant to us as it is to those community development workers in South Asia, to think in terms of what we humans really need. We can ask that of ourselves, we can ask it of each other and our elected officials. When we do, when we consider and acknowledge those needs and begin to act on them, we too might "wake up."

Overcoming Obstacles

No work, no eating.
                            —Pai Chang

If any man will not work neither let him eat.
                            —Paul the Apostle

The Greeks invented the idea of nemesis to show how any single virtue stubbornly maintained gradually changes into a destructive vice. Our success, our industry, our habit of work have produced our economic nemesis. In our current economic crisis we are driving to the poorhouse in new automobiles, spending our inflated dollars for calorie-free food, lamenting our falling productivity in an environment polluted by our industry. Work made modern men great, but now threatens to usurp our souls, to inundate the earth in things and trash, to destroy our capacity to love and wonder.
                            —Sam Keen

TARTHANG TULKU

Coping with Change

When we face our problems directly and go through them, we discover new ways of being. We build our strength and our confidence to deal with future difficulties. Life becomes a meaningful challenge leading us to greater knowledge and awakening. We discover that the more we learn, the more we grow; the more challenges we meet, the more strength and awareness we gain. When we live in accord with the process of change, we do something valuable simply by living.

Rivers flow, mountains erode, civilizations rise and fall. The cycles of change are endless. Geologic and evolutionary changes, the most gradual of all, have shaped the world as we know it today. Societies and cultures have appeared and vanished, each adding a new dimension to human life. In just two hundred years the United States has risen from a primitive frontier to the most technologically advanced and powerful nation on earth. World events reflect change as leaders and trends come into being—and move on to allow space for new leaders and trends. The value of money fluctuates, children are born, people die; nothing ever remains the same.

And yet, although all of us change from day to day, we seldom find it easy to change in the ways we want to or need to. Even when we are not happy, it often seems easier, even better, to hold on to what we have, to remain the same. We choose to ignore the opportunities for fulfillment and happiness that positive action can bring. We cling to the idea that we are not capable of adapting ourselves to the demands of our work and our lives; or we may believe that we have changed enough. If we are criticized for leading empty lives, we may become defensive, excusing ourselves, claiming that we are what we are, that we cannot change. It is easy to spend a whole life this way, refusing to take responsibility for our personal growth.

We do not wish to make the effort to change, but fighting change takes an even greater effort. Trying to prevent change in our lives is like trying to swim against the current of a flowing river. This way of being exhausts and frustrates us until a defeated quality begins to permeate our lives. But we could choose instead to take advantage of the transitory nature of existence and learn to participate in the vital flow of life, in tune with the process of change.

Change is natural and wholesome, not something to fear and avoid. By looking carefully at the changes that have happened in our lives, we can see that the process of change is what brings all good things about. When we allow ourselves to change, life swiftly carries us past difficult times and into times of joy and vitality. Once we see how change is continually acting on and within us, we can learn to use the energy of change to direct our lives.

It is helpful in learning to appreciate and develop your ability to change to think about how you have changed over time. You are not the same person you were ten years ago. How are you different? What were you like before? Would your present self and past self be friends if they met? What would they like and dislike about each other? How did you come to be the person you are now? Your ideals, thoughts, and opinions have changed; what has replaced the old ones and why? By reviewing the changes that have occurred, you can savor the growth and progress you have made, and appreciate the benefits the process of chance has brought to your life.

When you notice how much you have changed and developed even without consciously trying, you can see how much you could grow if you made a real effort to change. It may be helpful to think about your present life in relation to the future self you will become. Will your present actions improve your life, making it rich in growth and positive experience? What will you think when you look back ten years from today? How instrumental will you have been in making the changes that have taken place? By questioning your life in this way, you can gain a clearer perspective on your motivation to change and grow.

Bringing positive change into your life can be a simple matter, for it begins to happen as soon as you decide to expand your abilities. The next time you find yourself caught in a limiting pattern, let go of your fixed views and expectations, and open yourself to all that can be learned from a new way of being. Take the energy you once used to reinforce your old patterns, and use it to handle your difficulties quickly and well. When you assert yourself in this way, you will find no limit to your creative energy, to the fullness of your experience.

Calmly and steadily go through the day, quiet within yourself. When you are relaxed and peaceful within, you can recognize troublesome patterns as they arise, and allow them to teach you to change. Whenever you find yourself in a difficult situation, pause before reacting. Were your actions in any way a cause? Are you making excuses for yourself? If so, accept yourself instead—and at the same time, change your typical response. If you were about to respond emotionally, step back and take a quieter look at the situation. Choose a healthier response. Past habits can be changed, and positive qualities encouraged and developed. The option to change is always open, for your growth and development are a matter of choice. All you have to do is decide.

As we change our habits and patterns, we realize that problems can teach us to grow. Yet because our problems are often painful and disturbing, our natural tendency is to try to avoid them; we seek ways to get out of difficult situations, or to go around the obstacles we encounter. But our problems are like clouds: though they appear to disturb the serenity of a clear sky, they contain life-giving moisture that nourishes growth. When we face our problems directly and go through them, we discover new ways of being. We build our strength and our confidence to deal with future difficulties. Life becomes a meaningful challenge leading us to greater knowledge and awakening. We discover that the more we learn, the more we grow; the more challenges we meet, the more strength and awareness we gain. When we live in accord with the process of change, we do something valuable simply by living.

At the times when you become deeply discouraged and want to give up, or when you feel that it is too late in life to start making any changes, do not stop there. By encouraging yourself, you can support your motivation to learn, to grow, to use your potential creatively. Instead of allowing yourself to stay fixed in old patterns, you can challenge them and break them down. When you do this, you will extend your abilities and increase the richness of your experience more than you ever imagined. Instead of cutting your ambitions short, you can take the energy of your negative attitudes and consolidate it into a focused, purposeful force for change.

Once we have seen that we can choose to change, we can look forward to the future, really move forward into the future, and grow as quickly as we choose. Confident in our ability to develop our health and strength by our own efforts, we become an example for those around us, encouraging them to change as well. This support, this sharing of experience, is one of the greatest resources of mankind.

When we are open to change, we find that our minds are a creative source of joy and happiness, and our bodies are full of energy. Together the mind and body make a good vehicle; each is a wing enabling us to fly up to meet the challenges of life. We come to appreciate how fortunate we are to be able to use our minds and bodies to deepen and enrich our work, our relationships, and our lives.

Reflect on the values which are developing: an open heart, a willingness to confront life directly, confidence in ourselves. Life can be approached as if it were just another chore, but when we decide to make use of the many opportunities to change in positive ways, we can make our lives vital and healthy. We develop a genuine appreciation for ourselves, a sense of well-being which radiates through all our actions. When we accomplish change, we can see it, and take pride in it. Seeing the change in us, others too, will be encouraged. When we support one another's growth in this way, work is smooth and our hearts are joyful.

Even if our lives are basically happy and successful, we may still find ourselves having to cope with many problems. They demand our attention, and prevent the natural peace of mind that makes life a pleasure. At times these problems may overwhelm us, particularly when they arise from our inability to face our faults or failures. Powerful and disturbing feelings may arise within us, so that we come to feel that we just cannot cope with what is going on.

Occasionally we may sense trouble coming, and manage to avoid the worst of it; at other times, finding ourselves suddenly in the midst of difficulties, we may struggle through as best we can, perhaps seeking assistance from friends. Or we may attempt to escape the problem altogether, trying to find a way around it, rather than through it. Those in fortunate circumstances can at times find an escape from their difficulties by "getting away from it all," but most of us do not have this alternative. And we all have problems that just cannot be avoided.

There seems to be no way to guard against having problems. But while it is true that we have little control over many things that happen in our lives, even the most difficult of situations remains a problem only as long as we allow ourselves to be carried away by our emotional reactions. Generally, our problems are the result of our inner reaction to a situation; when we do not know ourselves clearly, we are like foreigners to our senses, our thoughts, and our feelings, and it is difficult to control our reactions. Thus problems recur in our lives because we have not learned to deal with them effectively. We may turn to others to help guide us through our difficulties, but while our friends may be well-meaning, they often do not have the answers we need.

We can learn to rely on ourselves to deal with our problems by paying attention to our patterns of response, and becoming aware of the motivations that can lead us into difficulty. When we recognize the quality of our feelings and emotions, and come to see clearly the results of our actions, we discover that our very lack of awareness has contributed to our problems.

Learning to recognize the way you respond to difficulties is the first step in increasing awareness. Bring to mind two or three times when you were upset by some circumstance you could not seem to cope with. Examine each incident in turn: just how did it arise? Who else was involved? What did you do? How did you eventually work the problem out? Have the same patterns repeated themselves? These questions give you room to stand back, to gain insight into what caused the problems, and to think realistically of new alternatives to cope with similar situations. When you begin to recognize the patterns in your reactions to problems, you can start to be your own counselor, and learn to prevent other such problems from arising.

Gaining a sense of how you respond in difficult times will help you to redirect your emotional energies. When you are depressed or upset, sit back and look at the pain you are experiencing. Do not try to interpret or judge what you are feeling; just locate the feeling and observe it attentively.

Confusion, tension, and depression all contain energy that can be used for us as well as against us. When we can calmly face our difficulties without trying to escape, without trying to manipulate or suppress our feelings, it is possible to see something that we have never seen before. We may realize very clearly that we simply do not want this pain any longer. We can then discover in ourselves the motivation to change the habits that lead us into difficulties.

We can use the energy of our emotions to skillfully cope with our problems, to rediscover the clear interplay of mind and senses that allows our energy to flow in more positive directions. Our emotions are really only energy; they become painful when we grow attached to them, and identify them as being negative. We can transform this energy into positive feelings, for ultimately, it is we ourselves who determine these reactions. The choice is up to us: we can dwell on negative emotions, or we can take their energy and use it to encourage a healthier response to our problems.

When you encounter obstacles within yourself, or difficulties in your work or your relationships with others, take a few minutes to sit quietly. Very gently open your eyes, and try to visualize the problem, allowing yourself to feel it fully. Then gently close your eyes, and go deeply into your feelings until they dissolve, and you are refreshed and relaxed.

Then slowly open your eyes, and without looking at anything specific, visualize aspects of the problem you may have overlooked. Close your eyes once again, and become immersed in these feelings as fully as possible until they, too, dissolve, and you feel completely fresh and new.

Repeat this process a few more times, until your negative feelings completely disappear. When you finish, open your eyes slowly, and let your breathing be very soft and gentle. Allow your breath, your awareness, and the light you see around you to merge and become balanced. As this happens, you will feel a light, clear, open quality. Develop and sustain this quality by continuing to breathe softly, balancing each inhalation and exhalation. When you do this, your body comes alive, your mind becomes concentrated, and your awareness expands.

Look on the day as if it were a new life you are about to begin. Do not carry any resistance into your new life; you are beginning afresh, with no problems or obstacles in your past or future. In your new life, all experience is alive with a rich and vital quality. You are fully connected to whatever is happening in each moment, in touch with a radiant clarity, aware of everything that is going on within and around you.

The clarity we gain when we use our energy in a positive way does more than lift us above our immediate difficulties; it teaches us about ourselves, and transforms unproductive reactions into channels for coping effectively. Once we begin to understand our negative patterns, we gain more confidence in our ability to deal with our problems ourselves. When we are inwardly clear and balanced, we have the ability to use our resources to deal with whatever may arise; we no longer need others to help us.

Once we learn to cope in this way, the ability stays with us, helping us to accept and face up to whatever happens in our lives. We develop important skills: how to sense our feelings accurately, and how to deal with them promptly. There is great satisfaction in seeing the improvement this brings about in our lives, in our relationships, in our work. Our sense of self-worth gradually begins to grow, and this in itself can alleviate many of the fears and anxieties that give rise to our difficulties.

Given a strong sense of being able to weather the storm, we can look beyond the moment, and gain perspective on our lives. We recognize that each day will bring a new experience. Our difficulties cease to appear so insoluble and never-ending, for we know that we can deal with whatever problems may arise, and we are stimulated to move through and beyond them capably and surely. As a wholesome, self-nourishing attitude grounds our being, we find that problems occur less frequently in our lives. Though we may still react to pressures outside us, we can control our responses and use our energy to move in healthy directions.

How abundant our potential is to live and act in positive ways! Our inner being has a power and dignity which can sustain us, lending strength to our lives, and inspiring those around us. When we reach the calm confidence that derives from our inner strength, our whole environment balances itself, becomes light, and grows enjoyable. This is what comes from learning to cope with the conflicts we all must go through. By discovering this strength in ourselves, we increase our abilities to find meaning and contentment in life.

It is really up to us. By opening to the potential our problems have for enhancing our self-understanding, we can change the quality of our lives and help to change the lives of those around us. We know that there will always be difficulties to face and problems to solve, but by taking responsibility, we learn to cope with them. By working on ourselves, by coming to know ourselves better, and then by sharing our growing strength with others, we create a base of support that helps to make our lives, and the world, a better place to be.

JOSEPH CARY

Free Time

Our stories say that once before time—our time—began, spring was the only season. Earth, our greathearted and unstinting mother, supplied us with all things needful. Days were sunny, evenings cool, the lion lay with the lamb. Unprompted by hoe or plowshare, fields broke spontaneously into amber waves of richly tasseled maize; mushrooms and strawberries abounded in the spacious woods, oaks groaned with the health-giving acorn. The rivers ran with nectar. At the heart of it all our first parents had dominion and kept a fabulous garden.

The thought of them stirs us still. What did they look like, newly made with all that free time in consumers' paradise, in that deathless, prenatal world our stories conjure? We call them "happy" but what can such a word signify applied to such persons in such a place? And what on earth did they do? "Not to irksome toil but to delight He made us," Milton conceives of Adam saying, and something wistful in us sighs assent and drowns in paradox. "Happy work," alas, is hardly work at all but play or recreation. Work is out of place in Eden. Or in any case, such tending and keeping, such lopping and pruning as we dream of in that enchanted plantation discovered in full bloom upon awakening must be understood as some sort of ritual or symbolic gesture—*noblesse oblige*—since in the nature of things it was not required for survival; it had no ecological function. For the rest they christened the birds and beasts and "had dominion" over every living thing.

In fact, before they fall into time and the only world we know, Adam and Eve are radiant enigmas: they lack feature and certifiable character. Indeed our stories have neither point nor plot until we recollect who tells them, and why—they are a measure of our discontent with what we are and how we live. The garden of delight grows out of our cursed, irksome ground, thick with weeds and thistles. The meaning of perpetual spring is that we are cold and tired. The man with the hoe, sweat on his brow, pictures a paradise of free time: the bright blank faces of Eve and Adam beguile his weariness. In an iron age we dream of gold.

Experience cannot imagine innocence except to say, deeply stirred, that it is infinitely precious and doomed. Adam and Eve are not our parents at all until the serpent stirs and they eat and hide and in the cool of the day the Lord walks one last time in the garden. It is time for time—our time—to begin. Our stories render the words of the second and final creation as: "In the sweat of thy face shalt thou eat bread, till thou return unto the ground; for out of it wast thou taken: for dust thou art, and unto dust shalt thou return."

In the garden, conditions were such that time was suspended, reward was immediate—there for the picking—and work as we know it did not exist. When the Lord later lifted his curse from the ground and made an everlasting covenant with Noah, He did not—that is to say, we cannot imagine that He could—undo or resuspend the condition of time. Eden cannot exist if, as the Lord says, "While the earth remaineth, seed time and harvest, and cold and heat, and summer and winter, and day and night shall not cease." This age is iron: you must work or starve. And work so regarded is one key consequence of what our stories call "the fall."

Yet even within a fallen—that is to say, an historical—world, our stories seek out comforting exceptions: the simple life, for example (the noble savage, the Sicilian shepherd with his flute, a home on the range, the village blacksmith), or golden ages of faith and faithful labor. In *The Need for Roots* Simone Weil is moved by what she judges to be traces of such times:

> There are numerous signs indicating…that long ago physical labor was preeminently a religious activity and consequently something sacred. The Mysteries—a religion that embraced the whole of pre-Roman antiquity—were entirely founded upon symbolical expressions

concerning the salvation of the soul, drawn from agriculture. The same symbolism is found again in the New Testament parables....There may perhaps have been a time when an identical truth was translated into different sets of symbols, and when each set was adapted to a certain type of physical labor in such a way as to turn the latter into a direct expression of religious faith.[1]

The myth of an age of faith, an age in which working is praying (*laborare est orare* is the old monkish phrase), is particularly poignant in times like our own. An age of faith would mean an age in which many of us could truly accept the living authority of the sacred in the world and in time and could wholeheartedly acknowledge that our relation to that presence was the single most vital relation in all our mortal lives. An age of faith might well imply a golden age of work since in such an age every act or gesture, no matter how secret or servile or burdensome, no matter how worldly or unworldly its context, would have also, inhering in it, a ceremonial function attesting to the individual worker's willing, more or less conscious, relation to the sacred. A hundred years ago the priest and poet Gerard Manley Hopkins, who did not live in such an age, meditated from the pulpit on the theme of "laborare est orare":

> It is not only prayer that gives God glory but work. Smiting on an anvil, sawing a beam, whitewashing a wall, driving horses, sweeping, scouring, everything gives God some glory if being in His Grace you do it as your duty....To lift up the hands in prayer gives God glory, but a man with a dungfork in his hand, a woman with a slop pail, give Him glory too. He is so great that all things give Him glory if you mean they should.[2]

> In an age of faith my work, that old hard sentence I labor out in the sweat of my face until the day I die, would be transformed into a duty owed to what I know I have most at heart. If I faltered, I would be surrounded and steadied by my brothers and sisters in God. Faith can move mountains by quarrying them and, as this witness by the Archbishop of Rouen shows (as cited by the historian Henry Adams), by bearing them miles over the plain to the village of Chartres. Who has ever seen! Who has ever heard tell, in times past, that powerful princes of the world, that men brought up in honour and in wealth, that nobles, men and women, have bent their proud and haughty necks to the harness of carts, and that, like beasts of burden, they have dragged to the abode of Christ these wagons, loaded with wines, grains, oil,

stone, wood, and all that was necessary for the wants of life, or for the reconstruction of the church?...When they halt on the road, nothing is heard but the confession of sins, and pure and suppliant prayer to God to obtain pardon. At the voice of the priests who exhort their hearts to peace, they forget all hatred, discord is thrown far aside, debts are remitted, the unity of hearts is established....When they have reached the church they arrange the wagons about it like a spiritual camp, and during the whole night they celebrate the watch by hymns and canticles.[3]

Such an age seems very far away. The medievalism of Hopkins' fellow and non-Catholic Victorians, such as Carlyle or Ruskin or Morris (or, in America, someone like Henry Adams), is very much an index of discontent with the signs of their own secular times (which are also ours) and, as such, more of a poem of longing than objective history. For Adams the sacred presence of the Virgin at Chartres some six hundred years ago had "acted as the greatest force the Western world [had] ever felt,"[4] and standing before the giant dynamo in the Gallery of Machines at the Paris Exposition of 1900 he could only be ruefully aware that there was no power in the modern world which could, like the Virgin, raise Chartres. And three quarters of a century later, with the energy of the split atom added to our means, we most likely agree.

We agree and at the same time recognize that an age of faith is not among our present options. If I had what William Butler Yeats called medieval knees I might well bow to the glorious yoke more willingly, but I am stuck with the stiff joints I have. To the infidel suspicious of his own nostalgia, even the old testimonies are suspect. What percentage of the cathedral builders, for instance, were assigned to the carving of those marvelous gargoyles about which Ruskin writes so eloquently? How many workmen got to grind and measure out the famous sapphire dust that gave those windows their heavenly blue? Labor was labor even in the Middle Ages, the infidel surmises, and most of our ancestors were not craftsmen but oxen and asses, not carvers but stonebreakers and haulers. Even the good Archbishop of Rouen seems primarily dazzled by the unique spectacle of "noblemen" drawing those laden carts and performing—for a limited period only, it must be remembered—serfs' work. But what about the serfs themselves who did this for their living? Were they blessed in their work? Not even Henry Adams can say; they could not write and left no diaries.

Still, standing in the presence of their surviving structures—not the cathedrals of Europe only, but the great heads of Easter Island, the pyramids of Mexico and Egypt, Stonehenge, the Parthenon, the "Wailing Wall"—something strange can happen. The stones speak an unfamiliar language that can touch us. Afterward we muse upon ages of faith and a mysterious way of working that would transform the worker as well as the work—upon a relation to a sacred authority lost, then dimly apprehended, now lost again. Our persisting and lovable stories tell the truth about us, at least: that we feel ourselves out of phase and inharmonious, lacking a center within and without; that even infidels feel a need for something sacred in their lives; that what we do for our living—our work—ought somehow to dignify, perhaps glorify, certainly not mock, that living.

The Concise Oxford Dictionary defines "work" as "an expenditure of energy, striving, application of effort to some purpose." For many, the purpose is subsistence or livelihood: short of starving we have no alternative. We work to subsist and such work is the price we pay, penal in nature, a necessary evil. Thus *ponos*, Greek for "work," has the same root as the Latin *poena*: "punishment," "penalty," "pain." Thus Karl Marx sees work as typically "an alienation of life since....I work in order to [provide] for myself the means of living. Working is not living."[5] Particularly since the Industrial Revolution and the coming of what Carlyle calls the Age of Machinery, work has seemed sterile and self-estranging. "The shuttle drops from the fingers of the weaver," he writes in *Signs of the Times* (1829), "and falls into iron fingers that ply it faster....Not the external and physical alone is now managed by machinery, but the internal and spiritual also." The French writer Simone Weil, speaking out of her brief but crucial experience on the assembly line at the Renault works in the 1930s, saw such work as meaning for most "a daily death": "To labor is to place one's own being, body and soul, in the circuit of inert matter, turn it into an intermediary between one state and another of a fragment of matter, to make of it an instrument...an appendage of the tool."[6]

For more fortunate others, on the other hand, work may be said to pay: that is, by means of my work I am able to buy free time, time during which I may do as I please. In such cases I sleep until noon, read *Paradise Lost*, do needlepoint, or fly south for the weekend, feeling my work was worth it. Here work is regarded as a currency, a means of exchange, and its value lies principally in what it is able to purchase above and beyond subsistence. The end consoles us for the means and the end will always involve not working. As Alasdair Clayre writes, "Work may be done without effort or reward; but what is done consistently without either tends to be called something else—a game or a hobby."[7] Or, nowadays, a "craft."[8]

St. Luke tells of two sisters, Mary and Martha, who receive the ministering Jesus in their home, along with his disciples and followers. But while Mary sits with the rest at the feet of the master, attentive to his word, Martha finds herself preparing and serving the meal for them all. And when at length her bitterness lends her courage and she complains to her chief guest of her sister's leaving her to drudge alone and asks him to bid Mary help her, she is gently but firmly reproved: "Martha, Martha, thou art careful and troubled about many things: But one thing is needful: and Mary hath chosen that good part, which shall not be taken away from her."

How is one to understand this? Certainly there is a parallel with the earlier lesson of the loaves and fishes, when troubled disciples feared there was not enough food to feed the assembled multitude and a miracle proved their fears unfounded. In the Sermon on the Mount we are urged to take no thought for food or drink and the priorities are clearly stated: "Seek ye first the kingdom of God, and His righteousness; and all these things shall be added unto you." So Mary has chosen the "needful" part: nourishing the understanding through an act of self-quieting and attention (if thus we might interpret her sitting at his feet and hearing his word) is a more urgent human concern than administering to the needs of the flesh. Or one might read this episode with the maxim "laborare est orare" in mind: the way of active service is as much a prayer, a turning toward the sacred, as is the way of contemplation or abstention from action. In this case Martha is rebuked for failing to see the potentialities of her own part and coveting another's.

And yet...the infidel's heart, troubled, goes out to Martha. The kitchen door swings shut but not before she has caught a last glimpse of her sister settling herself to listen. The bread needs slicing and the knife is dull. On no account must she rattle the plates and already she can catch—if she holds her breath and strains—the sound of his voice though not the words. And if Mary chose to stay and listen to them, Martha is here by default; she has no choice. If she does not serve, the guests will not be fed and the laws of hospitality are mocked. It is bitter. Her faith is not confident. She is not free to do what she would choose to do. Full of cares, she feels she lacks free time. And it is bitterer still when he turns to her with his look and says, "Martha, Martha, thou art careful and troubled about many things...."

"Our age," wrote Simone Weil just before her death in 1943, "has as its own particular mission, or vocation, the creation of a civilization founded upon the spiritual nature of work."[9] In the chapter to follow we try to explore the possibilities of such a creation, for ourselves if not for the age at large, amounting to an alternative understanding of, and means of participation in, the human condition of work. "A way of working" is one way of putting it. And the troubled and troubling presence of our sister Martha should never be forgotten. This chapter, at least, is dedicated to her.

NOTES

[1] Simone Weil, *The Need for Roots*, tr. Arthur Will (New York: Harper & Row, 1971).

[2] *A Hopkins Reader*, ed. John Pick (New York: Oxford University Press, 1953).

[3] Henry Adams, *Mont-Saint-Michel and Chartres* (Boston: Houghton Mifflin, 1933).

[4] Henry Adams, *The Education of Henry Adams* (Boston: Houghton Mifflin, 1933).

[5] Cited in Alasdair Clayre, *Work and Play* (New York: Harper & Row, 1975).

[6] Simone Weil, op. cit.

[7] Alasdair Clayre, op. cit.

[8] Jean-Jacques Rousseau recommends the way of the craftsman as the best of all ways of earning one's livelihood. But a craft for Rousseau is not regarded as a value in and of itself: it is a method of purchasing time and economic independence through a minimal expenditure of energy. In his ideological novel *Emile*, for example, Rousseau has his young hero learn a craft—carpentry in this case—on the grounds that it is "a purely mechanical skill where the hands work more than the head, and which does not lead to a fortune, but on which one can manage to live." For Rousseau a craft is a work condition that frees us from society and *makes fewer demands on us than usual*. It is good less for what it is than for what it isn't.

[9] Simone Weil, op. cit.

PAUL JORDAN-SMITH

Free Space

As Martha recrosses the threshold into the kitchen, what is she thinking? The words of apparent reproval sting, and there is more than a touch of resentment in her. Now, to all her troubles and concerns is added the turmoil of doubts and questions. Among them, one is uppermost: "But one thing is needed"—and what is that? What one thing is necessary, among ten thousand things all claiming necessity, all demanding one's attention? Should she turn back and try to imitate Mary? Should she just forget about the words of Christ and prepare dinner? What should she do? What is expected? How should she be? The words have touched a nerve, have awakened a longing so profound that her wish to listen, to hear and ponder, has risen and become uppermost. But how can she drop everything that must be done for the comfort of her guests and still remain herself? Mary has chosen the better part, but has Martha chosen hers? Or is she in that limbo between wanting and not wanting, between yes and no? It is Mary's nature, perhaps, to listen, to be always among the disciples, and Martha's to work, to prepare the meal, to serve. And yet for Martha another need is there, too: the need to hear, to learn, to receive the teaching.

Two possibilities appear: to shut the door and go about the business of preparing the meal, forgetting that other need; or, if possible, to include that need along with her essential nature: to work, prepare, and serve. But something still is necessary if one is to do both at once, and as Martha returns to the kitchen, she is in despair, not knowing how to be at once disciple and cook.

She sees, as she enters the doorway, the cake waiting to go into the oven, the knives and bowls that are her tools. She has turned from one demand only to find another. To turn back now, to sit with Mary among the others—that is not possible, for the concerns and troubles would only reappear and intrude themselves upon her attention, and again the words would be lost. But to turn away from the words, back to the clutter and clatter of the kitchen, seems impossible too. Her body is heavy with fatigue; she closes her eyes, and for a moment Martha the capable yields humbly to incapacity. In that instant something in her opens, and there comes a moment of pause, of stillness. Free time appears. She is now both Martha and Mary: but until now, how much of either has she been? She is in charge of the household, but she sees now that her usual attitude is to be troubled and concerned as if she did not know how to do all the countless things that need doing. But she does know: her hands know the making of bread, the mixing and carving and tasting that is the cook's business. Her eyes miss nothing that is out of place, and the sweeping and cleaning do not need the energy of worry. She opens her eyes, and she sees that with free time there is free space too, within and without. A new energy takes shape in her body, an energy that knows and, in knowing, can do. The guests will be fed. Her hands turn to the work before them with the certainty of skill and long experience. Her eyes observe, and whatever comes as a demand she turns willingly to meet, for there is space now in which to move. "But one thing is needed," and now the possibility exists of meeting that need—to be wholly Martha and wholly Mary, and not just fractions of herself.

It is this struggle that the craftsman faces, perhaps always, whenever work begins. I have seen carpenters work in what I thought was utter chaos: piles of wood shavings, tools scattered with abandon, no drawings or plans—or, if plans were there, they were buried in the shavings. Yet, when the need arose, the hand found the chisel without hesitation, and the shape of the wood conformed itself, as if by magic, to the mind's blueprint. Was there a moment just before work began in which the craftsman took stock of the workbench and of himself? Was there such a moment's pause in which the cares and troubles about many things gracefully took their proper place in the background so that a space could appear in front, so that the eye could see and the ear could hear and the hand could grasp with assurance the tool and material, and work could begin?

The turning of the attention to any new endeavor implies a change of direction and a moment in which that change could take place. One may liken the process, perhaps, to the trajectory of a ball thrown in the air: there comes a moment when the upward and outward direction changes and the return to earth begins. The masters of the Japanese Tea Ceremony, who drew on much of the experience of craftsmen in shaping the ceremony itself, gave a place of honor to just such a moment, called by them "the moment of no-choice": that moment when, the utensils of tea having been assembled in their proper places, the host pauses for an instant, takes stock of himself, and knows that, in the words of Rikyu, there is only one need: "to boil water, make tea, and serve it." There is no choice to be made, no "should I do this or that," but simply the following of the direction already chosen, the continuation of the process.

For this to take place, the craftsman needs knowledge, skill, craft—as well as his tools and materials. The need for things to be made—blankets, pots, or cabinets—can be seen in an inner as well as an outer sense. The outer sense—my need (or yours) for a blanket in which to keep warm, for a pot from which to eat, for a cabinet to hold the blanket or pot—is plain. But the craftsman must be in touch with another need: his need to work, his need to exercise the knowledge which he has spent his apprenticeship in getting, his need to follow with the attention not only the outward shaping of the thing but also the inward shaping of himself. For this he must have free time and space, in both the inner and outer senses. He must have a workshop and the time to work in it; he must have an inner freedom from the troubles and concerns of the rest of his life, time and space within so that the attention has room in which to follow the movements of the hands.

Well, my infidel self observes, even when on very rare occasions such a state of mind and heart and body is reached, it does not last very long. Soon I am back in my old rut, worrying and resenting and rattling the mental dishes as usual. Suddenly the wood shavings swallow up all my tools, the movement of the wheel falters, and the centered clay goes awry; the shuttle of red thread, which was in hand just a moment ago, has vanished entirely. At such moments, there are several possibilities. I can stop what I am doing, perhaps to begin again from the beginning. Or I can continue, try to find the thread again, center the clay again, take stock for a moment and try to find the space and time to work here and now. Not an easy thing: as hard—perhaps harder—than finding that state the first time. But now it may be that something is possible again because it has happened once before. Unfortunately, there is no formula and I must again find the possibility by searching for it. It may entail some suffering: suffering one's own emptiness, dryness, seeing its manifestation in the material results of my work.

It is necessary to begin again and again—to repeat the movement, but not for the sake of making it habitual, for that would be to betray the teaching of the craft. Rather, the repetition is necessary in order to know, in order to bring my fragmented and fugitive parts together under the set of laws that governs all craft and find the freedom in those laws. My inner nature will not suffer extinction by such obedience, except when I fall into the habitual. I need attention, in order to know my inner nature and to protect myself from the habitual, or just to observe when habit appears. In such a moment of real choice, I can find the free time and space in which to begin again.

Perhaps this is the meaning and purpose of apprenticeship. It has been said that the apprentice is the one who tries to remember the count-less things that his master has taught him; the master is he who knows only the one thing: his craft.

SAM KEEN

Work and Worth: The High Price of Success

One does not work to live; one lives to work.
                    —Max Weber

Have leisure and know that I am God.
                    —Psalm 65

The summer of 1950 I was eighteen, my brother was twenty, and we were fancy-free and broke. The only job we could get was as gandy dancers or trackmen on the Pennsylvania Railroad line between Wilmington and Marcus Hook. In those days the job of leveling the track had not yet been automated and was done by a large crew that used jackhammers to push gravel from the roadbed under the ties.

Monday morning we got up at five and dressed in the old Levis and faded shirts we had carefully calculated would not betray to the other men that we were college boys just on for the summer. Still sleepy, we ate all the breakfast we could manage, packed our lunch—four sandwiches apiece, carrots, fruit, cookies, and frozen V-8 juice—and drove off to work on my brother's motorcycle.

At the work depot the hiring agent took us over and introduced us to the foreman, Dan Pantelone. Our first surprise was that, with the exception of Dan and one other man, we were the only white guys on the gang. We tried to look casual but we stuck out like virgins in a harem. For one thing, the fact that we didn't have hats or gloves told everyone that we were not used to hard labor under the hot sun.

Once out on the track my anxiety began to rise. Confronted with picks, shovels, sledgehammers, bars, and jackhammers, I suddenly wondered if I would be able to work a full day. I felt sick to my stomach and wanted to go home. But before I could invent a face-saving excuse the foreman came over and told me to help the men who were replacing the steel plates that held the rail to the track. I was handed a sledgehammer and told to help Angel drive the spikes into the tie. It was supposed to go like clockwork—bam, bam, bam, bam, each of us hitting the spike alternately in a regular rhythm. The only problem was that I missed the damn thing more often than I hit it, and hit it with the handle of the hammer more often than the head. Angel, who was twenty-one, black, married with one child, and a four-year veteran of the railroad, looked at me with more tolerance than I expected and said, "Don't worry, boy, you'll get the hang of it." After half an hour blisters were beginning to form on my hands but I was hitting the spike two out of three times. "There, you're getting it, man," Angel said. I felt better, blisters and all.

In the afternoon, we were introduced to the joys of jack-hammering—without gloves. The notion was to use the fifty-pound hammer to force stone under the ties to keep the rails level. Since there were ten hammers connected to a single compressor, the gang had to move at a single pace. One slow man would hold up the whole crew, and I was determined not to be the drag. Revived by lunch, I grabbed the hammer hard and started to work. Before the hour was out my hands were battered and I could hardly lift the hammer. Thank God, a long freight forced us off the track. Lampkin, a large, slow-talking man, nearly sixty, came over and sat beside me. "Let me tell you something, boy. Don't grab that hammer so hard. Let it sit gentle in your hands. And don't lift it when you don't have to. Let it rest on the underlip of the tie and do the work for you. And I'm going to tell you something else. Don't ever start the day any faster than you intend on ending it. You take it easy. This railroad is going to be here when you are dead and gone."

Eons later, when quitting time arrived, we got on the motorcycle and blessed the delicious cool wind in our hair! At home we soaked in tubs of hot and cold water. Our hands, too sore to touch, floated by our sides like bloated bodies of dead soldiers. Immediately after supper, we fell asleep in the living room.

Somehow we got through the week. We learned to wear gloves, hold the hammer easy, walk slowly, and pace ourselves. Friday noon we put the hammers away, got the long bars from the tool box, and went along the stretch of track we had levelled during the week to line it. Sixteen men put bars under the track to lever it one way or the other until it was straight. Someone would begin a work chant, and we would all tap our bars in time and pull together on the beat. "I don't know [Pull]/Believe I will [Pull]/Make my home [Pull]/In Jacksonville [Pull]." The last half hour, we sat around waiting for quitting time, everybody in a good mood. "Now don't you boys spend all your money this weekend on pussy and wine," Lampkin told us. "What do you mean, Lampkin?" Angel said. "Them boys is pretty, not like you. They don't have to pay for pussy." "Shit, man," Lampkin shot back. "Just you ask your wife about me." And everybody laughed.

Quitting time. We raced home, bathed, and took off for the beach for the weekend. Every muscle was sore. The tattoo of the jackhammer still rang in our ears. The stigmata of broken blisters and new calluses marked our hands. But, oh, we did wear our wounds proudly, and cherished every ache like old soldiers fingering campaign ribbons. We had worked with the men, had money in our pockets, and were on our way to see the ladies.

THE BOTTOM LINE—WORK AND WORTH

Preparations for the male ritual of work begin even before the age of schooling. Long before a boy child has a concept of the day after tomorrow, he will be asked by well-meaning but unconscious adults, "What do you want to be when you grow up?" It will not take him long to discover that "I want to be a horse" is not an answer that satisfies adults. They want to know what men plan to do, what job, profession, occupation we have decided to follow at five years of age! Boys are taught early that they are what they do. Later, as men, when we meet as strangers on the plane or at a cocktail party we break the ice by asking, "What do you do?"

The first full-time job, like the first fight or first sex, is a rite of passage for men in our time. Boys have paper routes, but men have regular paychecks. Like primitive rites, work requires certain sacrifices and offers certain insignia of manhood. In return for agreeing to put aside childish dalliance and assume the responsibility for showing up from nine to five at some place of work, the initiate receives the power object—money—that allows him to participate in the adult life of the community.

Getting a credit card is a more advanced rite of passage. The credit card is for the modern male what killing prey was to a hunter. To earn a credit rating a man must certify that he has voluntarily cut himself off from childhood, that he has foregone the pleasure of languid mornings at the swimming hole, and has assumed the discipline of a regular job, a fixed address, and a predictable character. Debt, the willingness to live beyond our means, binds us to the economic system that requires both surplus work and surplus consumption. The popular bumper sticker "I owe, I owe, so off to work I go" might well be the litany to express the commitment of the working man.

After accepting the disciplines of work and credit, a whole hierarchy of graduated symbolic initiations follows, from first to thirty-second degree. Mere employment entitles one to display the insignia of the Chevette. Acquiring the executive washroom key qualifies one for a Buick or Cadillac. Only those initiated into the inner sanctum of the boardroom may be borne in the regal Rolls-Royce.

Within the last decade someone upped the ante on the tokens required for manhood. A generation ago, providing for one's family was the only economic requirement. Nowadays, supplying the necessities entitles a man only to marginal respect. If your work allows you only to survive you are judged to be not much of a man. To be poor in a consumer society is to have failed the manhood test, or at least to have gotten a D-. The advertising industry reminds us at every turn that real men, successful men, powerful men, are big spenders. The sort of man who reads *Playboy* or *The New Yorker* is dedicated to a life of voluntary complexity, conspicuous consumption, and adherence to the demanding discipline of style.

The rites of manhood in any society are those that are appropriate and congruent with the dominant myth. The horizon within which we live, the source of our value system, and the way we define "reality" are economic. The bottom line is the almighty dollar. Time is money, money is power, and power makes the world go round. In the same sense that the cathedral was the sacred center of the medieval city, the bank and other commercial buildings are the centers of the modern city.

Once upon a time work was considered a curse. As the result of Adam and Eve's sin we were driven from the Garden of Eden and forced to earn our bread by the sweat of our brows. Men labored because of necessity, but found the meaning and sweetness of life in free time. According to the Greeks, only slaves and women were bound to the life of work. Free men discovered the joys and dignity of manhood in contemplation and in the cultivation of leisure. Until the time of the Protestant Reformation the world was divided between the realm of the secular, to which work and the common life belonged, and the realm of the sacred, which was the monopoly of the Church. Martin Luther changed all of this by declaring that every man and woman had a sacred vocation. The plowman and the housewife no less than the priest were called by God to express their piety in the common life of the community. Gradually the notion of the priesthood of all believers came to mean that every man and woman had a calling to meaningful secular work.

In the feudal era manhood involved being the lord of a manor, the head of a household, or at least a husbandman of the land. As the industrial revolution progressed men were increasingly pulled out of the context of nature, family, church, and community to find the meaning of their lives in trading, industry, the arts, and the professions, while women practiced their vocations by ministering to the needs of the home and practicing charity within the community. Gradually, getting and spending assumed the place of greatest importance, virtually replacing all of the old activities that previously defined manhood—hunting, growing, tending, celebrating, protesting, investigating. As "the bottom line" became our ultimate concern, and the Dow Jones the index of reality, man's world shrank. Men no longer found their place beneath the dome of stars, within the brotherhood of animals, by the fire of the hearth, or in the company of citizens. Economic man spends his days with colleagues, fellow workers, bosses, employees, suppliers, lawyers, customers, and other strangers. At night he returns to an apartment or house that has been empty throughout the day. More likely than not, if he is married with children, his wife has also been away at work throughout the day and his children have been tended and educated by another cadre of professionals. If he is successful his security (*securus*—"free from care") rests in his investments (from "vestment"—a religious garment) in stocks, bonds, and other commodities whose future value depends upon the whims of the market.

Nowadays only a fortunate minority are able to find harmony between vocation and occupation. Some artists, professionals, businessmen, and tradesmen find in their work a calling, a lifework, an arena within which they may express their creativity and care. But most men are shackled to the mercantile society in much the same way medieval serfs were imprisoned in the feudal system. All too often we work because we must, and we make the best of a bad job.

In the secular theology of economic man, Work has replaced God as the source from whom all blessings flow. The escalating gross national product, or at least the rising Dow Jones index, is the outward and visible sign that we are progressing toward the kingdom of God; full employment is grace; unemployment is sin. The industrious, especially entrepreneurs with capital, are God's chosen people, but even laborers are sanctified because they participate in the productive economy.

As a form of secular piety Work now satisfies many of the functions once served by religion. In the words of Ayn Rand, whose popular philosophy romanticized capitalism and sanctified selfishness, "Your work is the process of achieving your values. Your body is a machine but your mind is its driver. Your work is the purpose of your life, and you must speed past any killer who assumes the right to stop you....Any value you might find outside your work, any other loyalty or love, can only be travelers going on their own power in the same direction."[1]

We don't work just to make a living. Increasingly, the world of work provides the meaning of our lives. It becomes an end in itself rather than a means. A decade ago, only twenty-eight percent of us enjoyed the work we did. And yet, according to a Yankelovich survey, eighty percent of us reported that we would go right on working even if we didn't need the money. By the 1980s this profile changed. We are just as attached to our work, but now we are demanding that the workplace provide an outlet for our creativity. Yankelovich reports in 1988 that fifty-two percent of Americans respond, "I have an inner need to do the very best job I can, regardless of the pay" and sixty-one percent, when asked what makes for the good life, say, "a job that is interesting."[2]

Something very strange has happened to work and leisure in the last generation. The great promise of emerging technology was that it would finally set men free from slavery and we could flower. As late as the 1960s, philosophers such as Herbert Marcuse, sociologists, and futurists were predicting a coming leisure revolution. We were just around the corner from a twenty-hour work week. Soon we would be preoccupied by arts, games, and erotic dalliance on leisurely afternoons. At worst we would have to learn to cope with "pleasure anxiety" and the threat of leisure.

Exactly the opposite happened. Work is swallowing leisure. The fast lane has become a way of life for young professionals who are giving their all to career. In the 1990s Americans may come more and more to resemble the Japanese—workaholics all, living to work rather than working to live, finding their identity as members of corporate tribes.

Recently the awareness has been growing that work, even good and creative work, may become an addiction that destroys other human values. A Workaholics Anonymous movement has emerged with a twelve-step program for men and women who feel their work lives have gotten out of control. According to a WA recruiting broadside, if you answer yes to three or more of the following questions you may be a workaholic:

1. Do you get more excited about your work than about family or anything else?
2. Are there times when you can charge through work and other times when you can't get anything done?
3. Do you take work with you to bed? on weekends? on vacation?
4. Is work the activity you like to do best and talk about most?
5. Do you work more than forty hours a week?
6. Do you turn your hobbies into money-making ventures?
7. Do you take complete responsibility for the outcome of your work efforts?
8. Have your family or friends given up expecting you on time?
9. Do you take on extra work because you are concerned that it won't otherwise get done?
10. Do you underestimate how long a project will take and then rush to complete it?
11. Do you believe that it is okay to work long hours if you love what you are doing?
12. Do you get impatient with people who have other priorities besides work?
13. Are you afraid if you don't work hard you will lose your job or be a failure?

14. Is the future a constant worry for you even when things are going very well?

15. Do you do things energetically and competitively, including play?

16. Do you get irritated when people ask you to stop doing your work to do something else?

17. Have your long hours hurt your family and other relationships?

18. Do you think about work while driving, while falling asleep, or when others are talking?

19. If you are eating alone, do you work or read during your meal?

20. Do you believe that more money will solve the other problems in your life?

Maybe the standards of WA for what constitutes a workaholic are a trifle high, or maybe they're an index of how consuming work has become, but (I confess) according to the above questions, I and most of my friends qualify as workaholics.

Part of the problem is that work, community, and family are getting mixed up and lumped together. Increasingly, Americans live in places where they are anonymous, and seek to find their community at work. Companies, with the help of organizational development consultants, are trying to make the workplace the new home, the new family. The new motto is: humanize the workplace; make it a community; let communication flourish on all levels. The best (or is it the worst?) of companies have become paternalistic or maternalistic, providing their employees with all the comforts and securities of home.

In short, the workplace is rapidly becoming its own culture that defines who we are. Like minisocieties, professions and corporations create their own ritual and mythology. Doctors share a common story, a history of disease and cure, a consensus about the means of healing with other doctors. Businessmen share the language of profit and loss with other businessmen and acknowledge the same tokens of success. As economic organizations have grown larger than governments, employees render them a type of loyalty previously reserved for God, country, or family.

To determine what happens to men within the economic world we need to look critically at its climate, its ruling mood, its ethos, its aims, and its method. We should no more accept a profession's or a corporation's self-evaluation, its idealistic view of itself (we are a family, a "service" organization, dedicated to the highest ideals of quality, etc.) than we would accept the propaganda of any tribe or nation.

A recent critical study of the climate of corporate culture suggests it may be more like a tyrannical government than a kindly family. Earl Shorris, in a neglected and very important book, suggests that the modern corporation represents a historically new form of tyranny in which we are controlled by accepting the definitions of happiness that keep us in harness for a lifetime. Herewith, in short, his argument:

> The most insidious of the many kinds of power is the power to define happiness....

> The manager, like the nobleman of earlier times, serves as the exemplary merchant: Since happiness cannot be defined, he approximates his definition through the display of symbols, such as expense account meals, an expensive house, stylish clothing, travel to desirable places, job security, interesting friends, membership in circles of powerful people, advantages for his children, and social position for his entire family....

> In the modern world, a delusion about work and happiness enables people not only to endure oppression but to seek it and to believe that they are happier because of the very work that oppresses them. At the heart of the delusion lies the manager's definition of happiness: sweat and dirty hands signify oppression and a coat and tie signify happiness, freedom and a good life.

> Blue-collar workers...resist symbolic oppression. One need only visit an assembly line and observe the styles of dress, speech, and action of the workers to realize the symbolic freedom they enjoy....They live where they please, socialize with whomever they please, and generally enjoy complete freedom outside the relatively few hours they spend at their jobs....No matter how much money a blue-collar worker earns, he is considered poor; no matter how much he enjoys his work, he is thought to be suffering. In that way, blue-collar wages are kept low and blue-collar workers suffer the indignity of low status.

> The corporation or the bureaucracy...becomes a place, the cultural authority, the moral home of a man. The rules of the corporation become the rules of society, the future replaces history, and the organization becomes the family of the floating man....By detaching him

from the real world of place, the corporation becomes the world for him.

> Men abandoned the power to define happiness for themselves, and having once abandoned that power, do not attempt to regain it....[3]

The new rhetoric about the workplace as home and family needs to be balanced by an honest evaluation of the more destructive implications of the iron law of profit. Home and family are ends in themselves. They are, or should be, about sharing of love to no purpose. They file no quarterly reports. Business is an activity organized to make a profit. And any activity is shaped by the end it seeks. Certainly business these days wears a velvet glove, comporting itself with a new facade of politeness and enlightened personnel policies, but beneath the glove is the iron fist of competition and warfare.

The recent spate of best-selling books about business that make use of military metaphors tell an important story about economic life and therefore about the climate within which most men spend their days. Listen to the metaphors, the poetry of business as set forth in David Rogers' *Waging Business Warfare*, from the jacket copy:

> Become a master of strategy on today's corporate killing fields—and win the war for success....How to succeed in battle: Believe it: if you're in business, you're at war. Your enemies—your competitors—intend to annihilate you. Just keeping your company alive on the battlefield is going to be a struggle. Winning may be impossible—unless you're a master of military strategy....You can be—if you'll follow the examples of the great tacticians of history. Because the same techniques that made Genghis Khan, Hannibal, and Napoleon the incomparable conquerors they were are still working for Chrysler's Lee Iacocca, Procter & Gamble's John Smale, Remington's Victor Kiam and other super-strategists on today's corporate killing fields....Join them at the command post! Mastermind the battle! Clobber the enemy! Win the war![4]

Or, maybe to succeed you need to know *The Business Secrets of Attila the Hun*? Or listen to the language of Wall Street: corporate raiders, hostile takeovers, white knights, wolf packs, industrial spies, the underground economy, head-hunting, shark-repellent, golden parachutes, poison pills, making a killing, etc.

When we organize our economic life around military metaphors and words such as *war, battle, strategy, tactics, struggle, contest, competition, winning, enemies, opponents, defenses, security, maneuver, objective, power, command, control, will power, assault* we have gone a long way toward falling into a paranoid worldview. And when men live within a context where their major function is to do battle—economic or literal—they will be shaped by the logic of the warrior psyche.

THE HIGH PRICE OF SUCCESS

At the moment the world seems to be divided between those countries that are suffering from failed economies and those that are suffering from successful economies. After a half century of communism the USSR, Eastern Europe, and China are all looking to be saved from the results of stagnation by a change to market economies. Meanwhile, in the U.S., Germany, and Japan we are beginning to realize that our success has created an underclass of homeless and unemployed, and massive pollution of the environment. As the Dow rises to new heights everyone seems to have forgotten the one prophetic insight of Karl Marx: where the economy creates a class of winners it will also create a class of losers; where wealth gravitates easily into the hands of the haves, the fortunes of the have-nots become more desperate.

On the psychological level, the shadow of our success, the flip side of our affluence, is the increasing problem of stress and burnout. Experts in relaxation, nutrition, exercise, and meditation are doing a brisk business.

But finally, stress cannot be dealt with by psychological tricks, because for the most part it is a philosophical rather than a physiological problem, a matter of the wrong worldview. Perhaps the most common variety of stress can best be described as "rust out" rather than burnout. It is a product, not of an excess of fire but of a deficiency of passion. We, human beings, can survive so long as we "make a living," but we do not thrive without a sense of significance that we gain only by creating something we feel is of lasting value—a child, a better mousetrap, a computer, a space shuttle, a book, a farm. When the requirements of our work do not match our creative potential we rust out. The second kind of burnout is really a type of combat fatigue that is the inevitable result of living for an extended period within an environment that is experienced as a battle zone. Like combat veterans returning from Vietnam, businessmen who live for years within an atmosphere of low-intensity warfare begin to exhibit the personality traits of the warrior. They become disillusioned and numb to ethical issues; they think only of survival and grow insensitive to pain. You may relax, breathe deeply, take time for R and R, and remain a warrior. But ultimately the only cure for stress is to leave the battlefield.

The feminist revolution made us aware of how the economic order has discriminated against women, but not of how it cripples the male psyche. In ancient China the feet of upper-class women were broken, bent backwards, and bound to make them more "beautiful." Have the best and brightest men of our time had their souls broken and bent to make them "successful"?

Let's think about the relation between the wounds men suffer, our overidentification with work, and our captivity within the horizons of the economic myth.

Recently, a lament has gone out through the land that men are becoming too tame, if not limp. The poet Robert Bly, who is as near as we have these days to a traveling bard and shaman for men, says we have raised a whole generation of soft men—oh-so-sensitive, but lacking in thunder and lightning. He tells men they must sever the ties with mother, stop looking at themselves through the eyes of women, and recover the "wild man" within themselves.

I suspect that if men lack the lusty pride of self-affirmation, if we say "yes" too often but without passion, if we are burned out without ever having been on fire, it is mostly because we have allowed ourselves to be engulfed by a metabody, a masculine womb—The Corporation. Our fragile, tender, wild, and succulent bodies are being deformed to suit the needs of the body corporate. Climbing the economic or corporate ladder has replaced the hero's journey up Mt. Analogue. Upward mobility has usurped the ascent of the Seven-Story Mountain, the quest to discover the heights and depths of the human psyche.

At what cost to the life of our body and spirit do we purchase corporate and professional success? What sacrifices are we required to make to these upstart economic gods?

Here are some of the secrets they didn't tell you at the Harvard Business School, some of the hidden, largely unconscious, tyrannical, unwritten rules that govern success in professional and corporate life:

Cleanliness is next to prosperity. Sweat is lower-class, lower status. Those who shower before work and use deodorant make more than those who shower after work and smell human throughout the day. As a nation we are proud that only three percent of the population has to work on the land—get soiled, be earthy—to feed the other ninety-seven percent.

Look but don't touch. The less contact you have with real stuff—raw material, fertilizer, wood, steel, chemicals, making things that have moving parts—the more money you will make. Lately, as we have lost our edge in manufacturing and production, we have comforted ourselves with the promise that we can prosper by specializing in service and information industries. Oh, so clean.

Prefer abstractions. The further you move up toward the catbird seat, the penthouse, the office with the view of all Manhattan, the more you live among abstractions. In the brave new world of the market you may speculate in hog futures without ever having seen a pig, buy out an airline without knowing how to fly a plane, grow wealthy without having produced anything.

Specialize. The modern economy rewards experts, men and women who are willing to become focused, concentrated, tightly bound, efficient. Or to put the matter more poignantly, we succeed in our professions to the degree that we sacrifice wide-ranging curiosity and fascination with the world at large, and become departmental in our thinking. The professions, like medieval castles, are small kingdoms sealed off from the outer world by walls of jargon.

Sit still and stay indoors. The world is run largely by urban, sedentary males. The symbol of power is the chair. With the exception of quarterbacks, boxers, and race car drivers, whose bodies are broken for our entertainment, men don't get ahead by moving their bodies.

Live by the clock. Ignore your intimate body time, body rhythms, and conform to the demands of corporate time, work time, professional time. When "time is money," we bend our bodies and minds to the demands of EST (economic standard time). We interrupt our dreams when the alarm rings, report to work at nine, eat when the clock strikes twelve, return to our private lives at five, and retire at sixty-five—ready or not. As a reward we are allowed weekends and holidays for recreation. Most successful men, and lately women, become Type A personalities, speed freaks, addicted to the rush of adrenaline, filled with a sense of urgency, hard driven, goal oriented, and stressed out. The most brutal example of this rule is the hundred-hour week required of physicians in their year of residency. This hazing ritual, like circumcision, drives home the deep mythic message that your body is no longer your own.

Wear the uniform. It wouldn't be so bad if those who earned success and power were proud enough in their manhood to peacock their colors. But no. Success makes drab. The higher you rise in the establishment the more colorless you become, the more you dress like an undertaker or a priest. The more a corporation, institution, or profession requires the sacrifice of the individuality of its members, the more it requires uniform wear. The corp isn't really looking for a few good men. It's looking for a few dedicated Marines, and it knows exactly how to transform boys into uniform men. As monks and military men have known for centuries, once you get into the habit you follow the orders of the superior.

Keep your distance, stay in your place. There are people above you, people below you, and people on your level, and you don't get too close to any of them. Nobody hugs the boss. What is lacking is friendship. I know of no more radical critique of economic life than the observation by Earl Shorris that nowhere in the vast literature of management is there a single chapter on friendship.

Desensitize yourself. Touch, taste, smell—the realm of the senses—receive little homage. What pays off is reason, willpower, planning, discipline, control. There has, of course, recently been a move afoot to bring in potted plants and tasteful art to make corporate environments more humane. But the point of these exercises in aesthetics, like the development of communication skills by practitioners of organizational development, is to increase production. The bottom line is still profit, not pleasure or persons.

Don't trouble yourself with large moral issues. The more the world is governed by experts, specialists, and professionals, the less anybody takes responsibility for the most troubling consequences of our success-failure. Television producers crank out endless cop and killing tales, but refuse to consider their contribution to the climate of violence. Lawyers concern themselves with what is legal, not what is just. Physicians devote themselves to kidneys or hearts of individual patients while the health delivery system leaves masses without medicine. Physicists invent new generations of genocidal weapons which they place in the eager arms of the military. The military hands the responsibility for their use over to politicians. Politicians plead that they have no choice—the enemy makes them do it. Professors publish esoterica while students perish from poor teaching. Foresters, in cahoots with timber companies, clear-cut or manage the forest for sustained yield, but nobody is in charge of oxygen regeneration. Psychologists heal psyches while communities fall apart. Codes of professional ethics are for the most part, like corporate advertisements, high-sounding but self-serving.

When we live within the horizons of the economic myth, we begin to consider it honorable for a man to do whatever he must to make a living. Gradually we adopt what Erich Fromm called "a marketing orientation" toward ourselves. We put aside our dreams, forget the green promise of our young selves, and begin to tailor our personalities to what the market requires. When we mold ourselves into commodities, practice smiling and charm so we will have "winning personalities," learn to sell ourselves, and practice the silly art of power dressing, we are certain to be haunted by a sense of emptiness.

Men, in our culture, have carried a special burden of unconsciousness, of ignorance of the self. The unexamined life has been worth quite a lot in economic terms. It has enabled us to increase the gross national product yearly. It may not be necessary to be a compulsive extrovert to be financially successful, but it helps. Especially for men, ours is an outer-directed culture that rewards us for remaining strangers to ourselves, unacquainted with feeling, intuition, or the subtleties of sensation and dreams.

Some feminists, who harbor a secret belief in the innate moral superiority of women, believe that women will change the rules of business and bring the balm of communication and human kindness into the boardroom. To date this has been a vain hope. Women executives have proven themselves the equal of men in every way—including callousness. The difference between the sexes is being eroded as both sexes become defined by work. It is often said that the public world of work is a man's place and that as women enter it they will become increasingly "masculine" and lose their "femininity." To think this way is to miss the most important factor of the economic world. Economic man, the creature who defines himself within the horizons of work and consumption, is not man in any full sense of the word, but a being who has been neutralized, degendered, rendered subservient to the laws of the market. The danger of economics is not that it turns women into men but that it destroys the fullness of both manhood and womanhood.

History is a game of leapfrog in which yesterday's gods regularly become today's demons, and the rectitude of the fathers becomes the fault of the sons. The Greeks invented the idea of nemesis to show how any single virtue stubbornly maintained gradually changes into a destructive vice. Our success, our industry, our habit of work have produced our economic nemesis. In our current economic crisis we are driving to the poorhouse in new automobiles, spending our inflated dollars for calorie-free food, lamenting our falling productivity in an environment polluted by our industry. Work made modern men great, but now threatens to usurp our souls, to inundate the earth in things and trash, to destroy our capacity to love and wonder. According to an ancient myth, Hephaestus Vulcan the blacksmith, the only flawed immortal who worked, was born lame.

Somehow men got so lost in the doing that we forgot to pause and ask, "What is worth doing? What of value are we creating—and destroying—within the economic order?" Work has always been our womb— the fertile void out of which we give birth to our visions. Today we need to stop the world for a while and look carefully at where our industry is taking us. We have a hopeful future only if we stop asking what we can produce and begin to ask what we want to create. Our dignity as men lies not in exhausting ourselves in work but in discovering our vocation.

Remembering Dr. Faust, it might be a good idea to pause and ask ourselves how much of our psyches we will trade for how much profit, power, and prestige. Maybe we should require graduate schools, professional organizations, places of labor, and corporations to put a warning over their doors. Caution: Excessive work may be hazardous to the health of your body and spirit.

I fear that something beautiful, terrible, and complex about work has escaped me. Some part of the mixed blessing I cannot capture in words.

A friend who is a successful entrepreneur asked me, "Are you anti-business? Business is where I create. It is where the excitement and juice is for me. I can hardly wait to get to my office." My literary agent, Ned Leavitt, tells me: "My work is my art. When I dress in my suit each morning I feel like a knight going forth to battle, and I love to fight hard and win in a hard bargaining session with a publisher and get the best deal for my clients."

I know. I know. I am also one of the work-driven men. And I am lucky to have work that fits skintight over my spirit. I hardly know how to separate work from self. Even when I subtract the long hours, the fatigue, the uncertainties about money, the irritation of having to deal with a million nit-shit details, the long hours in the limbo of jet planes and airports, the compromises I have to make, the sum is overwhelmingly positive. I don't know who I would be without the satisfaction of providing for my family, the occasional intoxication of creativity, the warm companionship of colleagues, the pride in a job well done, and the knowledge that my work has been useful to others.

But there is still something unsaid, something that forces me to ask questions about my life that are, perhaps, tragic: In working so much have I done violence to my being? How often, doing work that is good, have I betrayed what is better in my self and abandoned what is best for those I love? How many hours would have been better spent walking in silence in the woods or wrestling with my children? Two decades ago, near the end of what was a good but troubled marriage, my wife asked me: "Would you be willing to be less efficient?" The question haunts me.

NOTES

[1] Ayn Rand, *For the New Intellectual* (New York: Signet Books, 1961) p. 130.

[2] *American Health* (September 1988).

[3] Earl Shorris, *Scenes from Corporate Life* (New York: Penguin, 1990).

[4] David J. Rogers, *Waging Business Warfare: Lessons from the Military Masters in Achieving Corporate Superiority* (New York: Scribners, 1987).

PATRICIA RYAN-MADSON

Reality's Work

Effort is good fortune.
    —Shoma Morita

Masatake (Shoma) Morita was a very bright, extremely sensitive but sickly youth prone to insomnia and gastroenteric disturbances. He was studying psychiatry at the university and was accustomed to receiving a regular stipend for tuition, medical, and living expenses from his father. At one point the regular checks stopped arriving. His father had come upon financial difficulties and was forced to cut off his subsidy. Morita was extremely upset and felt betrayed by his family.

He decided to get back at his father for this treatment. To show off his "miserable state" he would cut off all medication (since he now couldn't afford it) and overexert himself. Or, as the story goes, he decided to "study himself to death." This would surely teach his parents the error of their ways in abandoning him financially.

But instead of dying the young Morita thrived. In fact, his physical symptoms all but disappeared as he applied himself to study full time. Not only did he appear to "get well" but his efforts produced spectacular academic marks! His own effort had inadvertently led to the relief of his suffering and the discovery of what he would come to describe as "the healing power of work." It laid the foundation for Morita's understanding of the relation of effort to mental health and became the basis of Morita Psychotherapy.

Morita Psychotherapy in combination with another Japanese form, Naikan "Reflection," are the foundations for an American Buddhist-based practice known as *Constructive Living*. Both Morita and Naikan have their origins in Buddhist thought.

The term "Constructive Living" was coined and developed by the American psychologist and anthropologist Dr. David K. Reynolds. Reynolds' creation of this paradigm was a result of decades of direct experience in Japan and a lifetime of study in Eastern thought and practice. He has written prolifically in English and Japanese on these themes in both the popular and scholarly presses. He is the acknowledged authority on Japanese psychotherapies in the United States. But his creative work in developing the clear language of the Constructive Living model is perhaps his most valuable contribution. By taking the essential teachings of the Zen-inspired Morita model and the Jodo Shinshu-inspired Naikan model, Reynolds has developed a simple prescription for living. The language is straightforward and secular, its advice easy to understand and humbling to practice.

PAY ATTENTION TO REALITY

I begin by noticing reality, things as they are. This is the practical exercise of paying attention. I notice that the screen of my computer is blue. The letters are pink. There is a hum from the printer and the computer itself. This hum is the sound of this machine working to support my efforts now. Attention for me now includes noticing the time, 9:35 a.m., as well as my thoughts (currently doubting if this paragraph could possibly be of use to anyone and while doubting, continuing to type). Remembering Natalie Goldberg's wise advice to writers: "Keep your hands moving."

NOTICE WHAT YOU ARE RECEIVING AND WHAT YOU ARE GIVING

The second principle informs my attention. It creates a particular lens through which I look. I am asked to notice what supports me, what I am receiving in this moment or have been receiving at other points in time. This lens cultivates the notion of interdependence, of noticing all the efforts that sustain me. Now I am receiving light from the sun, light from a desk lamp (which I observe is being used unnecessarily and so I turn it off). I am receiving help from the computer which records my thoughts, allows me to rearrange sentences, checks my spelling, and finally permits me to make a copy to send to my editor. The printer receives this information and creates pieces of paper which hold these words and permit their passage to you the reader. In literally hundreds of thousands of specific ways I am being supported at this very moment. The clock functions—ticking—giving me information about time.

KNOW YOUR PURPOSE

Observing reality, noting all I am receiving, my purpose emerges. As I write this now, I reflect on that purpose. I have an immediate purpose: to write for one hour this morning. To this end I "keep my hands moving." My purpose in writing is to spread information about Constructive Living in the hope that this practical advice may serve to relieve unnecessary suffering. This purpose seems to spring from an inner sense or desire I have to give something back to the world.

ACCEPT YOUR FEELINGS

So, knowing my purpose, I accept my feelings. Right now I am feeling antsy, wanting to get out of the house, wanting to jump up and make a cup of tea, wanting to be doing something physical other than sitting here with my hands moving over the keys. I am feeling insecure about this essay, doubting the form I am using now to write these personal immediate illustrations of how I use Constructive Living. There is no need to "fix" these feelings. I do not need to gain confidence as a writer in order to write. I do not "need" to jump up and make a cup of tea (although sometimes that is exactly what does need doing). I don't need to do anything at all with these sensations. I feel them, of course. They are my feelings. I accept them as part of me now. I do *need* to write, however.

DO WHAT NEEDS TO BE DONE

And so I act. Now, this means the action of writing. I sit at the computer. I keep my hands moving. Writing happens, through me. For me this is "right livelihood": doing what needs to be done. "What needs to be done" and "What I want to do" may coincide. However, my personal desires are not driving the inquiry. My personal needs are a subset of what needs to be done overall. Sometimes "my" needs lead, sometimes they follow. In reality there is no distinction. I return my attention again and again to reality to learn what needs to be done. And then I do it. In most cases "what needs to be done" is crystal clear, right in front of me. It is simply that I am not yet doing it. Constructive Living reminds me that I do not need to "get motivated," "gain confidence," "get psyched," or "get ready." I *do* need to act. It is in the doing itself that meaning is often revealed.

Both right livelihood and Constructive Living imply a principled standard. Everything we do has a consequence. No matter how small, there is no action which does not impact others in very practical ways. In Constructive Living the lens of Naikan (noticing what I receive and give) helps to replace the customary ego-centered perspective with a broader, more holistic view. This may discourage self-interest as the sole motivating factor. What needs to be done is never an abstraction, never theoretical. It is always specific, concrete. My awareness of interdependence can clarify and inform my actions. What needs to be done is always a more inclusive question than simply what I need to do now.

Constructive Living would view the question of right livelihood from the vantage point of purpose. Right livelihood occurs when work is purposeful. So if my purpose in life is "to benefit others and not to injure" then anything and everything I do which serves that end can be considered as right livelihood. My work as a drama teacher, my work on neighborhood committees, sweeping the street, volunteer work, making lunches for my husband, composing this article, washing dishes—indeed, whatever reality brings me that my mind tells me needs to be done qualifies.

If I accept that right livelihood is "doing what needs to be done," then the question arises: "How do I know what is right for me to be doing?" This question assumes that there may be some work that is *not* right for me to be doing. Further, it assumes that there may be some particular work that is right for me.

Reynolds has a quotation neatly typed and posted near the computer in his home office in Coos Bay, Oregon. It reads: "There is Reality's work that only you can do." If you ponder this for a few moments, it will be clear that this phrase contains at least two perspectives. From one perspective, everything I do derives from and returns to Reality. It's inescapable. The other perspective implies "specialness." Only I can do certain jobs. Another way of putting this is that there are some jobs, some kinds of jobs, which seem uniquely suited to my aptitude, abilities, and interests. How do I find them?

Constructive Living suggests two strategies: (1) Examine your purpose(s) and (2) pay attention to what Reality has placed in front of you.

The question of purpose is best studied in the clear light of Naikan reflection. To practice Naikan means to examine the self in relation to others by asking three questions: What did I receive from them? What did I return to them? What trouble and bother did I cause them? I begin the inquiry by recalling my earliest memories of my mother and father. As I sincerely reflect on these questions, I begin to discover the details of the thousands of meals that I was fed, the specific clothing bought for me, the rides I was given, the lessons, the times my mother sat by my bedside when I was sick. The specific answers to these questions provide me with a ledger. Naikan examination shows me that, even by my own standards, I have been receiving more than I have given back to others. These findings often bring about a personal realization of my debt to the world. I cannot find right livelihood by thinking only of myself.

The person in search of his purpose who is asking the question, "What would I really like to do?" isn't yet asking the instructive question. Starting with such a feeling based question is missing the mark. The question implies a loop between the questioner, the specific job, and that job's "ability" to please the doer. Further, it appears to promise that if I get the "right job," it will make me happy and I will after that be doing "work that I like." While this may appear reasonable, it makes my "happiness" the measure of my success.

Realistically, I know that I cannot "be happy" all the time. My feelings come and go, changing often like the weather. If I go in search of work that "excites me" I am likely to be disappointed at least some of the time. Even the most stimulating work contains tasks that must be done whatever my motivation. Reality doesn't bring work that is always pleasant to do. While it is unrealistic to seek work that will always make me happy, it is possible to seek and find work that consistently supports some purpose of mine.

For example, my purpose may be to make the world a more beautiful place. To that end, I may choose any number of jobs that focus my time and talents on creating aesthetic environments. I can serve that purpose, not only when I go to work as a graphic designer, but also in the way I set the breakfast table for my children. I can serve that purpose by picking up trash in the park or in my neighborhood. I may serve that purpose as well, when I refrain from rough language or gossip. Or my purpose may be to help relieve unnecessary suffering in the world. To that end, my choice to refrain from an unkind word to a colleague forwards that purpose no less than my job as a nurse or social worker. So the answer to the question of purpose precedes and informs all that follows in the search for my true work.

When Morita saw a patient who complained about his job, wishing to quit, he had a stock response. Before counseling or allowing the patient to quit, Morita asked him to examine his purpose. If, indeed, his purpose could not be served in this particular job then that was considered a sufficient reason to change. If it was possible to serve his purpose within the current job setting, then Morita would insist the client remain in the job and apply himself with greater attention and diligence. Morita saw that satisfaction in work came not so much from finding the "perfect job," but rather from "doing the job in front of you perfectly"—that is, with full attention.

As I grow to appreciate all that I have been given in my life a natural desire to return something emerges. Out of this desire comes my purpose and from this my work. It is clear also that right livelihood comes both from my own purpose and from Reality's purpose, achieved through my hands.

Awakening in Daily Life

Remember the sabbath day, to keep it holy.
Six days shalt thou labor, and do all thy work:
But the seventh day…thou shalt not do any work.
                    —Exodus 20:8-10

Does one scent appeal more than another?
Do you prefer this flavor, or that feeling?
Is your practice sacred and your work profane?
Then your mind is separated:
from itself, from oneness, from the Tao.

Keep your mind free of divisions and distinctions.
When your mind is detached, simple, quiet, then all
    things can exist in harmony, and you begin to
    perceive the subtle truth.
                    —Lao-tzu

ROGER PRITCHARD

Right Living in a Consumer Society

We feel alienated from our work. We don't love what we do, we merely tolerate it. We work only to earn money, and we use that money to consume more than we really want. We feel a dissatisfaction with our lives, and yet we feel powerless to change.

Our modern economic system is based on the manufacture of goods, the extraction of natural resources without regard for the consequences, the progressive elimination of meaningful work, and the constant increase of consumption. Consumption is insatiable: we want more and more and the economy has to grow and grow to meet our needs—just like some cancer.

We are materially wealthy beyond our own wildest dreams. Yet we feel uneasy. Studies have shown that there is no correlation between happiness and wealth, fulfillment and material possessions. People in our society regularly report that to be happy they "need" about double their current income.

"Right livelihood" offers us a positive alternative, a middle path between growth for its own sake and stagnation. An increasing number of Americans are following this path. Many of us are looking for ways to break out of the current system. We want to reduce consumption, conserve natural resources, cut down on pollution, eat more simply and nutritiously, bring more spirituality into our lives, and develop more of a sense of community. More and more of us are convinced that each generation should meet its needs without jeopardizing the life support system of future generations.

Those of us who start on path to right livelihood find that our lives are more balanced, simple, clear, and focused. We are no longer strung out in a meaningless cycle of material consumption.

The contemporary economy focuses on this cycle of consumption. It doesn't really support our efforts to find meaningful work. Today, work is a means to consume or to pay debt for consumption already indulged in. How many people do you know who really love the work they are doing? How many feel bored and alienated? How many are simply earning the money to spend it on material pleasures?

Right livelihood demands that you take responsibility for making your work more meaningful. Good work is dignified. It develops your faculties and serves your community. It is a central human activity. Work, in this view:

> makes you honest with yourself
> requires that you develop your faculties and skills
> empowers you to do what you are really good at and love to do
> connects you in a compassionate way with the outside world
> supports the philosophy of non-destructiveness and sustainability
> integrates work with personal life and community

In our time only artists have been given permission to look at work this way. So you might say you should consider your life a work of art. And whereas those who follow the way of the starving artist are expected to accept poverty as the price they pay, those who follow the way of right livelihood are not. Right livelihood gives material well-being a place, it simply does not put it on a pedestal. In right livelihood, material wealth is not the "bottom line." The true goals of work are, rather, self-fulfillment and wisdom—and, ultimately, enlightenment.

Those who pursue right livelihood are neither in poverty nor strung out in an overextended cycle of material consumption for which work is simply a means. They do work that feels and is right for them, for their community, and for the planet.

Most people find that it takes years to make the transition from the mainstream to this new way of life. First you have to admit that *you* are responsible for *your* self-actualization. Then you have to make the journey. This can be a painful process—to let go of the old and familiar ways always is—but most people are very satisfied with the results.

Don't think you have to take this journey alone. In fact, it's terribly important that you look around and find people and groups who support the right livelihood way of life. Giving and getting support while trying to meet the challenges of learning a new way is key. And sharing the journey with others of like mind ensures that you keep your motivation high.

You can start small, perhaps by recycling or using more public transit. As you gain experience and confidence you can begin planning larger steps such as a career change.

Most people find that it takes years to make the transition and settle into this new way of life. But once they have embarked most people report increased feelings of self-esteem and well being. They feel good that they no longer support the damage that the industrial era has done to the planet and to people. They have found a positive, balanced alternative through right livelihood.

MARSHA SINETAR

The Psychology of Right Livelihood

I'm looking for something more than money out of my work. I expect deep ful-
fillment and a little fun too.
                                        —Executive, major U.S. corporation

Work I disliked the most was work I wasn't suited for. Once, for example, I sold vacuum cleaners door to door. Now, there's nothing wrong
with that job, except I was painfully shy and basically introverted, and
knocking on doors in strange neighborhoods was, for me, an unnatural
act. But I was working my way through college and in desperate need of
tuition money, so I silenced my fears and told myself I could do it. The
money was good, and that somehow made it all right. The only catch
was, my heart wasn't in it. I lasted one day.

Looking back on that experience and others depressingly like it, I
realized that I am not cut out for some occupations. I have a specific
disposition and a given set of aptitudes that require an equally specific
type of work. I know now that work needs to fit my personality just as
shoes need to fit my feet. Otherwise I'm destined for discomfort. As an
organizational psychologist and educator, I have come to believe that
this is true for everyone. Our right work is just as important to personality, health, and growth as the right nutrients are for our bodies.

Almost any job has its benefits. "At least I don't have to take it home
with me," "It's only five minutes away," "It pays the bills," are some of
the advantages people identify in their otherwise uninteresting, tedious,
or unrewarding work. Moreover, even in situations not particularly suited

to them, people are able to develop new abilities. A shy person can learn to be more socially comfortable by selling vacuum cleaners, cars, or Tupperware. An extrovert can learn to work in solitary, focused settings. A technical specialist can become a good manager of people. Clearly we can see that people do grow through "staying the course," through facing difficulty, through self-discipline, through toughening their resolve and perseverance.

Yet, even though we are all fairly adaptable, elastic, and multidimensional, we are not born to struggle through life. We are meant to work in ways that suit us, drawing on our natural talents and abilities as a way to express ourselves and contribute to others. This work, when we find it and do it—even if only as a hobby at first—is a key to our true happiness and self-expression.

Most of us think about our jobs or our careers as a means to fulfill responsibilities to families and creditors, to gain more material comforts, and to achieve status and recognition. But we pay a high price for this kind of thinking. A recent national poll revealed that 95 percent of America's working population do not enjoy the work they do! This is a profoundly tragic statistic considering that work consumes so much time in our lives. In a few brief decades, our working life adds up to be life itself.

Such a nose-to-the-grindstone attitude is not even a good formula for success. When you study people who are successful, as I have over the years, it is abundantly clear that their achievements are directly related to the enjoyment they derive from their work. They enjoy it in large part because they are good at it. A bright client of mine once told me, "I'm at my best when I'm using my brain. My ideal day is when my boss gives me lots of complex problems to solve." Another client remarked, "I like people, and when I'm involved with them, time just flies by. Since I've been in sales, I find everyone I meet interesting and fun to talk to. I should be paying my company for letting me do this work."

"Right livelihood" is an idea about work that is linked to the natural order of things. It is doing our best at what we do best. The rewards that follow are inevitable and manifold. There is no way we can fail. Biology points out the logic of right livelihood. Every species in the natural world has a place and function that is specifically suited to its capabilities. This is true for people too. Some of us are uniquely equipped for physical work, athletics, or dance; some of us have special intellectual gifts that make possible abstract or inventive thinking; some of us have aesthetic abilities and eye-hand coordination that enable us to paint, sculpt, or design. Examples are numerous of nature's way of directing us to the path that will support us economically and emotionally; this is the path that we were meant to travel.

Any talent that we are born with eventually surfaces as a need. Current research on child prodigies—youngsters who, from an early age, are mathematical wizards, virtuoso musicians, brilliant performers—tells us that they possess a burning desire to express themselves, to use their unique gifts. In a similar fashion, each of us, no matter how ordinary we consider our talents, wants and needs to use them. Right livelihood is the natural expression of this need. Yet, many of us cannot imagine that what we enjoy doing, what we have talent for, could be a source of income for us or even a catalyst for transforming our relationship to work. But, indeed, it can be. Leaders in every walk of life (e.g. housewives, craftspeople, entrepreneurs, inventors, community volunteers, etc.) who have the drive, skill, and compelling vision to advance their ideas—despite obstacles—need to exert their influence as much as their solutions, energy, and enthusiasm are needed by others.

The original concept of right livelihood comes from the teachings of Buddha, who described it as work consciously chosen, done with full awareness and care, and leading to enlightenment. For many people today, alienated from both their talents and their labors, his injunction is food for considerable thought. We must begin to think about ourselves and our work in a larger sense than mere nine-to-five penance for our daily bread. However, this larger concept of work carries with it increased demands, demands not everyone is willing to meet.

Right livelihood, in both its ancient and its contemporary sense, embodies self-expression, commitment, mindfulness, and conscious choice. Finding and doing work of this sort is predicated upon high self-esteem and self-trust, since only those who like themselves, who subjectively feel they are trustworthy and deserving, dare to choose on behalf of what is right and true for them. When the powerful quality of conscious choice is present in our work, we can be enormously productive. When we consciously choose to do work we enjoy, not only can we get things done, we can get them done well and be intrinsically rewarded for our effort. Money and security cease to be our only payments. Let me discuss each of these qualities to illustrate my point.

CONSCIOUS CHOICE

The very best way to relate to our work is to choose it. Right livelihood is predicated upon conscious choice. Unfortunately, since we learn early to act on what others say, value, and expect, we often find ourselves a long way down the wrong road before realizing we did not actually choose our work. Turning our lives around is usually the beginning of maturity since it means correcting choices made unconsciously, without deliberation or thought.

The ability to choose our work is no small matter. It takes courage to act on what we value and to willingly accept the consequences of our choices. Being able to choose means not allowing fear to inhibit or control us, even though our choices may require us to act against our fears or against the wishes of those we love and admire. Choosing sometimes forces us to leave secure and familiar arrangements. Because I work with many people who are poised on the brink of such choices, I have come to respect the courage it takes even to examine work and life options honestly. Many pay lip service to this process; to do something about the truths we discover in life is no easy matter. However, more people live honest lives than we might imagine.

A Spanish proverb teaches, "God says, 'Choose what you will and pay for it.'" And so it is that as we weigh the yes/no possibilities of our choices, we learn more about our strengths and weaknesses and become more willing and able to pay the price of each choice. By choosing we learn to be responsible. By paying the price of our choices we learn to make better choices. Each choice we make consciously adds positively to our sense of ourselves and makes us trust ourselves more because we learn how to live up to our own inner standards and goals.

But the reverse is also true: When we unconsciously drift through life, we cultivate self-doubt, apathy, passivity, and poor judgment. By struggling, by facing the difficulties of making conscious choices, we grow stronger, more capable, and more responsible to ourselves. Once we see and accept that our talents are also our blueprint for a satisfying vocational life, then we can stop looking to others for approval and direction. Choosing consciously also forces us to stop postponing a commitment. In this way we move one step closer to being responsible, contributing adults.

Choosing our work allows us to enter into that work willingly, enthusiastically, and mindfully. Whatever our work is, whether we love it or not, we can choose to do it well, to be with it—moment to moment—to combat the temptation to back away from being fully present. As we practice this art and attitude, we also grow more capable of enjoying work itself!

WORK IS A WAY OF BEING

As a way of working and as a way of thinking about work, right livelihood embodies its own psychology—a psychology of a person moving toward the fullest participation in life, a person growing in self-awareness, trust, and high self-esteem.

Abraham Maslow, foremost to study and describe such healthy personalities, calls them "self-actualizing." The phrase simply means growing whole. These are people who have taken the moment-to-moment risks to insure that their entire lives become an outward expression of their true inner selves. They have a sense of their own worth and are likely to experiment, to be creative, to ask for what they want and need. Their high self-esteem and subsequent risk-taking/creativity bring them a host of competencies that are indispensable to locating work they want. They also develop the tenacity and optimism which allows them to stick with their choices until the financial rewards come. They are life-affirming. For them, work is a way of being, an expression of love.

A friend of mine is a furniture maker—a true craftsman and artist. Of his work he says, "I get great satisfaction from making fine furniture—the process enriches me, makes me feel that I am somehow in each piece." He believes, as I do, that part of the unique beauty of a lovely, handmade piece comes from its being part of the spirit that is brought to it during its making. He nourishes his creations with his care and attention and his work, in turn, nourishes him.

Self-actualizing persons follow the often slow and difficult path of self-discipline, perseverance, and integrity. No less is required of those of us who yearn to trade in our jobs or careers for our right livelihoods—work that suits our temperaments and capabilities, work that we love.

SELF-EXPRESSION

Work is a natural vehicle for self-expression because we spend most of our time in its thrall. It simply makes no sense to turn off our personality, squelch our real abilities, forget our need for stimulation and personal growth forty hours out of every week. Work can be a means of allowing the varied and complex aspects of our personality to act on our behalf, translating our attitudes, feelings, and perceptions into meaningful productivity.

It may help to think of yourself as an artist whose work is obviously a form of self-expression. His first efforts may appear to be experimental, scattered, bland, or indistinct. But as he applies and disciplines himself, as he hones his skills and comes to know himself, his paintings become a signature of the inner man. In time, each canvas speaks of the artist's worldview, his conscious and subconscious images, and his values. He can be understood through his works, almost as if he had written an autobiography.

Though the medium may be different, physicians, carpenters, salespersons, bicycle repairmen, anyone who uses his work as a means of self-expression, will gain the satisfaction of growth and self-understanding, and will single himself out from the crowd. Even entrepreneurs, who comprise a large part of my client base, tell me that there is "something within" that finds outer expression through their businesses. This expression allows their ventures to thrive. The remarkable thing about such self-expression, they say, is that it breeds confidence both in themselves and in their customers and employees, who quickly recognize someone whom they can count on.

COMMITMENT

When we are pursuing our right livelihood even the most difficult and demanding aspects of our work will not sway us from our course. When others say "Don't work so hard" or "Don't you ever take a break?" we will respond in bewilderment. What others may see as duty, pressure, or tedium, we perceive as a kind of pleasure. Commitment is easy when our work is our right livelihood. As social activist and former Secretary of Health, Education, and Welfare John Gardner once said, the best kept secret is that people want to work hard on behalf of something they feel is meaningful, something they believe in.

I met with a young man last year who had drifted into a far-from-satisfying but lucrative computer career. After much inner struggle he decided to leave his secure niche to return to school and study psychology. Recently, I received a letter from him and a copy of a straight-A transcript of his first semester courses. He was elated about his grades, but was having a hard time making ends meet, a condition he had never before encountered. Yet his certainty that he had found the right path for his life allowed him to excel and also gave him the power to respond resourcefully to the trials his new choice presented. He used his former skills and contacts to find part-time work and eventually decided to take a semester off to earn the lion's share of his tuition. "Once upon a time I would have quit when the going got rough," he reflected, "but now I'm eager to do what I must to stick to my choice." Because he is committed to his choice, he has gained a new level of vitality which fuels his ability to see it through to completion.

Successful people not only have goals, they have goals that are meaningful for them. They know where they are going and they enjoy the trek. Like this young man, when we are excited about what we are doing, when we are progressively moving toward the realization of meaningful goals, the difficulties become solvable problems, not insurmountable obstacles. I know that nothing will stop him from becoming a psychologist, and he will probably be a fine one at that. I knew it when he wrote in his recent letter, "The courses have been difficult and challenging, but I feel at home in this work and I am experiencing great joy for the first time in my life."

MINDFULNESS

If we think of what we do every day as only a job, or even as only a career, we may fail to use it fully for our own development and enrichment. When we are bored, frustrated, constrained, or dulled by what we do all day, we don't take advantage of the opportunities it offers. Moreover, we don't even see opportunities. The kind of relationship to work that is manifested in drifting attention, clock-watching, and wishing to be elsewhere also robs us of energy and satisfaction.

In contrast, anyone who has ever experienced active, concentrated attention knows the truth of the statement by well-known Quaker writer Douglas Steere: "Work without contemplation is never enough." You may have played a game of bridge, read a book, gardened, pieced together a ship in a bottle. Afterward, you realized that you had lost track of the passage of time and forgotten your cares.

What can be achieved in such momentary pursuits is the result of a quality of mind—a mind fully absorbed in its task, in the present—that can be available to us daily when we are working at our right livelihood. Absorption is the key to mindfulness—the deep involvement in the work itself and the way in which each task is performed. Mindfulness puts us in a constant present, releasing us from the clatter of distracting thoughts so that our energy, creativity, and productivity are undiluted. You become your most effective. Attention is power, and those who work in a state of mindful awareness bring an almost supernatural power to what they do.

ELLEN LANGER

Mindfulness and Work

The supreme accomplishment is to blur the line between work and play.
—Arnold Toynbee

The ability to shift contexts may be just as valuable to a manager or on the assembly line as it is to an artist or physicist. Fatigue, conflict, and burnout can all result from being mired in old categories, trapped by old mind-sets. For employer and employee alike, mindfulness may increase flexibility, productivity, innovation, leadership ability, and satisfaction. Since most of us, almost all day, almost all week, are either traveling to work, working, worrying about work, or planning the work ahead, the applications of mindfulness to the work setting are particularly useful.

A memo was circulated that said only, "Return this memo immediately." Most of those who received it did not notice its absurdity. Because it was in most respects similar to memos they saw every day, they mindlessly returned it. From this we can see how larger problems can result from initially small, unnoticed changes. When mindful, people tend to notice such problems before they become serious and dangerously costly. Whether it is a slight shift on a dial in a nuclear energy plant, or the first hint of what Theodore Levitt of the Harvard Business School calls the "shadow of obsolescence,"[1] the early signs of change are warnings and, to the mindful, opportunities.

The workplace is full of unexpected stumbling blocks that can get in the way of productivity. To a mindful manager or employee, these become building blocks. They don't impede progress because they are seen as part of an ongoing process, rather than disastrous deviations from past procedure. Take a situation in which, instead of the usual four people "required" to do a job, only three turn up, or one in which a piece of equipment routinely used in production is down for the week. If the employees in that department are locked in old mind-sets, the work will come to a screeching halt. A mindful employee, oriented to the present, might reassess the job as one for three people, or for whatever equipment was at hand.

SECOND WIND

Fatigue and satiation do not necessarily occur at fixed points. To a large extent, mental and physical exhaustion may be determined by premature cognitive commitments; in other words, unquestioned expectations dictate when our energy will run out.

As far back as 1928, psychologist Anita Karsten studied situations that at first feel good, but with repetition become neutral or uncomfortable.[2] She put subjects in "semi-free situations" in which they were given tasks to do but were instructed that they could stop working whenever they were tired. They were told to do the work as long as they enjoyed it. Tasks were of two types: continuous activities such as drawing, and tasks that come to a quick end but are repeated, such as reading a short poem again and again. (Tasks like chess that are long but come to an end were not used.)

For each type of task, the subjects worked until they grew weary. The investigator then changed the context. For instance, after the subjects had drawn until exhausted, the investigator asked them to turn the page over and redraw the last picture they had drawn, to show the experimenter how fast they could draw it. The "totally exhausted" subjects had no difficulty repeating the drawing in the new context. Rather, the change of context brought renewed energy.

When Karsten had subjects read poems aloud, after a while they became hoarse. When they complained to her how they hated the task, however, the hoarseness disappeared. Similarly, another subject, who claimed to be so fatigued that she could no longer lift her arm to make even one more hatch mark, was then seen casually lifting her arm to fix her hair.

New energy in a new context is known to most people as a "second wind." We see examples of it daily. Take a harried young scholar who has been working all day writing a book while also taking care of his rambunctious two-year-old daughter. By the time his wife comes home to help, he is too exhausted to move. But just then a call comes from a friend asking if he would like to play basketball. He leaps up and dashes off to play for four hours.

In each of these cases, a mind-set of fatigue was lifted by a shift in context initiated by someone else, the investigator or a friend. Mindful individuals use the phenomenon of second wind to their own advantage in a more deliberate way. Staggering different kinds of paperwork, changing to a different work setting, and taking a break to jog or make a phone call are all ways to tap latent energy by shaking free of the mind-set of exhaustion. (Mindfulness in itself is exhilarating, never tiring.) A self-starting, autonomous employee can do it for herself; a mindful manager can make it happen for others. The challenge for management is to introduce context changes within the required work load.

Another kind of mind-set that can lead to fatigue is the way we define a task. When we begin any undertaking, we have a mental picture of its beginning, middle, and end. In the beginning we tend to be energetic and mindful. In the middle phase, we may perform the task mindlessly or mindfully. If we are performing it mindfully, we are involved in creating new distinctions while we do it. We do not have a sense of ourselves as separate from the task. The task may seem effortless as long as we are involved in the process and distinctions are being created. If we do the task mindlessly, we rely on distinctions already made. As the task nears its end, we typically become focused on outcome and also expect fatigue to occur. We now notice the task as separate from ourselves as we evaluate the outcome. When we near the end of activities that we expect to be tiring, fatigue arrives. This mental picture of the end of a task is a self-imposed context and makes fatigue almost inevitable. Changing contexts *before* reaching this point may prevent fatigue. A simple change of activity will not necessarily bring this about, however. The change must be *experienced* as a new context. If a new physical exercise, for example, is still seen as exercise, the expectation of fatigue in that context may remain.

INNOVATION

Changing of contexts generates imagination and creativity as well as new energy. When applied to problem solving, it is often called *reframing*. A young musician recently told me of his long-standing inability to finish the songs he composed. This had bothered him deeply, and he felt like a failure as a composer until he reframed his "problem." Rather than seeing himself as incapable of finishing a song, he realized what a great gift he had for composing new themes. He then teamed up with someone who is great with musical detail and together they are highly prolific.

Changing contexts is only one path to innovation. Creating new categories, exploring multiple perspectives, and focusing on process all increase the possibility that a novel approach to a problem will be discovered. A tolerance for uncertainty on the part of management is also encouraging. If a manager can risk deviation from routine ways of doing things, creative employees can thrive and contribute. If not compelled only to make a product better and better, they may find ways to make a different, better product.

The imaginative use of "outsiders" can encourage each of the types of mindfulness just mentioned.[3] A man or two in an all-female company, a teenage board member, or a blind retiree can bring in new ideas. Independent consultants can fill the same role. Creating the position of outsider in a company, regardless of the characteristics of the person hired to fill it, can keep important questions flowing. Just as a traveler to a foreign culture notices what people indigenous to that culture take for granted, an outsider in a company may notice when the corporate natives are following what may now be irrational traditions or destructive myths. When routines of work are not familiar, they cannot be taken for granted and mindfulness is stimulated.

In *Getting to Yes*, Roger Fisher and William Ury suggest ways that negotiators can generate within their own minds the kind of perspectives brought by outsiders from different disciplines: "If you are negotiating a business contract, invent options that might occur to a banker, an inventor, a labor leader, a speculator in real estate, a stockbroker, an economist, a tax expert, or a socialist."[4] This openness to multiple perspectives—an essential ingredient in mindfulness—supports a policy of workers switching responsibilities, or switching career midstream. If the switch is within a field, rather than across fields, the benefits of a fresh perspective can outweigh the problems of having to learn a new technical jargon. For example, if an art historian became a vision psychologist, or vice versa, each might have something different to bring to the question, "How is a three-dimensional object rendered in two dimensions?"

Distance from the mind-sets of an industry is vital in designing products. Take a company that makes wheelchairs. Now that the elderly population is increasing, so should their business. Some people come to need wheelchairs the way others come to need eyeglasses. But unlike eyeglasses, wheelchairs have looked the same for years. There is no reason, other than habit, that wheelchairs must look so medical and ominous. Designers are now beginning to see wheelchairs as racing cars, as recreational vehicles, as colorful, comfortable, and zippy ways to get about. Eight years ago, in a nursing home where I consulted, we had residents decorate their own wheelchairs to make them more appealing and/or functional. The very word *wheelchair* seemed to take on a different flavor after this project. Just recently, I came across advertisements for the "Wildcat," the "Palmer 3," and the "Turbo"—three sleek new designs that seem to redefine what being in a wheelchair means.

As pointed out earlier, innovation can be dampened by too narrow an image of the task. People who make wheelchairs could see themselves in the transportation business or the recreation business in order to break out of the mind-sets associated with handicaps and hospitals. Theodore Levitt, whose famous phrase "marketing myopia" could be translated into "mindless marketing," came up with a delightfully poignant example of obsolescent mind-sets: the buggy whip industry. While one could argue that no amount of product innovation could have saved this business, a new self definition might have: "Even if it had only defined its business as providing a stimulant or catalyst to an energy source, it might have survived by becoming a manufacturer of, say, fan belts or air cleaners."[5]

Narrow definitions of competition go hand-in-hand with narrow mind-sets about a product. Small banks, for instance, see themselves in competition with other small banks, in the role of collectors and lenders of money to and from their communities. A bank like Citibank, which saw its function as an "information processing activity," was able to compete much more powerfully. In the same way, the maker of Royal or

Remington or Smith Corona typewriters would not have found their real competition by looking at one another. Over in another corner, a division of IBM was gearing up to knock them out of the running with the Selectric. This was a totally new concept for producing words on paper, later to be supplanted by the personal computer and word processors in all their forms.

THE POWER OF UNCERTAINTY

Ironically, although work may often be accomplished mindlessly and with a sense of certainty, play is almost always mindful. People take risks and involve themselves in their play. Imagine making play feel routine; it would not be playful. In play, there is no reason not to take some risks. In fact, without risk, the pleasures of mastery would disappear. Imagine mindlessly skiing or horseback riding; imagine going to the theater to see the same old play without searching for a new twist; imagine doing crossword puzzles already done, to which you remember all the answers. We tend to be more adventurous at play because it feels safe. We stop evaluating ourselves. Play may be taken seriously, but it is the play and not ourselves that we are taking seriously or else it is not really play at all. It would seem, then, that to encourage mindfulness at work, we should make the office a place where ideas may be played with, where questions are encouraged, and where "an unlucky toss of the dice" does not mean getting fired.

Many managers, however, become anxious when faced with a question for which there are no easy answers. At a nursing home where I consulted, an elderly woman wanted to make a peanut butter sandwich in the kitchenette instead of going to the dining room for dinner. The director said, "What if everyone wanted to do that?" If everyone did, the nursing home might save a lot of money on food. At the very least, it would have been useful information for the chef.

BURNOUT AND CONTROL

Burnout, a problem in a wide variety of workplaces from emergency rooms to corporations, is compounded by mindlessness. Rigid mind-sets,

narrow perspectives, the trap of old categories, and an outcome orientation all make burnout more likely. Conversely, as we have seen, changing contexts and mind-sets, or focusing on process, can be energy-
begetting.

Many of us know the energizing effects of a new job. There is an
excitement in learning new things, mapping out a new territory. As the
job becomes familiar, however, enthusiasm and energy wane. Burnout
sets in when two conditions prevail: Certainties start to characterize the
workday, and demands of the job make workers lose a sense of control.
If, in addition, an organization is characterized by rigid rules, problems
that arise feel insurmountable because creative problem solving seems
too risky. When bureaucratic work settings are of the "we've always done
it this way" mentality, burnout is no stranger.

In medical settings, where errors may cost lives, these conditions are
especially characteristic. Debra Heffeman and I tried to combat burnout
in Stevens Hall Nursing Home in North Andover, Massachusetts. We
introduced the staff to ideas of uncertainty and control so as to make
them more mindful. We demonstrated that the "facts" they used to guide
their care-giving were really probabilities and not certainties. We had
meeting after meeting in which we questioned how they could be so
sure of the rationale behind their policies. We paid particular attention
to those mind-sets that may induce dependency in the residents and rob
them of control. For example, a blind elderly resident wanted to smoke.
This was burdensome to the staff, who felt he must be accompanied to
prevent him from burning down the establishment. Their solution had
been to allow him to smoke only two cigarettes a day. But how could
they be sure that he needed help? Another patient's disease made it hard
for her to brush her hair. When a member of the staff brushed it for her,
he or she was unwittingly implying that she could not do it for herself.
One of the more dramatic cases was a woman who couldn't remember
to go to the dining room. The staff felt they had to escort her so that she
wouldn't starve. These cumulative and seemingly relentless responsibilities, seen as essential, contributed to feelings of burnout.

Once the staff understood that their justification for these solutions
was much weaker than they had thought, they were able to find other
ways of solving the problems. By returning some control to the residents, they made their own jobs easier. For example, they came to real-

ize that there was no firm reason to believe that a blind man couldn't learn to smoke safely. In fact, he already knew where and how to smoke without danger. They just had to give him a chance. The woman who had trouble brushing her hair was happier doing it herself as long as she approached the task in very small, incremental steps. And no one starved. Her hunger helped the forgetful woman remember where the dining room was. Seeing that problems may be solvable without relying on old rules made the staff feel more in control; seeking solutions made them more mindful. Records comparing the period before our intervention and a similar period of time afterward showed that staff turnover was reduced by a third. Less feeling of burnout meant less reason to leave. These results, though not experimentally derived, suggest that burnout is not inevitable.

Since the world of work confronts us with the same puzzles that face us in the rest of our lives, these observations about the effects of mindfulness on the job could become a book in themselves. It is probably also clear to readers familiar with business and management that the more progressive thinkers in this field have long been aware of the dangers of fixed mind-sets and outcome orientation and the advantages of multiple perspectives and shifting context, but under other labels. In the 1920s, Mary Parker Follett, a pioneer in management studies, anticipated certain of these ideas, emphasizing especially the value of a shift in mind-sets. Follett's warnings about an obsession with outcome are pertinent for any manager today: "A system built round a purpose is dead before it is born. Purpose unfolds and reflects the means."[6]

Certainty tends to develop with continued success. There is a tendency to continue doing whatever has worked, ironically making successful businesses more vulnerable to petrified mindsets. I spent part of a recent sabbatical at the Harvard Business School, where colleagues helped me streamline some of the ideas in this chapter. Some of us even made a game out of considering desk plaques for executives:

> Mindlessness is the application of yesterday's business solutions to today's problems.

> Mindfulness is attunement to today's demands to avoid tomorrow's difficulties.

NOTES

[1] T. Levitt, "Marketing Myopia," *The Harvard Business Review*, 38, no. 4 (1960): 45-56, reprinted in 53, no. 5 (1975): 26-174.

[2] A. Karsten (1928), "Mental Satiation," in *Field Theory as Human Science*, ed. J. de Rivera (New York: Gardner Press, 1976).

[3] Rosabeth Moss Kanter and Howard Stevenson, both of Harvard Business School, write about a version of this idea in business: R. Kanter, *The Change Masters: Innovation for Productivity in the American Corporation* (New York: Simon & Schuster, 1983); H. Stevenson and W. Sahlman, "How Small Companies Should Handle Advisers," *Harvard Business Review* 88, no. 2 (1988); 28-34. Also, Irving Janis describes a version of this idea in the political arena: I. Janis, *Victims of Groupthink* (Boston: Houghton Mifflin, 1972).

[4] R. Fisher and W. Ury, *Getting to Yes* (Boston: Houghton Mifflin, 1981).

[5] T. Levitt, "Marketing Myopia."

[6] M.P. Follett, *Dynamic Administration: The Collected Papers of Mary Parker Follett* (Bath, England: Bath Management, 1941), quoted in P. Graham, *Dynamic Management: The Follett Way* (London: Professional Publishing, 1987).

SAKI F. SANTORELLI

Mindfulness and Mastery in the Workplace:

21 Ways to Reduce Stress during the Workday

This article emerged out of a conversation initiated by Thich Nhat Hanh following the conclusion of a five-day mindfulness retreat in 1987. He had asked the participants to speak together about practical methods they used to integrate mindfulness into everyday life. Most people reported that this was a struggle and that the "how" of doing so was at best, elusive. Since this has been an explicit focus of our approach at the Stress Reduction Clinic, after talking about the clinic work and my own attempts to weave practice into the fabric of my everyday life, Arnie Kotler, who also participated in the discussion and is the editor of Parallax Press, asked me to write this article.

Over the past seventeen years, the Stress Reduction Clinic at the University of Massachusetts Medical Center has introduced more than 8,000 people to mindfulness practice. The clinic is the heart of an overarching community known as the Center for Mindfulness in Medicine, Health Care, and Society and offers medical patients a substantive, educationally-oriented approach we call *mindfulness-based stress reduction (MBSR)*.

As an instructor, I have had the good fortune of working with several hundred patients/participants each year. In the context of preventive and behavioral medicine, mindfulness practice is a vehicle that assists people in learning to tap deep internal resources for renewal, increase psychosocial hardiness, and make contact with previously unconceived-of possibilities and ways of being. Besides well-documented reductions in both medical and psychological symptoms, participants report an increased sense of self-esteem, shifts in their sense of self that afford them the ability to care for themselves while better understanding their fellow human beings, a palpable deepening of self-trust, and for some, a finer appreciation for the preciousness of everyday life.

In addition to this ongoing clinical work, I have the opportunity to teach in a wide variety of settings in both the public and private sectors. These programs are tailored to individual, corporate, or institutional needs with an underlying emphasis on the cultivation and application of mindfulness and mastery in the workplace. Out of one such program evolved: *21 Ways to Reduce Stress during the Workday*.

During a follow-up program for secretarial staff, I was moved by their struggle to practically integrate the stability and sense of connectedness that they sometimes felt during the sitting meditation practice into their daily lives while at work. In response to their struggle, "21 Ways" came into print. In developing these ways, I proceeded by simply asking myself: How do I attempt to handle ongoing stress while at work?—actually from the time I awaken in the morning until I return home at the end of the formal workday. How do I attempt to stitch mindfulness into the cloth of my daily life? What helps me to wake up when I have become intoxicated by the sheer momentum and urgency of living?

Mindfulness harnesses our capacity to be aware of what is going on in our bodies, minds, and hearts in the world—and in the workplace. As we learn to pay closer attention to what is occurring within and around us, one thing we begin to discover is that we are swimming in an unavoidable sea of constantly changing events. In the domain of stress reactivity, the technical term for this fluctuating reality is called a *stressor*. Stressors are ever-present events that we are continually adapting to. Some tend to be met with ease and others draw us away from our sense of stability. The crucial difference in our responses to stressors usually has to do with fear and our perception of feeling threatened or overly taxed by an event, be it either internal or external in origin. Seen from a psychological viewpoint, stress is a relational *transaction* between a person and her environment. From this transactional point of view, our perception and appraisal of the events as either being over-taxing to our inner and outer resources (threatening) or capable of being handled makes a tremendous difference.

Because many of our perceptions and appraisals are operating below the current threshold of our awareness, often we don't even know that our resources are being overly taxed. Conversely, because we have all been conditioned by habit and history, events that are not, or may no longer be threatening are often reacted to as if they are threatening. Therefore, developing our ability to see and understand what is going on inside and around us is an essential skill if we are to be less subject to these unconsciously-driven reactions.

Changing the way we see ourselves in relationship to events actually alters our experience of those events, their impact in our lives, as well as our capacity to maintain our well-being in the midst of such events. Given this viewpoint, the cultivation of mindfulness—our capacity to be aware and to understand ourselves and the world around us—is crucial to our ability to handle stress effectively.

Primarily, what the secretaries were struggling with was the gap between the awareness and stability they were beginning to touch in the domain of formal practice, and the dissipation of awareness and consequent dissonance experienced in the workday environment and their usual "workday mind." What they wanted was a vehicle for integrating "formal practice" into everyday life.

Although this need for integration is the same for all of us, notions about how to work in such a manner remain largely conceptual unless we develop concrete ways of practicing that transform theory into a living reality. This is exactly what the "21 Ways" provided. The participants got enthusiastic about these suggestions because it provided them something solid to work with when attempting to "bridge the gap" and integrate mindfulness into their workplace.

Since then, I have shared these "ways" with many workshop participants and continue to receive letters and telephone calls from people who have either added to the list or posted them as convenient reminders in strategic locations such as office doorways, restroom mirrors, dashboards, and lunch rooms. I've been gladdened to hear from them and happy that by its very nature, the list is incomplete and therefore full of possibility.

Each of these "21 Ways" can be seen as preventive—a strengthening of your stress immunity, or as recuperative—a means of recovering your balance following a difficult experience. Most importantly, they are methods for knowing, and if possible, modifying our habitual reactions in the midst of adversity. As you begin working with this list you'll notice that it includes pre-, during-, and post-work suggestions. Although arbitrary, these distinctions might be initially useful to you. Incorporating awareness practice into your life will necessitate a skillful effort that includes commitment, patience, and repetition. It may be helpful to think of yourself as entering a living laboratory where the elements of your life constitute the ingredients of a lively, educational process. Allowing yourself to be a beginner is refreshing. Give yourself the room to experiment without self-criticism. Allow your curiosity to carry you further into the process.

At the heart of workday practice is the intention to be aware of and connected to whatever is happening inside and around us (mindfulness) as well as the determination to initiate change when called for (mastery). A useful example of this process is revealed in the following story told to me some years ago by a physician friend. I call this story, *Little Green Dots*.

My friend told me that as his practice grew busier and more demanding, he began to develop minor, transient symptoms that included increased neck and shoulder tension, fatigue, and irritability. Initially, these symptom were benign, disappearing after a good night's rest or a relaxing weekend. But as his medical practice continued to grow, the symptoms became persistent and, much to his chagrin, he noticed that he was becoming a "chronic clock-watcher."

One day, while attending to his normal clinical duties, he had a revelation. He walked over to his secretary's supply cabinet and pulled out a package of "little green dots" used for color-coding the files. He placed one on his watch and decided that since he couldn't stop looking at his watch, he'd use the dot as a visual reminder to center himself by taking one conscious breath and dropping his shoulders.

The next day he placed a dot on the wall clock because he realized, "If I'm not looking at the one on my wrist, I'm looking at the one on the wall." He continued this practice and by the end of the week he had placed a green dot on every exam room doorknob. A few weeks after initiating this workday practice, he said that much to his own surprise, he had stopped, taken a conscious breath, and relaxed his shoulders one-hundred times in a single day. This simple, persistent decision to be mindful had been for him, transformative. He felt much better. Most importantly, his patients began telling him that he was "much more like himself." For him, that was the icing on the cake.

The story is simple and direct. Using what is constantly before us as a way of awakening to our innate capacity for stability and calmness is essential if we wish to thrive in the midst of our demanding lives.

Years ago, while working with a group of harried receptionists who described their reaction to the telephone ring as feeling much like Pavlov's dogs, I suggested that they use the first ring of the telephone as a reminder to take one breath, return to themselves, and then pick up the phone. For many, this simple practice became a powerful agent of change. Some said that people they had spoken with for years on the telephone didn't recognize their voices. Clients told them that they were speaking in a more measured pace and their voices had settled into the lower ranges. For the receptionists, the telephone no longer elicited the usual patterned reaction. They had learned to respond to this relentless, invasive, ubiquitous sound rather than to react. Through the action of awareness, the ring of the telephone had shifted from an object of unconscious threat and demand to a vehicle for cultivating greater awareness and skillful action.

Having experimented with the "green dots" on my own watch, I have found, that like any other method, they can quickly sink into the realm of the unconscious. Pretty soon, like the second hand, numbers, or date indicator, the dots become just another part of the watch face, completely unseen, of no help—actually perpetuating more unawareness.

No matter what is chosen as a reminder, our real work is to remember. This remembering is called mindfulness.

The following "21 Ways" are simply a road map. Allow your curiosity and the sense of possibility to unfold as you explore the territory, discovering your own "ways."

21 WAYS TO REDUCE STRESS DURING THE WORKDAY

1. Take five to thirty minutes in the morning to be quiet and medi-tate—sit or lie down and be with yourself...gaze out the window, listen to the sounds of nature, or take a slow quiet walk.

2. While your car is warming up—try taking a minute to quietly pay attention to your breathing.

3. While driving, become aware of body tension, e.g. hands wrapped tightly around the steering wheel, shoulders raised, stomach tight, etc., consciously working at releasing, dissolving that tension.... Does being tense help you to drive better? What does it feel like to relax and drive?

4. Decide not to play the radio and be with your own sound.

5. On the interstate, experiment with riding in the right lane, going five miles below the speed limit.

6. Pay attention to your breathing and to the sky, trees, or quality of your mind, when stopped at a red light or toll plaza.

7. Take a moment to orient yourself to your workday once you park your car at the workplace. Use the walk across the parking lot to step into your life. To know where you are and where you are going.

8. While sitting at your desk, keyboard, etc., pay attention to bodily sensations, again consciously attempting to relax and rid yourself of ex-cess tension.

9. Use your breaks to truly relax rather than simply "pausing." For in-stance, instead of having coffee, a cigarette, or reading, try taking a short walk—or sitting at your desk and renewing yourself.

10. For lunch, try changing your environment. This can be helpful.

11. Try closing your door (if you have one) and take some time to con-sciously relax.

12. Decide to stop for one to three minutes every hour during the work-day. Become aware of your breathing and bodily sensations, allowing the mind to settle in as a time to regroup and recoup.

13. Use the everyday cues in your environment as reminders to "center" yourself, e.g. the telephone ringing, sitting at the computer terminal, etc.

14. Take some time at lunch or other moments in the day to speak with close associates. Try choosing topics that are not necessarily work related.

15. Choose to eat one or two lunches per week in silence. Use this as a time to eat slowly and be with yourself.

16. At the end of the workday, try retracing today's activities, acknowledging and congratulating yourself for what you've accomplished and then make a list for tomorrow. You've done enough for today!

17. Pay attention to the short walk to your car—breathing the crisp or warm air. Feel the cold or warmth of your body. What might happen if you open up to and accept these environmental conditions and bodily sensations rather than resist them? Listen to the sounds outside your workplace. Can you walk without feeling rushed? What happens when you slow down?

18. At the end of the workday, while your car is warming up, sit quietly and consciously make the transition from work to home—take a moment to simply be—enjoy it for a moment. Like most of us, you're heading into your next full-time job—home!

19. While driving, notice if you are rushing. What does this feel like? What could you do about it? Remember, you've got more control than you might imagine.

20. When you pull into the driveway or park on the street, take a minute to orient yourself to being with your family members or to entering your home.

21. Try changing out of work clothes when you get home. This simple act might help you to make a smoother transition into your next "role"— much of the time you can probably "spare" five minutes to do this. Say hello to each of your family members or to the people you live with. Take a moment to look in their eyes. If possible, make the time to take five to ten minutes to be quiet and still. If you live alone, feel what it is like to enter the quietness of your home, the feeling of entering your own environment.

JEAN KINKEAD MARTINE

Working for a Living

What has the relative quiet or, at least, the more disciplined move-ment of the workshop to do with me in my untidy office? I am at my desk early today, with a moment to sit quietly and listen to the question. Is there a craftsmanlike way of working that is available not only to the worker in his workshop, but to the worker wherever he works, whatever his work is—in a factory or bank, in an executive office or house full of children; even here in a noisy advertising agency?

For a long time these have been academic questions for me, at times interesting me seriously; at other times merely piquing my curiosity, of-ten degenerating into mere doodlings in my mind. Today something is different.

Today I want to know for myself if there is still a way of working that would not only support me physically, but would also support this inner hunger that I feel now: a hunger actually to be here at my job, more awake, instead of dreaming at it, swept along from one minor crisis to the next, from paycheck to paycheck.

The New York drama critic Walter Kerr seems to be speaking my thoughts when, in *The Decline of Pleasure*, he writes: "The work we are doing is more or less the work we meant to do in life [but] it does not yield us the feeling of accomplishment we had expected....If I were re-quired to put into a single sentence my own explanation of the state of our hearts, heads, and nerves, I would do it this way: we are vaguely wretched because we are leading half-lives, half-heartedly, and with only one-half of our minds actively engaged in making contact with the universe about us."[1]

This is part of my concern right now: this half-heartedness, half-mindedness with which I live my one and only life. It seems related to the triviality of the work I do, and I would like to place the blame for my dissatisfaction squarely there. I begin to dream about fulfilling work: in a hospital, perhaps; in some use of myself that would satisfy this hunger. Still, what I am doing is the work at hand. It is my livelihood; it needs doing. I would wish to find a way to attend to it more creatively, or at least more carefully, so that it felt more like an exchange: a giving as well as a taking.

I remember the story of two Zen monks, both prodigious smokers. Concerned about the question of smoking during their prayer time, they agreed to consult their superiors. While one received a stern reprimand from his abbot, the other was given a pat of encouragement. The unlucky one, greatly puzzled, asked his friend exactly how he had framed his question. "I asked," the second monk replied, "whether it was permissible to pray while smoking."

Maybe this is the kind of care my work needs. To pray while typing, while answering the phone—would it require a very different way of praying; a way that Zen monks must come to through their training— something like that wordless beseeching one discovers in trying to guide a car along an icy road or in performing any exacting piece of work under all but impossible conditions?

I once looked up the origin of the word "prayer" and found its root is in the Latin *precarius*, "obtained by entreaty," hence implying uncertainty, risk. The plain truth is that in my usual way of working I feel nothing precarious or risky. Nothing is really at stake. Today, for reasons I don't understand, I feel that something vast and mysterious is at stake, something known only to me, important only to me. I can only call it my being. It's as if my usual way of working serves to sever me from my me-ness, from this new and fragile sense of myself at this typewriter right now.

Before I can go any further with a study of my own work, perhaps I need to ponder the meaning of work in general—in other times as well as in our own—and as I ponder, I sense a kinship between the words "work" and "worship." I begin to suspect that man is physically organized in exactly the way he is, just so that he will need to work in order to live; and it seems possible that the substance required for his own transformation and for the maintenance of the universe is created as a direct result of his work.

"In the sweat of thy face shalt thou eat bread," God told Adam, and if man did not actually need to work to feed, shelter, and clothe himself, actually in order to survive, perhaps this essential substance, whatever it is, would never be created. Perhaps, since man was created precisely as he is—exactly this kind of breathing, digesting, thinking, feeling organism—there is a precisely ordered way for him to work and to live in order to serve a universal purpose.

For me this is a fresh thought, this idea that it is man-at-work that serves the universe in a special way; and it sheds new light on the possible meaning of the way of the craftsman. However distracted the cathedral builders must have been, upon occasion, from the spiritual aspect of their work (for surely illness, family problems, all the continuing vagaries of the human condition beset these men as they do us), their inner hunger must have been fed by their way of working, a way indicated by their priests and guild masters who constantly reminded them that they were in the service of something higher, that their work was their means of service and not an end in itself.

With what heart they must have worked then, entrusting themselves to this higher authority!—this same "heart," perhaps, that set the golden harp (surely a symbol of joy in work) side by side with the tools of gold that were unearthed by archaeologists in the Sumerian city of Ur. The dweller in a golden age or an age of faith seems to have understood that he was living a kind of double life, one in the visible world and one in the invisible. Traditional man was apparently taught from infancy that all that he manifested in his everyday living vibrated invisibly in another dimension, and that it was his voluntary attempts to participate in this hidden dimension that set him apart from other living creatures— that made him, in fact, a transformer, a Man.

But today where are such teachers? Where are our priests? Our wise men? I try now to imagine what it would be like to be a member of a guild; to be an apprentice in a workshop at the head of which was a master in the original sense of the word: a man whose craft was truly his own, in his hands and heart and in his bones; a man who could impart the inner as well as the outer element of this craft to those working under him, not just by words and example, but by his very presence.

Guild members, we are told, would begin their day with the master in prayer to the guild's patron saint before turning to the work, and prayers of one kind or another punctuated the whole day. Throughout the day there was the closeness of man to man, the sense of one another's existence, and the exchange between the experienced workers and the novices: the meeting of eyes, the showing and the watching, the speaking and the listening. How different from the usual factories and workplaces of today, where little is "handed" from man to man, where eyes rarely meet, and the human voice cannot always rise above the noise of machinery; where men in their isolation from one another begin to feel a kinship only with their particular machine—a truck driver with his truck, a printer with his press, even a copywriter with her typewriter.

There is an instant now in which I feel the limitation of this kind of kinship, and I wonder how we ever lost touch with one another and with our sacred heritage. How did we become separated from that other dimension in which our forebears felt their common humanity and the common authority for their lives? Our discontent as workers today must stem from this incredible lapse: this mass forgetfulness that we are under any authority higher than that of our boss, whether he be the factory foreman, the president of the company, or oneself.

Oh, for the ordered structure of the guild workshop! The strong clear voice of the master "re-minding" me, in the real sense of that word, to return to the silence. Another completely fresh thought comes to me now. So many of the rituals of the traditional societies must have been created for just this call to inner silence. The beating of drums, the tolling of the Angelus, the sounding of the ram's horn, the repetition of the sacred syllables in whatever language, the ceremonial dances—all these mysterious activities that until this moment have appeared to me like so many quaint customs must have been designed for just this reminding. And at this moment I am shocked to discover the life going on inside me: the breath coming and going; the amazing heartbeat. I am here; the thought is here; and a kind of feeling that I am here in this very ordinary place with a minute, mundane advertisement to write, but it is my work and it requires me.

What I constantly forget is that I always have my place. It is here exactly where I am. Where else could it be? Here is this life that is uniquely mine, one whole unit of creation that is entirely my place and my responsibility.

I feel a great desire not to lose touch with this feeling-thought that is with me this morning. I have felt it before: a wishing for something more for myself or from myself. Is there a master in me to whom I can turn, if—like people in fairy tales—I can wish hard enough? I don't know, but something I have read comes alive for me now: "Wood and stone will teach me what cannot be heard from the master's teaching."

I have no wood or stone, but I have my job; that is my reality for now. "To take what there is and use it," Henry James wrote many years ago, "without waiting forever in vain for the preconceived—to dig deep into the actual and get something out of that—this doubtless is the right way to live."[2] A thought from Father Robert Capon's writing stirs vigorously in me. "Adam," he wrote, and he was speaking of twentieth-century Adam, of the likes of you and me, "is the priest of Creation. His truest work is to offer up reality itself, not just a head full of abstractions about it."[3]

It seems as if it could be right here, even in this super-automated, super-franchised, polluted, synthetic age, that I might begin my apprenticeship; right here, now, in this attitude of seeing what is. Perhaps this is the elusive way of working that makes all the difference between the craftsman and the slave—just this reordering of my energies because I want to work this way, because I need to, because I must. The authority is still there. We are not forgotten in spite of our forgetfulness, for natural laws, unlike the ordinances of temporal authority, are never changing. It is the very constancy of these laws that offers us a challenge and a hope. It leaves something up to me; it is for me to seek a way to reconnect with these laws. It is even an obligation, if Simone Weil was right in saying that it is the work of our age to create a civilization "founded upon the spiritual nature of work."[4]

Perhaps it would be just in a daily lifelong attitude of "seeing" that the noisy, chaotic activity I call my job could become a support for my attention instead of a distraction. Perhaps, if I attend to the reality that is in front of me moment by moment—phone, machine, pencil, boss, coffee—constantly failing, accepting to fail and to begin again—this perfectly ordinary work I do might become extraordinary work, might even become my craft.

The phone is ringing now. The first of my coworkers has arrived and is answering it. The question I began with remains: Is there a way of working that would support this need I feel actually to be here at my work?

The answer, I am sure, is not to be found in my head or in any book, but quite simply in an ever-deepening of the question itself.

I confront the outline I left on my desk last Friday, and I get to work.

NOTES

[1] Walter Kerr, *The Decline of Pleasure* (New York: Simon & Schuster, 1962).

[2] Henry James, *The Notebooks of Henry James* (New York: Oxford University Press, 1947).

[3] Robert Capon, *Bed and Board* (New York: Simon & Schuster, 1965).

[4] Simone Weil, *The Need for Roots* (New York: Harper & Row, 1971).

THICH NHAT HANH

The Art of Living

Life is an art. The way we live our lives is an expression of our deepest understanding and our whole being. Many years ago I met a young American named Jim Forest. Jim is an intelligent man, and he asked me to teach him about the practice of mindfulness. One time when we were together, I offered him a tangerine. Jim accepted the tangerine, but he continued talking about the many projects he was involved in—his work for peace, social justice, and so on. He was eating, but, at the same time, he was thinking and talking. I was there with him. I was really there, that is why I was aware of what was going on. He peeled the tangerine and tossed the sections of it into his mouth, quickly chewing and swallowing.

I said to him, "Jim, stop!" He looked at me, and I said, "Eat your tangerine." He understood. So he stopped talking, and he began to eat much more slowly and mindfully. He separated each of the remaining sections of the tangerine carefully, smelled their beautiful fragrance, put one section at a time into his mouth, and felt the juices surrounding his tongue. Tasting and eating the tangerine this way took several minutes, but he knew that we had the time for that. When he finished eating this way, I said, "Good." I knew that the tangerine had become real, the eater of the tangerine had become real, and life also had become real at that moment. What is the purpose of eating a tangerine? It is just for eating the tangerine. During the time you eat a tangerine, eating the tangerine is the most important thing in your life.

In Buddhism, there is a word, *apranihita*. It means wishlessness, or aimlessness. The idea is that we do not put anything ahead of ourselves and run after it. When we practice sitting meditation, we sit just to enjoy the sitting. We do not sit in order to become enlightened, a buddha, or anything else. Each moment we sit brings us back to life, and therefore, we sit in a way that we enjoy our sitting the entire time. Walking meditation is the same. We do not try to arrive anywhere. We take peaceful, happy steps, and we enjoy them. If we think of the future—of what we want to realize—or if we think of the past—our many regrets— we will lose our steps, and that would be a pity.

The next time you have a tangerine to eat, please put it in the palm of your hand and look at it in a way that makes the tangerine real. You do not need a lot of time to do it, just two or three seconds. Looking at it, you can see a beautiful blossom with sunshine and rain, and you can see a tiny fruit forming. You can see the continuation of the sunshine and the rain, and the transformation of the baby fruit into the fully developed tangerine in your hand. You can see the color change from green to orange and you can see the tangerine sweetening. Looking at a tangerine in this way, you will see that everything in the cosmos is in it— sunshine, rain, clouds, trees, leaves, everything. Peeling the tangerine, smelling it, and tasting it, you can be very happy.

This is an exercise in the art of living. Everything we do can be like this. Whether we are planting lettuce, washing dishes, writing a poem, or adding columns of numbers, it is not different from eating a tangerine. All of these things are on equal footing. We can enjoy each task the same way we enjoy our tangerine. I myself am a poet. One day an American scholar told me, "Don't waste your time gardening, growing lettuce. You can write more poems instead. Not many people write poems the way you do, but anyone can grow lettuce." That is not my way of thinking. I know very well that if I do not grow lettuce, I cannot write poems. Eating a tangerine, washing dishes, and growing lettuce in mindfulness are essential to me to write poetry. The way someone washes the dishes reveals the quality of his or her poetry.

After one retreat in Los Angeles, a painter asked me, "What is the best way to look at the moon and the flowers so that I can use them in my art?" I said, "If you think that way, you will not be in touch with the flower or the moon. Please abandon your notions and just be with the flower, with no intention of getting anything from it." He said, "But when I am with a friend, I want to receive the benefits of our friendship.

Isn't it the same with a flower?" Of course, you can benefit from a friend, but a friend is more than a source of support, help, or advice. Just to be with him or her is enough. We are in the habit of doing things in order to get something. We call this "pragmatism." We even say that truth is something that pays.

The practice of mindfulness is the opposite. We practice just to be with ourselves and with the world. When we learn to stop, we begin to see, and when we see, we understand. Peace and happiness are the fruit of that. In order to be with our friend, a flower, or our coworkers, we need to learn the art of stopping.

How can we bring peace to a society that wants each thing to be a source of profit? How can a smile bring deep joy and not just be a diplomatic maneuver? When you smile to yourself, that smile is entirely different from a diplomatic smile. Smiling to yourself is proof that you are deeply at peace. We need to live in a way that demonstrates this. When we do, each moment of our life is a work of art. We may not think of it this way, but it is truly so. We are pregnant with joy and peace, and we make life beautiful for others.

The way we earn our living can be a source of peace, joy, and reconciliation, or it can cause a lot of suffering. When we know how to be peace, our work can be a wonderful means for us to express our deepest self, the foundation of our being. Our work will take place one way or another, but it is the being that is essential. First of all, we must go back to ourselves and make peace with our anger, fear, jealousy, and mistrust. When we do this, we are able to realize real peace and joy, and the work we do will be of great help to ourselves and the world.

What about techniques? Each endeavor and craft has its own techniques, but techniques are not enough. One young man in Vietnam who wanted to learn how to draw lotus flowers went to a master to apprentice with him. But the master just took him to a lotus pond and instructed him to sit there and look at the lotus flowers all day, without doing anything else. The young man watched one flower bloom when the sun was high, and he watched the flower return into a bud when night fell. The next morning, he practiced in the same way. When one flower wilted and its petals fell into the water, he just looked at the rest of the flower, and then he moved on to another lotus.

He did that for ten days and then went back to the master. The master asked him, "Are you ready?" and he answered, "I will try." Then the master gave him a brush, and he painted like a child. But the lotus he drew was very beautiful. He had *become* a lotus, and the painting just came forth. You could see his naïvete concerning technique, but real beauty was there.

The way we live our daily lives, whether we are mindful or not, has everything to do with peace. Bringing our awareness to every moment, we try to have a vocation that helps us realize our ideal of compassion. We try our best to have a job that is beneficial to humans, animals, plants, and the Earth, or at least minimally harmful. We live in a society where jobs are hard to find, but if it happens that our work entails harming life, we should try our best to find another job. Our vocation can nourish our understanding and compassion, or it can erode them. We should try not to drown in forgetfulness. So many modern industries are harmful to humans and nature, even the production of food. The chemical poisons used by most modern farms do a lot of harm to the environment. Practicing right livelihood is difficult for farmers. If they do not use chemical pesticides, it may be difficult for them to compete commercially, so not many farmers practice organic farming. This is just one example.

Right livelihood has ceased to be a purely personal matter. It is our collective karma. Suppose I am a schoolteacher and I believe that nurturing love and understanding in children is a beautiful occupation. I would object if someone were to ask me to stop teaching and become, for example, a butcher. But when I meditate on the interrelatedness of all things, I can see that the butcher is not the only person responsible for killing animals. He does his work for all of us who eat meat. We are co-responsible for his act of killing. We may think the butcher's livelihood is wrong and ours is right, but if we didn't eat meat, he wouldn't have to kill, or he would kill less. Right livelihood is a collective matter. The livelihood of each person affects us all, and vice versa. The butcher's children may benefit from my teaching, while my children, because they eat meat, share some responsibility for the butcher's livelihood.

Any look at right livelihood entails more than just examining the situation in which we earn our paycheck. Our whole life and our whole society are intimately involved. Everything we do contributes to our effort to practice right livelihood, and we can never succeed one hundred percent. But we can resolve to go in the direction of compassion, in the direction of reducing the suffering. And we can resolve to work for a society in which there is more right livelihood and less wrong livelihood.

Millions of people, for example, make their living in the arms industry, helping directly or indirectly to manufacture both "conventional" and nuclear weapons. The U.S., Russia, France, Britain, China, and Germany are the primary suppliers of these weapons. So-called conventional weapons are then sold to Third World countries, where the people do not need guns, tanks, or bombs; they need food. To manufacture or sell weapons is not right livelihood, but the responsibility for this situation lies with all of us—politicians, economists, and consumers. We all share responsibility for the death and destruction that these weapons cause. We do not speak out. We have not organized a national debate on this problem. We have to examine and discuss this issue more, and we have to help create new jobs so that no one has to live on profits from weapons' manufacture. If you are able to work in a profession that helps realize your ideal of compassion, please be grateful. And please try to help create proper jobs for others by living mindfully—simply and sanely. Please use all your energy to try to improve the situation.

To practice right livelihood means to use the practice of mindfulness to address social and political problems and also the problems of daily life. Telephone meditation, for example, is a very important practice. Every time the telephone rings, you can hear it as a bell of mindfulness, stop what you are doing, and breathe in and out consciously three times, before proceeding to the telephone. That is the practice of right livelihood. I know a man who practices walking meditation between business appointments. He walks mindfully between office buildings in downtown Denver. Passersby smile at him, and his meetings, even with difficult people, are very pleasant, and usually successful. We need to discuss among ourselves how to practice mindfulness in the workplace and how to practice right livelihood. Do you breathe between telephone calls? Do you practice smiling while cutting carrots? Do you relax after hours of hard work? Do you live in a way that encourages everyone to have a job that is in the direction of peace and compassion? These questions are very practical and very important. If we can work in a way that encourages this kind of thinking and acting, a future will be possible for us, our children, and their children.

Using Mindfulness to Find Meaningful Work

*The ancient followers of the Tao were subtle, mysterious and
penetrating. They were too deep to be fathomed.
All we can do is describe their appearance.
Hesitant, as if crossing a winter stream.
Watchful, as if aware of neighbors on all sides.
Respectful, like a visiting guest.
Yielding, like ice beginning to melt.
Simple, like an Uncarved Block.
Open, like a valley.
Obscure, like muddy water.*

*Who else can be still, and let the muddy water slowly become clear?
Who else can remain at rest, and slowly come to life?
Those who hold fast to the Tao
    do not try to fill themselves to the brim.
Because they do not try to be full,
    they can be worn out and yet, ever new.*
                                        —Lao-tzu

CLAUDE WHITMYER

Using Mindfulness to Find Meaningful Work

The essays in this book represent the shared human experience available to help us understand the concept of "right livelihood." However, the primary source of anyone's knowledge of right livelihood is their own experience. Our ability to understand right livelihood is also greatly influenced by working with others who are also seeking it.

My experience of working with others seeking right livelihood began in 1984 when I became coordinator of the Briarpatch. Working closely with members of the Briarpatch exposed me to the possibilities of right livelihood. And, as my Briar clients began growing their businesses and hiring employees, I was increasingly called upon to help them apply the values of community service and caring to the problems and concerns of their workers.

Instead of simply dismissing a worker who didn't measure up, or who had difficulty getting along with others, we discovered ways to help them engage in self-reflection and self-development. This allowed them to learn how they could do what they really loved and still pay the bills.

In addition to these direct experiences I also sought information from anthropology, economics, psychology, and sociology, as well as from various religious and metaphysical treatises.

So, working on my own right livelihood, working with others, and studying what the experts and wise ones have said allowed me to develop a consulting process that I could offer to people at large. I call this process Good Work Guidance and it has proven extremely helpful, if I am to judge by the testimonies of my clients and students. To close this collection, I would like to summarize what I have learned.

BEGIN WITH MINDFULNESS

What you must do is simple. Begin with mindfulness. Proceed with mindfulness. End with mindfulness.

Mindfulness means creating new categories, welcoming new information, tolerating more than one view. It also means letting go of the demand for categories, disassociating from the craving for information, detaching from the need for a point of view. Mindfulness means present moment appreciation of our inner states of being and the world around us. As psychologist Jon Kabat-Zinn puts it, "...mindfulness is moment-to-moment awareness. It is cultivated by purposefully paying attention to things we ordinarily never give a moment's thought to. It is a systematic approach to developing new kinds of control and wisdom in our lives, based on our inner capacities for relaxation, attention, awareness, and insight."[1]

Those of us who live in the Judeo/Christian/Islamic cultures have clear support for this. We believe in a God-given responsibility to use mindfulness to find our calling. This belief says that we each have an individually unique calling to do God's work. Jew, Christian, or Muslim, it matters not. God wants his children to be conscious, to help one another, to live in peace. Don't take my word for it. Ask any cleric for the references in the Torah, Bible, or Koran.

Christians, for example, are told in many places of the importance of their calling: "The Eyes of your understanding being enlightened; that ye may know what is the hope of his calling...." (Ephesians 1:18) Add to this Luke 10:25-27, where Christ is confronted by a lawyer who asks him, "Teacher, what shall I do to inherit eternal life?" Christ answers with a question of his own, "How is it written in the law? How do you read?" And the lawyer answers by quoting the Old Testament, "Thou shalt love the Lord thy god with all thy heart, and with all thy soul, and with all thy strength, and with all thy mind; and thy neighbor as thyself." It becomes obvious that the Bible gives us a clear directive to use mindfulness to find right livelihood while practicing compassion towards our neighbors.

Mindfulness is how "the Eyes of your understanding" become enlightened. Mindfulness is how you love yourself. Loving your neighbor is done through mindful acts of compassion.

The Bible also provides many clear-cut directives about how to behave. "Thou shalt not kill." "Thou shalt not commit adultery." "Thou shalt not steal." "Thou shalt not bear false witness against thy neighbor." "Thou shalt not covet thy neighbor's house; thou shalt not covet thy neighbor's wife, nor his manservant, nor his maidservant, nor his ox, nor his ass, nor anything that is thy neighbor's." (Exodus 20:13-17)

How similar this all is to the wisdom of the Buddha.[2] Buddhists are guided in their pursuit of right livelihood by the five precepts for the layperson to voluntarily take training in the abstention from lying, stealing, killing, intoxicants, and inappropriate sexual behavior, such as rape, incest, or adultery.

As the Buddhist concept of right livelihood was adopted in the West, it also came to mean work that was personally fulfilling, work that made a difference, work that served others, but work that also paid the bills. And why not? Sympathy for the concept existed, even if only subliminally, because it was already part of the Western Judeo/Christian/Islamic cultural milieu.

As Buddhism has become increasingly visible in the West, it is clear that the predominant form it is taking here is that of the lay practitioner or householder. According to the Buddha there are several things conducive to the happiness of the layperson: the practice of moral behavior, such as honesty, compassion, and ethics; philanthropy and gift giving; having good friends; mastering a profession; financial security; and freedom from debt. As Buddhist monk and scholar Walpola Rahula points out in the first Chapter, the Buddha believed that poverty was the root of crime, while economic stability was the foundation of the contemplative life.

Both Buddhist and Judeo/Christian/Islamic ideas are reflected in the more comprehensive meaning of right livelihood as it is used in the West today. Right livelihood has come to mean work that is morally correct and personally fulfilling, work that makes a difference, work that helps and is supported by our neighbors or "communities," work that honors the spirit of mastery, work that provides a decent living, work that is done with mindfulness.

WHAT CHARACTERIZES PEOPLE WITH RIGHT LIVELIHOOD?

Some people know all their lives what right livelihood is for them. But, for most of us, that kind of clarity is hard to come by. We can begin to understand what it takes to find and maintain right livelihood by looking at the people who already have it. There is sure to be something about the way that they live that might help us in our own quest.

In the twenty years I have spent as a business owner and consultant, I have had the opportunity to observe more than 1,000 different individuals who considered themselves to be pursuing their right livelihood and I have found a number of characteristics they have in common.[3]

On the top of this list is "persistence," the trait of sticking with a project or goal until either it is accomplished or it becomes very clear that it should be dropped.

Not every job we have in life is right livelihood. When we first begin examining the work we do, we may discover that it does not really qualify as right livelihood and we must begin the process of fixing it or finding other work. Even if we have found our right livelihood, it may require care and nurturing over a long period of time before it becomes self-sustaining. In any of these cases, it is persistence that will see us through.

In looking at our current work, we may discover that it is not right livelihood. Or we may identify what we think is our right livelihood and begin down the path of encouraging its development. In either case a moment may arrive in which we see clearly that we can no longer tolerate doing "wrong" work or that it is futile to continue putting effort into what we thought was going to be our right work. When that moment arrives, we need the wherewithal to stop and find something else to try. This is the ability to "face the facts"—to recognize when something is not going to work out—to let it go without wasting any further time or attention on it.

Persistence and the ability to face the facts are the foundation upon which the third of the character traits exhibited by practitioners of right livelihood is built. This is the overall strategy of "minimizing risks." Minimizing risks is demonstrated through thorough planning and preparation. For example, it is a commonly held belief that entrepreneurs are big risk takers. Interviews with entrepreneurs, however, reveal that they don't see themselves that way. The common observer sees what an entrepreneur does as risky because that observer doesn't understand the marketplace in as much detail as the entrepreneur does. The entrepreneur has familiarized him or herself with the market to such an extent that they see what they are going to do as a nearly sure thing. They have studied the marketplace, potential clients, customers, and multiple aspects of the product in great detail and have a well developed strategy for proceeding. When the moment comes to move forward, there is very little risk as far as they are concerned.

This is what all practitioners of right livelihood do as well. They don't passively move from one job to another. Rather they create a plan of action. They research the job market or the prospective employer. They know so much about their field and the demand for their skills that when they seek new work they are usually in the top few applicants.

The fourth trait on our list is the desire to be a "hands-on learner." Practitioners of right livelihood do not sit back passively, waiting for someone else to tell them what to do. They get involved in even the most mundane parts of their jobs in order to understand how everything works and how it all functions together. They actually enjoy going out into the world to learn what it takes to do the best possible job. Such active participation means they really understand the work they are doing, and it is much easier for them to judge its merits as right livelihood.

"Self-starting energy" is the fifth of the character traits of people with fulfilling work. Self-starting energy comes from a sense of physical well-being and a desire to live life to its fullest. Self-starting energy makes it possible for you to get up in the morning, even when you are feeling blue or don't really have anything you have to do.

Right livelihood is interesting, absorbing work. Not so much because it is exciting, glamorous work, but more because the mindfulness practice involved makes it possible to be fully present in the work, whatever its day-to-day reality might be. When you are fully present in your work you also become fully present in the problems and personality difficul-

ties that are an inevitable part of any job. Being aware of these compli-
cations makes it possible to deal with them in a more immediate and
effective way. It becomes unnecessary to repress or avoid them out of
fear or confusion. So they don't build to a point of eruption and you are
less prone to the fatigue of work stress and more likely to wake up energetic and happy to go to work rather than tired and resentful. This is
how self-starting energy is accumulated.

Probably one of the most important things on this list of character
traits exhibited by practitioners of right livelihood is a "community of
support." This means that you are surrounded by like-minded people, or
"neighbors" if you will, who encourage and nurture you, and you, in
turn, encourage and nurture them. Responsiveness to your community
extends beyond your family and friends to include an overall ethic of
social responsibility. Right livelihood practitioners demonstrate this
ethic, as right livelihood guide Roger Pritchard points out, by "involving themselves in reducing consumption, conserving natural resources,
cutting down pollution, eating more simply and nutritiously, opposing
nuclear war, bringing more spirituality into their lives, and developing
personal support networks to help each other do these things."

It is almost impossible to have right livelihood if it does not arise
from the encouragement of a community of friends and if it is not responsive to the needs of the local community and the global community alike.

The seventh item on the list of character traits of people with fulfilling work is what we usually call "emotional stability." But, in fact, emotional stability is not really possible. One thing we can know for sure, as
we observe our emotions, is that they are not stable. They rise up and
fall away constantly. From moment to moment we are filled with worry,
fear, anger, hatred, confidence, courage, patience, or love. Sometimes
we can identify a cause for our feelings and sometimes we cannot—sometimes they are just there.

While you have very little real control over your emotions, you have
absolute control of your behavior. So what we are talking about is actually stable or constructive behavior. We call this emotional stability because, to an outside observer, we demonstrate steady behavior. As
Constructive Living guide Patricia Ryan-Madson points out, regardless
of how we feel, we do what needs to be done to fulfill our personal pur-

poses, and we therefore appear to be emotionally stable. Even when we have an emotional storm going on, we choose to act in a way that is consistent with our values and leads us to our goals.

The final item on our list of character traits exhibited by practitioners of right livelihood is "mindfulness." While mindfulness is a process, it is also the context in which we develop and exhibit all the other character traits. Mindfulness helps us keep our personal purpose in front of us. Mindfulness makes it possible to see the goals that are implied by our personal purpose. Mindfulness keeps us informed of the necessity and the results of persistence, of facing the facts, of minimizing our risks.

Engaging in hands-on learning and becoming involved with a community of supporters provide many opportunities to practice mindfulness. Regular, persistent practice of mindfulness actually increases our self-starting energy and leads to emotional stability. Mindfulness is the *sine qua non* of right livelihood. Without mindfulness there can be no right livelihood.

The main thing that holds us back from our right livelihood is the absence of these seven character traits. Beyond their absence, however, the two most frequent barriers to practicing right livelihood are poor time management and poor money management. Consequently, right livelihood practitioners tend to pay very close attention to time and money.

The character traits just recounted (with the exceptions of mindfulness and a community of support), along with attention to time and money, are not limited in importance to the small population of right livelihood practitioners I have described. They are also echoed in the mainstream literature about what it takes to succeed on the job or as an entrepreneur. They are frequently accompanied by a list of other factors that reflect the mainstream values of social status and wealth, but they are usually included as fundamental considerations, nonetheless.

HOW IS RIGHT LIVELIHOOD DIFFERENT FROM JUST FINDING A JOB?

First of all, there is a difference in strategy. When your goal is to just get a job, you might start by taking some kind of test that will measure your skill level or personality strengths, such as the Strong Vocational Interest Blank or the Meyers-Briggs Personality Types test, or any of a number of others. With or without the help of a career or job placement counselor, you then try to identify the types of jobs that will utilize your strengths and skills. The theory is that if you do something you're good at, you will be happy.

Or, you might use a different strategy in which you seek work that is identical to the work you've had before. You might stay in the same industry and move to another company doing the same job, or you might try to move to another industry doing work that is similar. If you are really desperate, you might take any job at all as long as it brings in some money.

If your goal is right livelihood, however, your strategy is quite different. You start by clarifying your values. By illuminating what you really *believe in*, what your *vision of life* is, what your *personal purpose* is, you make it possible to clarify your goals. Clear vision and purpose lead to clear goals—goals you can feel passionate about rather than goals that society or others think should be yours.

In right livelihood, whether or not you have been tested, you look for work that is aligned with your vision and purpose. Generally that means you'll take work that you have a keen interest in—work that is "right" for you.

Another difference between just finding a job and seeking right livelihood is that you start from the beginning with a careful consideration of finances. It is important to be intimate with your financial condition. When you know where you stand you're better prepared to take advantage of the opportunities that present themselves to you. What is the value of what you own? What do you owe? The difference is your net worth. How much does it cost you to live each month? Divide your net worth by your monthly budget and you get a rough estimate of what we can call "financial security." Sometimes it is necessary to "finance" your move from one kind of work to another. It is difficult to feel safe about doing that if you have no idea whether you can afford to stop working long enough to make the move or not.

In calculating your monthly budget, avoid putting yourself in a state of deprivation. Many people are tempted to put themselves on a very low budget by cutting out everything that isn't absolutely necessary. They make these cuts in a moment of enthusiasm about the future. Then when the demands of day-to-day living cause their enthusiasm to wane, they begin to feel deprived. They become resentful and find themselves with an uncontrollable urge to splurge in order to make themselves feel better. Afterwards they feel contrition and guilt and return to an even more severe budget in the hope of making up for their mistake. This is akin to the "binge/purge" cycle that many people experience around dieting.

It would be better to start by calculating the level of deprivation you think you can tolerate and then increase that by a small factor. So, if you've been taking your clothes to the laundry instead of doing them yourself, don't cut it out entirely. Just cut it by half or two-thirds. The same goes for life's little luxuries, such as massages or special desserts, the things that you think you should do without.

This is especially true for time off. One of the first things to go when we are trying to conserve money is our vacation. That's a big mistake. When you eliminate a vacation you eliminate an important source of rejuvenation. Without adequate rejuvenation, it is difficult to weather hard times or accomplish demanding tasks. It is very important to take time off, so look for less expensive ways to take a vacation, shorter chunks of time off near where you live, or time away in places where you know people to visit who would be glad to have you drop by for a few days. But don't eliminate time off altogether.

THE IMPORTANCE OF SIMPLE LIVING

Another way that right livelihood differs from just finding a job is the reliance on simple living, the purposeful strategy to lower your expenses and reduce your consumption. In addition to lowering your impact on the environment, and hence, your harm to other living things, reduced expenses and consumption lead to a life with fewer distractions and responsibilities. So you have more time and more flexibility about how you spend that time. In addition you can finance changes in your work more easily if your lifestyle is inexpensive.

A simpler life brings with it less caretaking of laborsaving devices and property. And it often means an enhanced aesthetic experience because of the simplifications you make to your living and work spaces.

After all, a room full of precious objects is nothing more than a junk shop. So right livelihood practitioners make purposeful choices about what level of lifestyle they really want to pay for.

THE IMPORTANCE OF THE PRESENT MOMENT

The present moment is when and where you are when you practice mindfulness. It is only possible to make your best choices about right livelihood in the present moment. Take a look at your thoughts right now. How many things are competing for your attention? You are reading this book and perhaps you are trying to understand what possible relevance my ramblings could have to your life. You might hear the sounds of people, the noise of traffic, a dog barking in the distance, a clock ticking nearby. What do you hear? Every few moments you might be thinking about what you must do later in the day or tomorrow—what you will have for dinner, what you will say to a friend when you call her tomorrow. And so forth. What are *you* thinking? What else are you attending to?

Please take a minute to bring your attention to this very moment. Notice your body where it contacts the furniture or the ground. Feel your breath as it moves in and out of your lungs. Spend a moment taking in the whole space that surrounds you, without judging or naming anything. Now, watch as your concerns rise up again. What really needs to be done? What can wait? Which concerns arise from the pursuit of your vision and purpose? Which are actually the concerns of others?

As you get swept up in your observations and the rising of your concerns, notice what is going on. Notice how you lose your awareness of the present moment. Bring yourself back to the present moment by beginning this exercise again. Focus on your breathing first. Then extend your attention again to notice where you are and what is going on. Look again at your concerns as they arise. Repeat this exercise whenever you wish to clarify what is important to you.

Practitioners of right livelihood continually return to the present moment. The present moment is where they tend to live. As we have said repeatedly, present moment awareness is the foundation of right livelihood.

WHAT IS "RIGHT" WORK?

What do we mean when we say that right livelihood means "right" work? What *is* right work? Many of the ways you can measure "right" work have been enumerated throughout this collection. But, there are two additional concerns that must be addressed if we are to find work that allows, even encourages, us to put everything our contributors recommend into practice. These are, not surprisingly, time and money.

How you manage time and money can have a significant effect on how successful you are at finding and maintaining right livelihood. Whether or not you have found right livelihood, you still need to pay the bills. You also need the time to practice mindfulness and the other steps that lead to right livelihood. To ensure that you have enough time for self-realization while still paying the bills, it is important to judge all the work you do by the degree of control it gives you over your time and the amount of money it gives you to pay the bills.

The ideal work gives you a lot of control over your time and high pay. You have a lot of time for self-examination and the seeking of right work, and plenty of money to pay the bills.

Work that gives you low control over time but high pay is all right too, from an investment standpoint. If you take, for example, a middle level management position in which you work fifty or sixty hours a week for a set salary, that would be okay if the salary was high enough to pay your bills and still save some to finance a later switch to work with more control of your time.

But this would only work if you set a specific milestone. You can't work at a job that demands so much of your life without knowing there will be an end to it. In my experience, without an endpoint you will be miserable; with an endpoint, the sacrifice becomes tolerable. So it helps a lot to say to yourself, "I'm going to do this for a year," or "two years," or "I'm going to do this until my net worth is equal to two years' expenses." But at the point that you've met your goal, you need to dump the low time-control, high-pay job and move on to the task of identifying and perfecting your right livelihood.

Another type of work gives you low pay but high control over your time. This is what I call the "starving artist." A job like this gives you all the time you need to practice mindfulness and pursue your personal purpose, but you live in poverty. This is an okay lifestyle if you don't have any responsibilities. A single person can afford to live like this with little difficulty. For some this can be the perfect way to right livelihood. But when you have a family, this type of work becomes harder to justify. And, if you've taken on any kind of financial responsibility, such as a car payment or a mortgage, this type of work is simply impossible until you have fulfilled those responsibilities.

Finally, there are the low pay, low control over time jobs. This is working two or more jobs for long hours at minimum wage. This is work you take if you're really desperate and you simply must bring some money in. But you have to be very clear with yourself that you're going to leave work like this as soon as possible. And that's not always easy because when you're working a lot of hours you're going to come home tired and unmotivated to work on changing your life. If you find yourself in this situation it requires cultivating that self-starting energy to keep doing what it takes to find another, more suitable job. That cultivation, of course, begins with practicing mindfulness on the job.

This is also where your community of support can play an important role. They can encourage you and help you remember what your goals are, even though fatigue and boredom may temporarily blind you.

Regardless of which kind of work you choose, the opportunity to practice mindfulness is always present. So even though you may feel that you are not doing work that is true to who you are, even though you are doing work that leaves you fatigued, you can still develop the character traits that will be the foundation of whatever work you choose to do. You can practice persistence in following your goal of finding the best work for you. You can continue to take things into your own hands and you can practice facing the facts about your current work. With mindfulness as your core practice, your right livelihood will come to fruition in the present moment.

IS RIGHT LIVELIHOOD REALLY POSSIBLE?

Whether right livelihood is actually possible, given the complexities of life in the modern world, is a question that many people ask. It seems clear, upon close examination, that most of the work we do today fails in one way or another to meet all of the criteria, especially the social criteria of responsibility for the long-term consequences of our work. But we *can begin* to take responsibility for the consequences of our work, which includes the activity of making things right.

As we go about protecting and cleaning up the environment, making food, shelter, and basic health care available to everyone, working toward peace between nations and tribes, and whatever else seems to need doing, we will always have the opportunity to practice mindfulness and to work on clarifying our personal values.

And that's how, we have said, right livelihood differs from just finding a job. The process is one in which you clarify your personal vision of life and your personal purpose. And then you pursue the goals that are implied by that vision and purpose. It may require that you take less than perfect work that is a compromise in order to pay the bills. But regardless of the job you can still begin the process of practicing mindfulness.

THE IMPORTANCE OF TRUST

Right livelihood, we have said, is impossible without a community of support. Trust is key to building that community of support. You trust yourself when you believe in your ability to make judgments about what will be good for you. You demonstrate trust for others when you believe in their judgment and integrity. Others learn to trust you when you show that you are open to their input, willing to listen, and concerned about the impact your decisions will have on them.

When you and those with whom you work and live trust one another, you create an atmosphere where people can be open and honest. You learn to depend on each other without the fear of having to pay later. You build a strong team spirit that permeates all your work and play together.

How can you begin to build trust or improve the level of trust in an existing situation? Beyond honesty and openness, beyond the willingness to listen, and a concern for the future welfare of those around you, it is important for you to get clear about your own goals and to communicate your goals to your friends and supporters. The single most important factor in building and maintaining trust is consistency. It is difficult to build trust and extremely easy to lose it. If you want people to trust you, you must remember never to leave them out of the loop. If you make just one decision that you expect others to carry out or support you on and you fail to give them the opportunity for input, expect the worst.

The greatest enemy of trust is failing to keep your commitments. When you make a promise to yourself and fail to keep it you undermine *self*-trust. When you make promises to others and don't keep them, you undermine *their* trust in you. When others make promises to you and don't keep them, you stop trusting them. A simple rule to remember is "Life works best when we keep our promises."

Next time you make a promise to yourself, write it down. Then look at the promise in detail until you see its smallest parts. Every time it occurs to you to do what you have promised, make it a habit to do some small part of it. Even though you don't feel like it—even if you are tempted to just sit there—do something. For example, if you make a promise to yourself to start exercising each day, write it down. With only a few moments of thought, it is easy to see that exercise is made up of a lot of little movements: movements of your head, arms, legs, and so forth. From the moment you write your promise down, you are committed. To keep your commitment, you must follow this simple procedure. Every time you think of exercising, get up and move. Even if all you do is turn your head from side to side, or lift your arms up parallel with the floor, that is okay.

The secret here is that if you think of exercising and then do even the simplest movement, you will be creating an experience of movement associated with the thought of exercising. If you don't get up and move you will be creating the association of lethargy with the thought of exercise. Which do you think will work to get you into an exercise program? Starting with even the simplest movements, one at a time, you can gradually build a complete exercise program.

The same thing is true when you make a promise to others. Even if you can't complete the whole promise, try to do some tiny part of it, or at least, make an appointment with yourself to do it. After all, setting aside time is one of the small parts of keeping any commitment.

GIVING BACK MORE THAN YOU GET

The most important step in building support for right livelihood is giving back more than you get. It's not really a matter of keeping track in some kind of ledger book. It's more a function of the attitude that you adopt in caring for yourself and those around you. People tend to mirror the way that they are treated. If you show an interest in helping and sharing, those around you will start helping you and sharing more with you. If you empathize with other people's situations, they tend to empathize more with yours. If you work with others to solve a personal problem by sharing information and creating a collaborative solution, they will start including you in their own problem-solving efforts. If you give those around you the latitude to solve problems their own way rather than telling them how to do it, they will start letting you solve problems in your own way. If you give others factual descriptions of what bothers you, rather than blaming, they will respect you more and be a great deal less defensive.

The key is to be active about it. Look for opportunities to cooperate. With a proactive attitude of supporting others, you will seldom experience a shortage of support from others.

A simple caution is in order, however, when it comes to giving to others. It is possible at times to find yourself in relationships that seem one-sided. You give and give and the other person never seems to get into the spirit of giving back. This needn't concern you too much as long as you remember to stay true to your vision and purpose. If someone seems to be needlessly dependent upon you and you find yourself feeling fatigued and worn out from taking care of them, clarify your boundaries. What are the commitments you've made to this other person that fit in with your vision, purpose, and goals? Self-protection is not the same thing as self-centeredness or selfishness. Try to remember this simple aphorism: Give more than you get, but not more than you've got.

Engaging in mindful, meaningful work is simple and difficult. It is simple because what I must do is quite clear and difficult because it requires faith in myself, perseverance, and most important, diligent, regular effort.

A close look at the complexities of life today makes me sometimes think there really isn't a single job left on the planet that doesn't somehow violate one or more of the tenets of right livelihood. In other more hopeful moments, I realize that the work of those who are sincere in their efforts to do right must somehow qualify as right livelihood, even if the influence of modern commerce causes some part of what they are doing to be harmful to others.

It is difficult for me to condemn the organic gardening store that carries the greensand I might use to rebuild the worn-out San Francisco soil in my backyard. True, a diesel-powered truck hauls that greensand from Tennessee, spewing carbon monoxide and other pollutants all the way. As a consumer of the greensand, I am equally responsible. I might instead choose to purchase soil amendments that come from nearby or, better yet, start my own compost pile.

When I was growing up, no one even hinted that I was going to have to look at every detail of my life with a magnifying glass. But that may well be what is required if I am to stay true to my values and maintain my right livelihood.

This is why practicing mindfulness and simple living is so important. By living simply I create an immediate reduction in the impact I have on the environment. The more simply I live, the fewer choices I have to make about what will and won't hurt the environment and others. So simple living helps me avoid being swallowed up in the complexity of issues about what does and does not qualify as right livelihood.

My mindfulness practice helps me with the remaining choices by encouraging an ongoing awareness of my personal purpose. Choosing what to do next, with my personal purpose in mind, is much less effortful. There is no easy way to identify what is right livelihood and what isn't, but, for me, the guiding light has been this simple maxim: *If you're not working on yourself, you're not working.*

It is my hope that this collection of essays has helped introduce you to the importance of right livelihood and to the relationship between mindfulness and meaningful work. I also hope that it has helped you see how to go about finding your own right livelihood and how to overcome the obstacles in your path. If these hopes are met, I will have achieved my purpose.

NOTES

[1] Jon Kabat-Zinn, *Full Catastrophe Living* (New York: Dell, 1990), p. 2.

[2] In spite of this similarity, we should note the difference, as Professor Steven D. Goodman points out in Chapter 5, between the nomothetic traditions, whose laws are handed down from a supreme being in the form of "Thou shalt not kill" or "Thou shalt not steal" and the Buddhist traditions, where the formula is "I voluntarily take training in the abstention from...."

[3] Much of my exposure to individuals pursuing right livelihood comes from my ten years as coordinator of the Briarpatch Network. In their book, *Honest Business*, Salli Rasberry and Michael Phillips first reported the four traits common to right livelihood entrepreneurs: persistence, facing the facts, minimizing risks, and hands-on learning. Their report was based on observation of individual members of the Briarpatch during the first three years of its existence. In our continued work with Briars, Salli, Michael, and I have confirmed that these characteristics are still present and important after twenty years. Salli and I have subsequently verified the importance of these additional factors: self-starting energy, having a community of support, emotional stability, and the practice of mindfulness. And I have also confirmed the importance of all these character traits to the nearly 200 workers seeking right livelihood who have come to me for "Good Work Guidance" during the last five years.

Glossary

Bodhi tree - *Ficus religiosa;* the tree in India under which the historical Buddha, Siddhartha Gautama, sat until he attained enlightenment.

bodhisattva - Skt., lit., "enlightenment being"; a being who engages in the systematic practice of the "perfect virtues" of generosity, discipline, patience, effort, meditation, and wisdom but who forsakes entry into nirvana in order to help all other beings to attain enlightenment.

gassho - Jap., lit., "palms together"; the expression used in Zen for the ancient greeting of placing your hands together and bowing in mutual respect and reverence.

jiriki - Jap., lit., "one's own power"; an expression that refers to the attainment of enlightenment through one's own practice efforts.

joriki - Jap., lit., "power of the mind"; the power or force of concentration that arises from the practice of zazen.

kalpa fire - kalpa (Skt.), world cycle; kalpa fire is the term used to describe the conflagration at the end of time that is a natural part of the regenerative cycle of the universe.

Kannon - Jap., another name for Kuan Yin, the Boddhisattva of Compassion.

karuna - Skt., compassion.

koans - Jap., the Zen phrases used to help students transcend their logical minds; koans come from teachings or episodes in the lives of ancient masters and are used to point to the nature of ultimate reality.

mana - Skt., the latent passion of arrogance.

metta - Pali, loving-kindness.

mindfulness - a state in which one is aware of what is going on in the present moment.

mudita - Pali, joy.

nirmanakaya - Skt., "body of transformation"; the earthly body in which buddhas appear to human beings in order to fulfill the buddhas' resolve to guide all beings to liberation.

nirvana - Skt., lit., "extinction"; a state of liberation or illumination beyond the reach of the thinking mind.

samu - Jap., lit., "work service"; the manual labor that is part of every-day maintenance of life in a monastery.

satori - Jap., Zen term for the experience of awakening.

sumi-e - Japanese brush painting; a highly refined art integrating the practice of mindfulness into the execution of each movement.

sunyata - Skt., lit., "emptiness, void"; the key idea of Buddhism which states that all the things that make up the cosmos are empty and imper-manent, devoid of a separate, independent existence.

tariki - Jap., lit., "power of the other"; an expression that refers to the attainment of enlightenment by relying on power outside of oneself.

upekkha - Pali (Skt. **upeksha**), equanimity.

vajra - the diamond-sword symbol in Tibetan Buddhism that stands for the true reality or emptiness of being.

zazen - Jap., the Zen practice of sitting meditation.

zendo - Jap., a Zen meditation hall.

The Householder's Bookshelf

BOOKS ON MINDFULNESS

Mindfulness is the state of being aware in the moment. It is the foundation upon which right livelihood is built. When we practice mindfulness, our lives become richer and more meaningful, and we get closer to an understanding of who we are and what life can offer us.

Davis, Bruce. *Monastery Without Walls: Daily Life in the Silence* (Berkeley: Celestial Arts, 1990). We yearn for perfect peace, yet we live in a high-speed rush to see "who can die with the most toys." This book speaks to the monk or mystic within every one of us, affirming our place in the sacred silence of inner reflection and showing how everyday life is filled with opportunities to live as if the world itself were a holy monastery and our work a sacrament.

Ellwood, Robert. *Finding the Quiet Mind* (Wheaton, IL: Theosophical Publishing House, 1983). A simple, but powerful instructional text on the practice of mindfulness.

Fields, Rick, with Peggy Taylor, Rex Weyler, and Rick Ingrasci. *Chop Wood, Carry Water: A Guide to Finding Spiritual Fulfillment in Everyday Life* (Los Angeles: Tarcher, 1984). An excellent basic guide to the development of spirituality in everyday life.

Foster, Richard J. *Celebration of Discipline: The Path to Spiritual Growth* (San Francisco: Harper & Row, 1988). An excellent book on modern Christian spirituality, with chapters on meditation and prayer as mindfulness practices.

Gach, Michael Reed. *Greater Energy at Your Fingertips* (Berkeley: Celestial Arts, 1990). Approaches mindfulness through the body, teaching how to use posture, acupressure, and breathing techniques to heighten awareness.

Nhat Hanh, Thich. *Being Peace* (Berkeley: Parallax Press, 1987). Considered by many to be the bible of engaged Buddhism.

Nhat Hanh, Thich. *The Miracle of Mindfulness: A Manual on Meditation* (Boston: Beacon Press, 1987). A classic manual on meditation, concentration, and relaxation, containing an appendix with specific mindfulness practices for everyday living.

Nhat Hanh, Thich. *The Sun My Heart* (Berkeley: Parallax Press, 1988). Draws from Buddhist psychology, epistemology, and contemporary physics and uses many anecdotes to illustrate the journey from mindfulness to insight contemplation.

Reynolds, David K. *Constructive Living* (Honolulu: University of Hawaii Press, 1984). Clear and concise lessons on overcoming shyness, depression, fear, stress, grief, and chronic pain. You *can* make substantial changes in your personality and character so that life simply works better. A summary of the author's work bringing the Japanese psychotherapies of Naikan and Morita to America in a way that is easy to understand.

Suzuki, Shunryu. *Zen Mind, Beginner's Mind* (New York: Weatherhill, 1970). A collection of deeply meaningful "Dharma talks."

Tulku, Tarthang. *Skillful Means: Patterns for Success* (Berkeley: Dharma Publishing, 1991). An excellent guide to applying mindfulness in everyday life, especially at work.

BOOKS ON COMPASSION

Compassion is mindfulness in action. As we proceed with our practice we begin to apply mindfulness to the planet and her people through everyday acts of compassion.

Badiner, Allan Hunt, editor. *Dharma Gaia: A Harvest of Essays in Buddhism and Ecology* (Berkeley: Parallax Press, 1990). Eric Utne described this book as "source documents for the emerging environmental era, written by a pantheon of postindustrial visionaries."

Callenbach, Ernest and Michael Phillips. *Citizen Legislature* (Berkeley: Banyan Tree, 1985). What if the U.S. House of Representatives were made up of people drawn from a random lottery of all the nation's citizens? What kind of laws would such a body propose? Read this book to get a glimpse of the answer. This book has been called *The Federalist Papers* of our time.

Eppsteiner, Fred, editor. *The Path of Compassion: Writings on Socially Engaged Buddhism* (Berkeley: Parallax Press, 1988). An impressive collection for those who wish to take mindfulness from the meditation hall into everyday life.

Nhat Hanh, Thich. *Touching Peace: Practicing the Art of Mindful Living* (Berkeley: Parallax Press, 1993). A book on practicing peace in everyday life, showing how mindfulness can help us see the roots of war, violence, substance abuse, and social alienation.

Peavey, Fran. *Heart Politics* (Philadelphia: New Society Publishers, 1986). Reads like a combination of Mark Twain, Thomas Jefferson, and Erma Bombeck. Peavey takes us along on her personal journey as she helps elderly tenants facing eviction from their residential hotel, alcoholics and street people longing for self-respect, prostitutes in Bangkok, Indians cleaning the Ganges River, and civilians coping with the tragedy of the Middle East conflict.

Plant, Christopher and Judith, editors. *Green Business: Hope or Hoax?* (Philadelphia: New Society Publishers, 1991). A well-researched critique of "shallow green" consumerism, with examples like biodegradable plastics and dolphin-safe tuna. It explores how changes in the way we do business can help create a sustainable economy.

Schumacher, E.F. *Good Work* (New York: Harper & Row, 1979). A wonderful collection of essays by the founder of the "intermediate technology" movement. This books rejects speculation about what technology may do for us in the future and focuses instead on what human beings can do now, both personally and collectively.

BOOKS ON RELATIONSHIP[1]

Relationship is the essence of what it means to be human. It makes work possible. Unless you've retreated to a mountain cave or a cloister, relationship is the means by which your life takes place. Together, mindfulness, compassion, and relationship are the basic building blocks of right livelihood.

Barnett, Frank and Sharon. *Working Together: Entrepreneurial Couples* (Berkeley: Ten Speed Press, 1988). Wisdom and insights gained through interviews with entrepreneurial couples dispels the myths, addresses the social biases, looks at the benefits and risks, and outlines the steps to becoming successful co-entrepreneurs.

Greenleaf, Robert K. *Servant Leadership: A Journey Into the Nature of Legitimate Power and Greatness* (New York: Paulist Press, 1977). Deals with important social questions such as: Who is a leader? Who is a follower? How does one effectively lead others?

Johnson, Robert. *We: Understanding the Psychology of Romantic Love* (New York: Harper & Row, 1983). Shows how we can overcome the illusions we often have about love and create a deeper, longer-lasting, more meaningful relationship based on a new understanding of true love.

Leonard, Linda Schierse. *On the Way to the Wedding: Transforming the Love Relationship* (Boston: Shambhala, 1986). Uncovers the inner obstacles to love and creativity as experienced by both men and women. Shows that whether one seeks an inner or an outer wedding, it is the work of transformation within that provides the transcendent ground for the attainment of enlightened relationship.

McGlaughlin, Corinne and Gordon Davidson. *Builders of the Dawn: Community Lifestyles in a Changing World* (Summerton, TN: The Book Publishing Co., 1990). Real-life stories from eighty-seven intentional communities that are alive and well in today's world, from Arcosanti in the Arizona desert to Findhorn in Scotland.

Moore, Thomas. *Soul Mates* (San Francisco: HarperCollins, 1993). A new volume dealing with relationships, frequently recommended by friends and associates, but too late for review.

Morrison, Roy. *We Build the Road As We Travel* (Santa Cruz: New Society Publishers, 1991). The compelling story of 21,000 workers who built their own businesses, schools and banks—taking control of their own communities and lives. Beginning forty years ago, a humble parish priest and a handful of students motivated the people of the town of Mondragon in the Basque region of Spain to build what is now a vital, successful, and resilient network of more than 170 worker-owned-and-operated cooperatives that serve well over 100,000 people.

Peck, M. Scott. *The Different Drum: Community Making and Peace* (New York: Simon & Schuster, 1987). "In and through community lies the salvation of the world." Author of the best-selling *The Road Less Traveled* and *People of the Lie*, Peck explores the spiritual journey toward self-acceptance, true belonging, and world peace. This book makes it easy to see that we have within our grasp the power to experience a new connectedness and wholeness through community.

Whitmyer, Claude, editor. *In the Company of Others: Making Community in the Modern World* (New York: Putnam Publishing Group, 1993). Brings together a range of voices singing the praises of community, offering guidance for starting one, and practical solutions for the economic and emotional difficulties that may arise.

BOOKS ON WORKING: FOR YOURSELF AND FOR OTHERS

Whether we work for ourselves or somebody else, the growing self-awareness that arises through the practice of mindfulness, compassion, and relationship makes our life more fulfilling.

Anderson, Nancy. *Work with Passion: How to Do What You Love for a Living* (New York: Carroll & Graff, 1984). One of the most practical and motivating guides to finding your right livelihood, including excellent self-assessment tools and instruction in goal setting, building personal support networks, researching potential jobs, approaching potential employers, using a resume, and overcoming negative emotions.

Bolles, Richard Nelson. *What Color Is Your Parachute? A practical manual for job-hunters and career changers* (Berkeley: Ten Speed Press, updated annually). The definitive life/work planning manual, a perennial best-seller because the exercises and advice actually work.

Ekins, Paul, with Mayer Hillman and Robert Hutchinson. *The Gaia Atlas of Green Economics* (New York: Anchor, 1992). Explores a new concept of wealth and wealth creation and outlines what government and individuals can do to repair the environment and build a sustainable society.

Fadiman, James. *Unlimit Your Life: Setting and Getting Goals* (Berkeley: Celestial Arts, 1989). Takes us through the steps necessary to set and achieve life's goals—personal, economic, career, and spiritual.

Hwoschinsky, Paul. *True Wealth* (Berkeley: Ten Speed Press, 1990). A new approach to money, based on understanding of financial and nonfinancial assets and goals.

McMakin, Jacqueline and Sonya Dyer. *Working from the Heart: For Those Who Hunger for Meaning and Satisfaction in Their Work* (San Diego: LuraMedia, 1989). A moving description of how to find success through serving others, with a balanced emphasis on introspection, seeking the help of others, clarifying personal values, creating a work environment that fosters "heart work," and allowing spiritual nourishment to be a part of work.

Phillips, Michael and Salli Rasberry. *The Seven Laws of Money* (New York: Random House, 1974). An eye-opening look at how money actually works. The source of the often misquoted *first law of money*: "Do what you love. *If you're doing the right thing*, the money will follow." There is a 1993 condensed miniature version of this book, but I prefer the original.

Phillips, Michael and Salli Rasberry. *Honest Business: A Superior Strategy for Starting and Managing Your Own Business* (New York: Random House, 1982). Day-to-day, practical advice, with highly motivating anecdotes. If you've always wanted to own your own business but are afraid you might have to compromise your integrity, this book is a must.

Rasberry, Salli, editor. *The Briarpatch Book* (Volcano, CA: Volcano/New Glide Publications, 1978). A compilation of the first eight issues of *The Briarpatch Review*, a journal of "right livelihood and simple living."

Sher, Barbara with Anne Gottlieb. *Wishcraft: How to Get What You Really Want* (New York: Ballantine, 1979). The sub-subtitle says it all: "A unique, step-by-step plan to pinpoint your goals and make your dreams come true."

Whitmyer, Claude and Salli Rasberry. *Running a One-Person Business* (Berkeley: Ten Speed Press, 1994, 2d ed.). A practical guide, written for the single-person operation, but helpful to any business. Chapters on bookkeeping, financial management, time management, ways of organizing information, how to lay out a work space, the special concerns of working from home, choosing technology, emotional support systems, and how to stay a one-person business.

There are many good biographies and autobiographies about people who are making a difference in the world by the way they run their businesses. Among the best are:

Ausubel, Kenny. *Seeds of Change: The Living Treasure* (San Francisco: HarperCollins, 1994). The story of the "Seeds of Change" mail-order business that promotes biodiversity through the cultivation and distribution of organic heirloom varietal seeds.

Chappell, Tom. *The Soul of a Business* (New York: Bantam, 1993). The story of "Tom's of Maine" natural toiletries company.

Roddick, Anita. *Body and Soul: Profits with Principles* (New York: Crown, 1991). The story of the Body Shop and its founder.

Ziegler, Mel, Bill Rosenzweig, and Patricia Ziegler. *The Republic of Tea: Letters to a Young Zentrepreneur* (New York: Doubleday, 1992). The story of the "Republic of Tea" packaged tea company.

NOTES

[1] I apologize to the gay community for the absence of good books on same-sex relationships. None had come to my attention by press time. Please send me your recommendations.

Organizations that Support Right Livelihood

Businesses for Social Responsibility
1850 M Street N.W., #750
Washington, DC 20036
202-872-5206
Trade association for businesses concerned about right livelihood, worker ownership, environmental impact, community service, etc. Can provide contact information of local chapter in your area, if one exists.

Center for Business and Democracy
Goddard College
Plainfield, VT 05667
802-454-8311
Provides management and leadership training for socially responsible and alternative businesses. Goddard College itself also offers an External Masters Degree program that can focus on the issue of right livelihood.

Center for Good Work
P.O. Box 77086
San Francisco, CA 94107-7086
415-648-2667
Offers vocational guidance with an emphasis on right livelihood and the use of mindfulness to find meaningful work. The editor of this volume is director.

Masters of Business Administration Program
Dr. William Sadler
Department of Business and Economics
Holy Names College
3500 Mountain Boulevard
Orinda, CA 94619
510-436-1346
MBA program offering an emphasis in socially responsible business practices.

The New Careers Center, Inc.
1515 23rd Street
P.O. Box 339-CT
Boulder, CO 80306
303-447-1087
Offers "The Whole Work Catalog," a mail-order list of books on alternative careers, new work options, self-employment, and home business.

Project on Spirituality in the Workplace
Dr. Richard Snyder
34 Invincible Court
Alameda, CA 94501
510-521-3183
Think tank-like group of academics and business people working on the issues of spirituality in the workplace, what it is, how to nurture it.

Right Livelihood Award
Michelle Syverson
P.O. Box 680
Manzanita, OR 97130
503-368-7652
A yearly award to support those working on practical and exemplary solutions to the real problems facing the world today. Recipients are nominated by a special worldwide committee.

Contributors

Robert Aitken is the founding teacher of the Diamond Sangha in Honolulu. He is author of *A Zen Wave*, *Taking the Path of Zen*, *The Mind of Clover: Essays in Zen Buddhist Ethics*, *The Dragon Who Never Sleeps*, and *Encouraging Words*.

Joseph Cary is Professor Emeritus of English and Comparative Literature at the University of Connecticut and author of *Three Modern Italian Poets: Saba, Ungretti, Montale* and *A Ghost in Trieste*.

Ernest Callenbach is author of *Living Cheaply with Style*, *Ecotopia*, and *Ecotopia Emerging*, and coauthor of *A Citizen Legislature* and *Eco-Management: The Elmwood Guide to Ecological Auditing and Sustainable Business*. He founded *Film Quarterly* and served as its editor until 1991.

Rick Fields, editor of *Yoga Journal*, is author of *How the Swans Came to the Lake: A Narrative History of Buddhism in America*, and *The Code of the Warrior: In History, Myth, and Everyday Life*. He coauthored *Chop Wood, Carry Water* with Peggy Taylor (editor of *New Age Journal*), Rex Weyler (founder of Greenpeace), and Rick Ingrasci, a holistic health physician.

Shakti Gawain is author of *Creative Visualization, Living in the Light, Return to the Garden, Awakening,* and *The Path of Transformation: How Healing Ourselves Can Change the World.*

Robert Gilman is the founding editor of *IN CONTEXT: A Quarterly of Humane, Sustainable Culture,* which in 1991 won the *Utne Reader's* Alternative Press Award for "Best Coverage of Emerging Issues." He is coauthor of *Global Action Plan's Household EcoTeam Workbook.*

Steven D. Goodman is Assistant Professor of Indo-Tibetan Buddhism and Comparative Philosophy at the California Institute of Integral Studies and adjunct faculty at the Institute of Buddhist Studies, Graduate Theological Union, Berkeley. He is coeditor of *Tibetan Buddhism: Reason and Revelation.*

Thich Nhat Hanh, a Vietnamese Zen monk, is the author of *Being Peace, The Miracle of Mindfulness, The Sun My Heart,* and many other books.

Paul Jordan-Smith is coeditor of *I Become Part of It: Sacred Dimensions in Native American Life,* and a contributing editor to *Parabola.*

Sam Keen is author of *Your Mythic Journey, The Passionate Life,* and *Fire in the Belly: On Being a Man,* and *Faces of the Enemy.*

Ellen Langer is a Professor of Psychology and Chair of the Social Psychology Program at Harvard University. Her books include *Personal Politics, The Psychology of Control,* and *Mindfulness.*

Gene Logsdon works a small farm in Wyandot County, Ohio, and is author of *At Nature's Pace: Farming and the American Dream.*

John Daido Loori is teacher at Zen Mountain Monastery in Mount Tremper, New York. He is author of *Mountain Record of Zen Talks, Eight Gates of Zen,* and *Two Arrows Meeting in Mid-Air.*

David Loy is Associate Professor in the Faculty of International Studies, Bunkyo University, Chigasaki, Japan.

Joanna Macy is Adjunct Professor in the School of Transformative Learning at the California Institute of Integral Studies. She is author of *Despair and Personal Power in the Nuclear Age*, *Dharma and Development*, *Thinking Like a Mountain*, *Mutual Causality in Buddhism and General Systems Theory*, and *World As Lover, World As Self*.

Jean Kinkead Martine is a partner in an advertising agency and a short story writer.

Carolyn Meyer is author of *People Who Make Things: How American Craftsmen Live and Work*.

Toni Packer conducts retreats at Springwater Center, Springwater, New York, in California, and several European countries. She is the author of *Seeing without Knowing* and *The Work of This Moment*.

Fran Peavey is author of *Heart Politics*, *A Shallow Pool of Time* and *By Life's Grace*.

Michael Phillips is moderator of American Public Radio's "Social Thought." He is coauthor of *The Seven Laws of Money*, *Honest Business*, *Marketing without Advertising*, and *Citizen Legislature*.

Roger Pritchard is a right livelihood guide and socially responsible financial consultant.

Walpola Rahula is author of *What the Buddha Taught* and *The Heritage of the Bhikkhu*.

James Robertson is author of *Future Wealth: A New Economics for the 21st Century*, *Future Work: Jobs, Self-Employment and Leisure after the Industrial Age*, and *The Sane Alternative: A Choice of Futures*.

Patricia Ryan-Madson is Senior Lecturer in Drama and Head of the Undergraduate Acting Program at Stanford University, the American Coordinator of the Oomoto School of Traditional Japanese Arts, and coleader of the San Francisco Center for Constructive Living.

Saki F. Santorelli, Ed. D., is an Associate Professor of Medicine, Associate Director of the Stress Reduction Clinic, and Director of Clinical and Educational Services at the Center for Mindfulness in Medicine, Health Care, and Society at the University of Massachusetts Medical Center. He has written and coauthored a number of articles and book chapters on meditation in both the scientific and popular press. He is currently writing a book about mindfulness in the helping relationship.

E.F. Schumacher was instrumental in the creation of the "intermediate and appropriate technology" movement. He is author of *Small Is Beautiful* and *A Guide for the Perplexed*.

Marsha Sinetar is an organizational psychologist, mediator, and writer whose books include *Ordinary People as Monks and Mystics*, *Do What You Love, the Money Will Follow*, and *Developing a 21st Century Mind*.

Sulak Sivaraksa, author of *Seeds of Peace: A Buddhist Vision for Renewing Society*, is a prominent and outspoken Thai social critic and activist.

Gary Snyder is a Pulitzer Prize winning poet and teacher of literature and wilderness thought at the University of California at Davis. His poetry collections include *Turtle Island*, *Axe Handles*, and *Earth Household*, and his essay collections include *The Real Work* and *The Practice of the Wild*.

Shunryu Suzuki-roshi was founder of the San Francisco and Tassajara Zen Centers. He is author of *Zen Mind, Beginner's Mind*.

Janet Tallman teaches culture and communication at John F. Kennedy University in Orinda, California. She has just completed a book on conversational styles in everyday life.

Tarthang Tulku is a religious teacher from the Tarthang Monastery in East Tibet. He is a prolific author and among his many books are two that are important to anyone interested in the subject of right livelihood: *Ways of Work: Dynamic Action* and *Skillful Means: Patterns for Success*. He lives and teaches at the Nyingma Institute in Berkeley, California, and the Odiyan retreat center in northern California.

Appreciation

To the entire membership of the Briarpatch community for the unique opportunity to learn about right livelihood from those who practice it. Especially to my core supporters and advisors: Sara Alexander, Andy Alpine, Charmian Anderson, Kristen Anundsen, Cathy Beaham, Clarke Berry, Barbra Blake, Joni Blank, Bart Brodsky, Ernest Callenbach, Anisa Cieply, Jo Anne Coates, Saundra Durgin, Jack Fitzwater, Andora Freeman, Anthony Giovanniello, Kathleen Gorman, Gordon Grabe, Lynn Gravestock, Tom Hargadon, Judith Jenna, Willa Kacy, Irene Kane, Fenton Kay, Sharon Kehoe, Dyanne Ladine, Vicki Lee, Moses Ma, Chris Mays, Patricia-Ryan Madson, Jack McCurdie, Joan McIntosh, Karen Moawad, Peggi Oakley, Sophie Otis, Fran Peavey, Norman Prince, Shali Parsons, Harry Pasternak, Roger Pritchard, Carole Rae-Watanabe, Salli Rasberry, Maureen Redl, Deborah Reinerio, Tom Rose, David Rowley, Morgan Rowley, David Sibbet, Portia Sinnott, Valerie Skonie, Lee Spiegel, Randall Sugawara, Michael Stein, Joan Leslie Taylor, Paul Terry, Judy Vasos, Nancy Vernon-Burke, Jake Warner, Goran Wiklund, Arek Whitmyer, Lyla Wilson, and my students in the MAB program, Shelley Arrowsmith, David Ferrara, Mark Hughes-Weissman, Tara Mann, Jessalyn Nash, Mary Schmidt, Michael Stein, James Williams, and Nonnie Welch.

To my clients both vocational and entrepreneurial who also made it possible for me to create an anthology informed by personal experience. To the authors in this volume for understanding the relationship between mindfulness and meaningful work and the issues that affect it.

Special thanks to my publisher, Arnie Kotler, who has the uncommon virtue of an almost infinite measure of patience and who helped me clarify my thinking, remember my focus, and attempt to meet my deadlines. Credit also goes to Marianne Dresser, Judy Hardin, Phil Wood, and the staff at Parallax Press, who were invisible most of the time but whose presence was deeply felt and appreciated at key moments. I also want to thank Jerry Horovitz and Gaetano Maida for their support of the idea for this book and their ongoing interest in its progress.

Thanks also to Torbert McCarroll for his wonderful translations of the *Tao Te Ching*.

I am particularly indebted to Tarthang Tulku Rinpoche and Thich Nhat Hanh. It was through my efforts to apply the words of these two great teachers that I awoke to the necessity of balance between mindfulness and meaning in the context of everyday work. Both have made penetrating contributions to the development of Dharma in the West and to an understanding of the profoundly spiritual role that work can play in our lives.

I wish to give a special thanks to my partner in life and love, Gail Terry Grimes. She has guided me in writing and editing the entire book. Her continued encouragement and support in the face of sometimes overwhelming circumstances in both of our lives continues to amaze me.

Permissions and Copyrights

About the Editor

Claude Whitmyer's maternal grandmother taught him the Christian Science practice of "knowing the truth" when he was still a child. When he was ten years old his mother joined the Baha'i World Faith where he was first introduced to Buddhism and Buddhist meditation. Over the past thirty years he has studied a variety of Christian contemplation and Taoist/Buddhist meditation techniques as a foundation for his personal mindfulness practice. In the last decade he has focused his practice on learning to carry mindfulness with him, from the meditation cushion to the workplace.

Mr. Whitmyer pursues his own right livelihood as a writer and teacher and as an advisor to individuals seeking a more meaningful work life. He is coordinator of the Briarpatch, a worldwide network of several hundred businesses and community organizations that practice right livelihood. He is author of *Running a One-Person Business* (with Salli Rasberry) and editor of *In the Company of Others: Making Community in the Modern World*. Claude is founder and director of The Center for Good Work, which offers guidance to individuals seeking personally fulfilling work and to businesses and nonprofits that advocate community service, environmental preservation, and worker participation in management decisions.